Northern Ireland: Society Under Siege

Northern Ireland: Society Under Siege

Rona M. Fields

Foreword by
Alfred McClung Lee

Transaction Books
New Brunswick (U.S.A.) and London (U.K.)

 Library of Congress Catalog Number: 80-80316
ISBN: 0-87855-806-3
Printed in the United States of America

Library of Congress Cataloging in Publication Data
Fields, Rona M.
  Northern Ireland.

  Reprint of the 1977 ed. published by Temple University Press, Philadelphia,
under title: Society under siege.

  Includes bibliographical references and index.
  1.   Northern Ireland—Social conditions.
2.   Irish question.   3.   Stress (Physiology)—Case
studies.   4.   Violence—Northern Ireland.   I.   Title.
HN398.N6F53   1980   941.6   80-80316
ISBN   0-87855-806-3   (pbk.)

Contents

To the children of my body

For the children of my spirit,

In the name of Peace

Who understands
before communicated with
Knows
as only the oppressed
Know.

MICHAEL O HUANACHAIN, 1973

Understand that you yourself
are guilty of every atrocity
however far from you
it seems to be happening

GUNTER EICH

The scorched cloth smell and smell of burnt flesh
From morning, a bomb in one of the parked cars,
The gulls, glinting like an ice on asphalt in April
The sun, in a smog of cheap petrol exhaust
Fumes: all bring on the sinusy nightmare . . .

PADRAIC FIACC, 1974

Foreword

Even when they are superficial, dramatic events get center-stage attention in the mass media and preoccupy policymakers. Such events, as reported, often give a biased view of what is happening in a civil conflict, with Northern Ireland since 1968 being a case in point. Partisan editors and politicians present selected news accounts easily as evidence that the "benign peace-keeping" troops from the United Kingdom actually do devote themselves exclusively to preventing "Protestants" and "Roman Catholics" from murdering each other for purely "religious" reasons. As in so many other situations of this sort around the world, the case for the oppressors overshadows any semblance of a case for the oppressed.

The troops, with their dehumanized image of the Irish "paddies," have a record that often is not at all benign; they add to the tolls of violence. The local Royal Ulster Constabulary, heavily representative of the "Protestant" ethnic group, is similarly regarded as a participant in violence rather than a preventive force.

Religious labels block "Roman Catholics" from obtaining economic and political opportunities equal to those of so-called "Protestants" in this colony. Those tagged "Protestants" try to continue to benefit from the ethnic conspiracy—encouraged by employers and politicians—that gives them special privileges in the underprivileged colony.

In Northern Ireland, the controlling English, imbued as they are with racist imperial traditions, cannot accept that any "colonials"—whether "Protestant" or "Roman Catholic"—can possibly govern themselves. As a result, as Rona M. Fields so aptly points out in this book, both groups are oppressed, and both are suffering from a species of psychological genocide. As multinational corporations have taken over control of larger and larger sections of the British political economy, they have found this fragmented social situation a profitable one in which to carry on a part of their operations.

The blood in Northern Ireland's streets, the bombings and shoot-outs, the men and women "lifted" from their beds in the night on suspicion and imprisoned, and the destroyed property are all allotted TV time and newspaper headlines. Some 2,000 people have been killed and more than 14,000 wounded since 1968 in a province with a population of only 1.5 million. This is a disastrous enough picture, but it is incomplete. It consists of symptoms. What are the causes? What are the rest of the costs—costs even greater in continuing human suffering than physical maiming and slaughter? What is happening to children growing up in this conflict situation? To what extent are their lives distorted and deeply scarred not only by the conflict but also by the exploitative conditions that created the conflict situation? How and why is Northern Ireland (for that matter the whole of the British Isles) so dedicated to bitter ethnic—miscalled "racial" and "religious"—and class deprivation and struggle?

These are questions for which Rona Fields sought answers through years of intimate exploration in the six counties of Northern Ireland and in the twenty-six of the Republic. She indicates that even if the hostilities in this three-sided civil war were to stop today, and even if that cessation of open strife were miraculously to be on terms accepted as fair by all parties, years and even generations of careful repair work would be needed to heal the psychic and social wounds and dislocations afflicting the whole population. The situation is similar to that of the blacks and whites in the United States, whose minds and social structures are distorted by the long experiences of black oppression.

The damages in Ireland are not only deep, they are wide-spread. As Fields points out in this wide-ranging and perceptive book, in all of Ireland she "seldom met anyone who was not a victim" (p. xii) of the struggle. In a very real sense, she could have said as much about the people of the whole of the British Isles. English imperialism, nurtured for almost a millenium by British exploitation of the Celtic fringe in Wales, Scotland, and Ireland, developed racism and patricianism as a way of life. It is a way of life to which the English are still committed in spite of its counterproductive consequences in colony after colony around the world.

Fields views many dimensions of the Northern Irish "under siege." She understands the relevance of the long historical record of efforts at the physical and psychological genocide of the Irish people. She then relates to this broader canvas her participant observations in families, organizations, and street scenes, her sample surveying, her studies of evidences of group process and dynamics and of social structure. As an American professional, she was able to establish rapport with people on all three sides of the struggle. As a woman, she was able to get the most intimate data and assessment I have read of those "slaves of slaves," the Irish women, and of their children. At the same time, she does as well in describing the "very ambiguous British army situation as a peace-keeping force" (p. 133).

Fields' discussion of psychological and social control procedures and practices gives a significant thrust and is a major contribution to this book.

She outlines the many ways in which colonialism, prejudice, and racism, strengthened by the puritanical rigidity characteristic of that colony, work toward the goal of psychological genocide. As she notes, "In Northern Ireland all the institutions contrive a 'set' through which no one in the social system may perceive the dissonance inherent in the authoritarian, rigid oligarchical social ordering imposed under the rhetoric of democracy." She sees this as exemplified, among many other ways, "by the consistent use of corporal punishment in the schools" (pp. 236-37).

Fields vividly raises more questions, focuses on more human problems, than she can possibly answer. In doing so, she does make the substantial contribution of brushing aside the news-fiction "descriptions" of the struggle so common on both sides of the Atlantic. She describes real people in anguish and desperation. She looks with horror at "the manipulation of an entire population toward its destruction" as a social entity. She wanted to know for herself "what will happen to these children, their families, and their tortured country" (p. xii). She has candidly recounted what she found. Her report is a challenge to humanity and an indictment of English patricianism, racism, and imperialism.

ALFRED MCCLUNG LEE

Preface

During the period in which this book was written many of the persons whose lives and efforts inspired its writing were murdered and mutilated. Too often those who have been marked for destruction in Northern Ireland are men and women who are advocating a nonsectarian solution to the troubles. They are working-class, grass-roots leaders who have stepped from the ranks of their peers to express their position in order to initiate steps toward new understanding. There were two such men, Billy McMillen and Sammy Smith, about whom I had already written before they were killed and whose deaths represent further regression from a just resolution of the conflict. Besides these murdered leaders, there are hundreds of children, Protestant and Catholic, into whose lives I wandered in the pursuit of my research. Many of them became my friends during the six years of my frequent visits to Ireland. I've watched them grow up— some of them. Others I've known haven't lived to grow up or have become crippled bodies and damaged minds. During this time, also, I've shared the agonies of the thousands of people in Northern Ireland whose suffering in interrogation and internment has aged them before their time. I endured a small sample of that experience myself and afterward realized that this "soft guillotine," which separates the spirit from the person and alienates the individual from himself or herself, is indeed psychological genocide. Often I've asked myself why go back? I could argue that it is the commitment to my research; the necessity for maintaining a longitudinal "sample"; but I know that is not sufficient reason to explain my persistence. Sometimes I think the answer is that because every time I have completed one or another part of my research and articulated my findings there has been such a massive effort on the part of the governments involved to suppress them, even to the extent of shredding ten thousand copies of a two-hundred-page book (*A Society On The Run*—my report on two years of research findings). But I think that my reason for going back and continuing this work is not the superrational, or even the rebellious. Rather, it is because every time I walk from Belfast City Center toward Leeson St. in Lower Falls, some children rush to my side shouting "Rona's home again!" Oftentimes I don't even recognize the children because they've grown so much within the few months of my absence. Sometimes there are new children who had been still in their prams on my previous visits to their neighborhood. I think that I have carried on and will continue this study because I need to know for myself what will happen to these children, their families, and their tortured country. The experience of it carries a special responsibility for dissemination and action and that's why putting the research into this book has been so terribly important to me.

I used to think of myself as a pacifist. In fact, I found it so hard to understand violence and prejudice that I kept focusing my disciplinary "microscope" on such circumstances in the expectation that by finding out why violence happens I or someone else might find a way to end it. In the course of this research I have learned that I am not a pacifist. I have felt deep anger and desperately wanted to hit back at those who bullied and abused me. I felt my human dignity threatened, which hurt more deeply than the threat to my life itself.

When I started these studies I also had a commitment to the "underdog," which characterized much of my earlier work. But in all of this research in Ireland I have seldom met anyone who was not a victim; which is not to suggest that a victim cannot in turn victimize someone else.

In my earlier book, I thanked a lot of people by name, only to find that this public acknowledgment of our connection endangered them. This time although I shall be more judicious, I shall regret that some of the individuals to whom I owe much cannot be named. In that book I explained my entrance into the problems of Northern Ireland, as well as the connection I recognized between the troubles in Northern Ireland and conflict and social prejudice I had earlier researched in the black ghettos of Chicago and Chicano barrios of Los Angeles. But now I see a more sinister relationship, in fact, because it is not purely a phenomenological similarity. The roots of racism as we have experienced it in the U.S. are embedded in the colonial enterprise that has over the past eight hundred years all but destroyed the Irish people. That's why this book is not intended as a unique case history, but rather as an examination of generalizable consequences of the manipulation of an entire population toward its destruction. Studies of former concentration-camp inmates are relevant to this work not only in assessing the effects of the torture and internment experience on former internees but also for understanding the society, which is captive in its entirety.

If you go to Northern Ireland looking for villains, heroes, and victims, you will find that among the one and a half million persons each is a composite of the three. If you extend your search to Whitehall, Westminster, and Dublin, you will find in their archives the record of villainy and corruption as it proceeded from the greed of old men into the spilled blood of young men and women for some thirty generations down to our time. The historical process of viewing human lives as commodities of exchange and bodies for exploitation; the process by which one people is subjugated for the specious rationale of the survival of another people: these processes are the omnipresent villains. Those who espoused them in the past and who do so today are the archfiends. But those who uphold and enforce the codes protecting these processes, though victims themselves of a kind of subliminally conducted "thought reform" program, have become the medium for the conduct of atrocities accessory to the processes. As long as this haunted reality does not arouse the concern of those who, by virtue of geographical distance, turn away from its perspective, they too contribute to its perpetuity.

In recognizing the reality of Northern Ireland, one must remember that here are people no different in their human dimensions from people in London, Boston, Los Angeles, or Dublin. In each of these places, the potential is present, as are the social and political dynamics, for conflagration as fearsome as anything existing in Belfast. Indeed, there have been times in recent history when similar people have attacked one another across picket lines and killed one another on prolonged strikes in Kohler, Wisconsin, and Detroit, Michigan. There have been times when such people have set fire to their own homes and neighborhood shops in Watts in Los Angeles and in Spanish Harlem. Neither their white skins nor their fluency in the English language separate these people of Northern Ireland from any other oppressed peoples in the world; nor are they different from any of similar color and feature in any suburb of America or town in England. That is, with one exception: they have been marked for a peculiar kind of destruction—psychological genocide.

My research in Northern Ireland, both in conception and treatment, has been concerned with social action as viewed by a psychologist. The objectives—methods of investigation and of reporting the findings—have been through the use of the "tools of the psychologists' trade." They include a variety of personality or projective tests, clinical interviews, studies of cognitive development, and analysis of group dynamics and group process. It has been conducted through my involvement as a participant observer during nearly six years of escalating conflict in Ireland—North and South. As a sociologist, I could and did bring to the work background and training in participant-observation field research; survey sampling; group process and dynamics; and social structure.

Probably because of my dual disciplinary training and outlook, the sociological perspective compels a differentiation between "psychologizing" and "psychology in social action." The former, which may or may not imply action, refers to the too common application of theories and techniques of psychology to social and political problems. By analyzing these larger conflicts in terms of individual dynamics and interaction theories, psychologizing makes plausible an interpretation of events and societies as the microcosm of human behaviors in a vacuous context, lacking regard for political and social systems. This is an error perpetuated by the laboratory approach to studying social problems in a controlled environment rather than *in situ*. Social action psychology proceeds from the assumption that the psychologist, along with everyone else, is functioning in a larger sociopolitical arena and may be an actor in any of the power relationships within the milieu. As an outsider, I was able to straddle many of the otherwise rigid and insurmountable fences between segments of the population in Ireland, where social class barriers are as strong as any sectarian barriers and political boundaries are more ferocious than the street barricades. While doing my research I lived in homes ranging from the working-class ghettos of Lower Falls and Sandy Row to the Malone Road areas in which reside the upper and middle classes of Belfast. In the south, I have been a guest in the homes of a wide variety of Irish people in Dublin, Wexford, Galway, Donegal, and points in between. This close contact was essential for me, as a social scientist and fourth-generation American, to understand the frightening perspective of the view from within. And it is frightening indeed when the subject is violence. The violation of life is itself a horrendous enough prospect, but the ultimate violence has been done to the human dignity of the people whom I grew to know and love. Now, as before in Ireland, the major victim of violence and assassination has been the truth. This places on me a particularly heavy and even awesome responsibility. I am dealing not merely with figures in a compilation of empirical data but also with people who are most often accounted for only in numbers and not encountered as integral human beings; often voiceless amid the shouting, and too often exploited by their heroes as much as by their enemies. They allowed me into their homes and thoughts, trusting that I'd be fair and understanding. The more I shared with them the more I realized how often their trust had been betrayed and the more afraid I became lest I would, unwittingly, become a source of further betrayal.

This book, based on social research, like any other of its kind, could not be the product of one individual's thesis, design, and productivity. It is the cumulative experience and effort of many individuals made concrete by the author and attested in print. It is, nonethelelss, no one's fault but my own if I have articulated these experiences inadequately. So I must start back to acknowledge and recognize some of the major contributors to this work. Magda B. Arnold provided me with knowledge and facility in many of the tools of research through her work with me as my major advisor in graduate school and in the many years since then, as friend and colleague. Alfred McClung Lee, sociologist and Irish scholar, has for many years encouraged me to persist in my Irish efforts, as well as provided me with collegial advice. My colleagues in Psychologists for Social Action—Ned Opton, Marc Pilisuk, Bob Buckhout, Serena Stier, Milt Wolpin, and Howard Gruber—have, through the years before and since I started these studies in Ireland, contributed, encouraged, citicized (always constructively), and goaded me on in the name of conscience and commitment. My colleagues in the British Society for Social Responsibility in Science— Tim Shallice, Hugh Sadler, Chris Ryan, Andy Solandt, and Dorothy Griffiths—shored and shared my efforts. The Honorable Sean MacBride, in his leadership of Amnesty International, as well as through his profound contributions to human welfare in Ireland and Africa, has been for me a model from whom I continue to learn the lessons of commitment and responsibility.

In Ireland many have helped me. Patrick Oliver Snoddy, President of the Gaelic League, has been advisor and friend, directing me through the fabulous riches of Irish culture. Eoin McKiernan has through the Irish American Cultural Institute enabled me to meet and learn from some of the outstanding scholars in Ireland today. Kevin Danaher provided me with essential background information on early Irish law. Margaret Mac-Curtain, Mary Maher, Maureen Johnson, Mairin de Burca, Moira Woods, and Mary Anderson were invaluable colleagues in my research on women, particularly, and Irish society in general. Doctors Stewart, Lane, Plunkett, and Fraser, all of Northern Ireland, enlightened and inspired me with their own courage and moral conviction.

My Irish family, Peg and Mick Darcy, Catherine Darcy, their mother, their children (David, Mary Louise, Michael, John, and Nicole) and Wexford relations, provided me with warmth, hospitality, friendship, encouragement, and a sense of rootedness in Ireland.

In the north, Joe Mulvenna, Kevin Boyle, Sean McCann, Geoffrey Morris, Donal and Pauline Murphy, Madeline Stewart, Edwina Stewart, Eilis MacDermot, Madge Davidson, Brendan Harrison, Bridget and Johnny Bond, Louis Boyle, Tommy Stitt, Jim Sullivan, Jimmy Drumm, Gerry O'Keefe, Emily Gibson, the Kerr family and many others housed, fed, entertained, instructed me, introduced me around, and otherwise incorporated me into their lives even at time of enormous difficulty. For too brief a period I enjoyed the help of Elaine Patrick, my student research assistant. Kathleen O'Connell, another student, helped index the book.

At home and in the field, my children, Marc, Shawn, Cathy, and Miriam, accompanied me and contributed their valuable insights and aid. All of them derived unique and important kinds of maturity through their Irish experiences. My father has stood ready to encourage and help me despite his anxieties about my safety and his terrible disappointment about the fate of my earlier book.

My editor, Ken Arnold, and his predecessor, Maurice English, have been valuable friends, as well as technicians for this work.

Finally, this book owes its existence and I owe my gratitude to all the people who offered me a place in a bed in their tiny crowded houses, a cup of tea in their parlors, and their inner perspective for my understanding; to all the children who eargerly lined up for the dull business of psychological testing and stayed on afterward to play and talk and cuddle with a stranger; the sad-eyed men who stumbled out of internment camps and away from interrogation centers shamed and hurt and yet trusting that perhaps the extra burden of my testing would in some way bring surcease from their nightmares and pain.

To all of these people I am indebted and grateful. I am proud to be considered a part of their lives, as they are now so much the fabric of my own life.

R. M. F.

Introduction

Ireland—The Victim

There is a saying in Ireland—"fighting like a couple of Kilkenny cats"—which implies a kind of mortal combat undertaken by desperate individuals. The saying arose from an incident that, like most incidents of several hundred years ago, was either historical, apocryphal, or mythical. It was the seventeenth-century siege of Kilkenny, an old and small city near the center of Ireland that held fast against the invading English armies half a dozen times or more between the fifteenth and seventeenth centuries. This time it was Cromwell's army, it is said, which, when they had finally broken through the defenses of the besieged town, set out to slaughter every living thing. Not a person nor a cow was to be left alive, for they were all Irish, and by order everything Irish was to be "extirpated." They slaughtered the priests, every one they could find, in terrible ways. Then they set about with sword and with their bare hands and with fire to massacre the men, women, and babies. When they'd finished with the human inhabitants, the soldiers, despite their weariness, went to work slaughtering the cattle and then the dogs and the sheep. When they came to the cats, they were tired and a little bored, so they invented something new: they strung a line between two trees and, having gathered up all the cats, tied them by their tails, two by two, and flung them over the line. Well, cats being cats, they clawed and chewed each other to death.

The story is historically uncertain, but the slaughters and scorched-earth policies of successive English invasions are not only historical facts, but also a feature of contemporary social psychology of Ireland. The Irish people have a psychohistory predicated on siege, manipulation, victimization, wanton destruction and self-destruction like that of the Kilkenny cats.

It is currently out of vogue to relate the history of Ireland in terms of colonial oppression, bloody revolutions, foiled struggles for liberation, economic devastation, and martyrdom. The current Irish Minister for Posts and Communication, Conor Cruise O'Brien, a noted literary critic and historian, has eloquently argued that this kind of history has been self-defeating and worse—self-deluding. The current "troubles" in the north, as they are called, are but another evidence, he says, of the reality of two Irelands.[1] If this is so, then writing about the Irish past must acknowledge a discontinuity predicated on the geopolitical border fixed in 1922 as a compromise to terminate years of bloodshed on that island. But in spite of that separation, the death toll by political violence has persisted north and south of the border to this date. The political imprisonment of thousands of men and women, north and south, during the past decade would also suggest that the history of Ireland before 1922 is not merely an archaic myth.

There can be room for argument on the issue of premeditated, organized, schematic destruction of the Irish people versus happenstance.[2] But the evidence of destruction stands clearly by itself. The partitioning of the island is more a symbol of the social dynamics unleashed by centuries of oppression and colonial rule than it is a measure of the level of destruction. The solution for the "troubles" remains as ephemeral and unreachable as the mists and rainbows hovering over the Irish countryside.

Woodrow Wilson labeled the "Irish question" "the great metaphysical issue of all time . . ." and then proceeded to ignore it in setting forth the tasks of the League of Nations for assuring self-determination by all other European peoples.[3] But precisely because the Irish problem has persisted for so long, and because the various solutions attempted have so often presaged application to other parts of the world (with equivalent failure), it becomes imperative to examine the case of the Irish people.

In terms of twentieth-century history, Ireland was the first colony granted independence; it was the first nation partitioned into two separate political units; urban guerrilla warfare, which has marked the independence campaigns of later liberation movements, started in Ireland. Whether directly or indirectly, twentieth-century liberation movements have emulated the tactics and often the black beret uniform of the Irish Republican Army.

Earlier, many other strategies and tactics for social movements originated in Ireland, too. The boycott, a tactic frequently utilized by labor and nationalist groups during the twentieth century, has Irish origins in the Land League movement for agrarian reform during the latter half of the nineteenth century.[4] The hunger strike, a tactic adopted by groups as diverse as the Suffragists and the Gandhians, originated in early Celtic practice and twentieth-century Irish prisoners' protest.[5] Such tactics and programs emanated from the earlier applications of colonialism, racism, and cultural genocide to the Irish people by their British conquerors from at least the fourteenth century. The Irish were the first to experience British colonial policy as racism and genocide. These policies were later incorporated in the practices against the American Indian populations of North

America (who were frequently likened to "wild Irishmen" by their colonial persecutors).[6]

The most recent period of conflagration on the island has taken more than sixteen hundred lives within half a decade. It has featured an apparently fratricidal campaign that is variously interpreted by those unfamiliar with the history of colonialism in Ireland as an archaic residue of Reformation religious rivalries, as a sectarian feud, or even as a revolt of the working class.[7] Outside Ireland, the struggles in its northern six counties are seldom correlated with the national liberation struggles of former African colonies; nor are they compared with the insurgency campaigns of Basques and Catalonians against the fascist Franco government of Spain. Even less often are the historical experiences of the Irish people compared with the genocidal enactments against European Jews and against Armenians under the Ottoman Empire, or with the decimation of the American Indian population.

Yet the Irish were among the first to experience victimization from fascism, genocide, national liberation struggles, and colonial exploitation. Ethnically, the population called "Irish" is a mixture of Celts, Picts, Angles, Saxons, Normans, Norsemen, Spaniards, Portuguese, and Dutch. There is not even an appropriate definition of the Irish as an ethnic group. Despite cartoon depictions of the Irish Savage Buffoon in *Punch* cartoons of the nineteenth and early twentieth century, and romanticized descriptions of the dark-haired, fair-skinned, blue-eyed beauty of Kathleen Ni Houlihan, there is no anthropologically accurate format for measuring Irish ethnicity. For the Irish are an ethnic blend of nearly all European peoples. Their far island was early inhabited by a people referred to by the Romans as *Scotti* (fierce fighters) and then invaded by the Gaelic Celts who had migrated from the mountains and shores of northern Portugal and Spain, while other Celtic tribes found their home in Britain and Brittany. Latins and Phoenicians found the island of Ireland not long after the Celts, but did not stay there in any great numbers during the early centuries. The Vikings raided and then settled mostly on the south coasts of Ireland; their names and genes were assimilated with the mainstream and some of the Viking habits and culture were carried by that mainstream.[8] The next invasion and settlement was Norman—an ethnic combination not unlike that which already inhabited the place, since the Normans themselves were descendants of Celts, Vikings, and other west European strains. The invasion of the Normans marked a different kind of turning point. Although they too became Irishized in later years, they brought a feudal system, which was superimposed on a pastoral communal economic system in which not even property rights issued by automatic inheritance, but rather through a combination of individual choices and group consensus, defined through a complex legal system, propounded by oral tradition until the sixth century.[9]

But that was not the last ethnic invasion. Scots, themselves for long so close as to be almost indistinguishable, persisted in crossing back and forth over the island chain separating Ireland from Scotland, continually adding their genetic and cultural stock into the pool. And it was not long before small groups of Spaniards, Portuguese, and a smaller proportion of Italian and French sailors and soldiers, either through shipwreck or battle alliances with the Irish against the British, also settled in Ireland. The English themselves—a mixture of Anglo-Saxon and Celt, Norman and Dutch, settled in Ireland or adventured in Ireland, leaving their mark with considerable genetic intermingling. A few Spanish and Portuguese Jews, fleeing the Inquisition, found safe refuge in the south of Ireland and joined the earlier settlement of English Jews who had formed a community in Dublin.[10]

The late President of the Irish Republic, Erskine Childers, was himself a descendant of the combination of Gaelic Celt, Anglo-Saxon, and Sephardic Jewish, which epitomized the ethnic mixture of the island. Ireland had indeed achieved a genuine melting pot long before the colonization of the Americas. Over and over again, new immigrants—whether they came as invaders, as settlers, or as slaves, like St. Patrick himself—became Irish and welcome.

Perhaps the cultural abyss between the Irish and their captors was a product of the persistence of the Gaelic Celtic ways into the sixteenth and seventeenth centuries, standing in sharp contrast with the English (and other Europeans') feudal systems and mercantilism. The Irish, like the American Indians and the Siberian natives later subdued by the Russians, existed for the most part in a pastoral communal economy and tribal society that contradicted the entire concept of civilization and order then prevalent in Europe. Most important, their persistence in this pattern defied the English determination to "develop the resources" of Ireland, to the advantage of the English economy, by providing from it taxes to support their government.

In the historical experience of the Irish people are some of the earliest recorded successful guerrilla warfare operations against the regular forces of Elizabethan England and against which some of the most prominent English military scholars and leaders, such as Humphrey Gilbert and Thomas Gainsford, devised "pacification" actions, which consisted of burning down people, homes, pastureland, and crops.[11]

The earlier Irish liberation movements, climaxing with the one led by the Great O'Neill, were terminated in the seventeenth century through the *complete* destruction of the Irish countryside and most of its *population.* Whereas in 1366 to be Irish was to be outside the law,* by the second

---

*The Statutes of Kilkenny, enacted in 1366, consisted of thirty-five acts that forbade the use of the Irish language, Brehon (Irish) law, Irish surnames, costume, Irish

half of the seventeenth century, everything Irish was outlawed—the language, the legal system, the clerics, and religion—even the relationship of the person to the land of his or her birth.

This constitutes one of the earliest examples of the relationship between ascription of "race" and prejudicial treatment by law. It is also an early example of the definition of ascription of difference of human capacities by virtue of inherited superiorities. The statutes also incorporated one of the earliest European formulations prohibiting miscegenation. As we shall see in later chapters, the social distancing prescribed by such statutes would ultimately provide the framework for the destruction of masses of people by virtue of their race as much as of their religion.

During the fifth through the thirteenth centuries, the Irish wandered the face of the earth as scholarly missionaries and as mercenary soldiers.[12] From the time of Cromwell's invasion to the present, the Irish have wandered as refugees and emigrants—and even as slaves. For Cromwell's executives shipped off thousands of Irish children, aged eight through twelve, to become slaves in Barbados and other British Caribbean holdings.[13]

Until the reign of Henry VIII, in the latter part of the sixteenth century, the Anglo-Normans, established in Ireland as the ascendancy but assimilated with the native Gaels, focused their political attentions on the monarchy, and on their battles with one another and against the Gaelic chiefs for lands and titles. Henry's disestablishment of the Church, the papal reaction to his schism, and the resulting rift between adherents of the two communions set the stage for the pseudo-religious wars that turned Ireland into a battlefield during the seventeenth century. Ironically, the Anglo-Irish aristocracy that rebelled against Elizabeth I found common cause with the Stuart kings against the parliamentarians.

Queen Elizabeth proved more determined than her father to excise Catholicism from her kingdom.[14] Her military commanders, some of whom had served at the Spanish court, extended her colonial aspirations to the western hemisphere and saw the political instability of the Irish territories as a serious threat to the continuity of the new empire. Ireland's disloyalty to Elizabeth posed a threat from two directions. First, it threatened to prevent access to the New World colonies and trade. Second, the Spaniards, who had supported the claim of Mary to the throne, were in league with the dissident Catholic aristocracy of Ireland, and indeed, in the final battle of the last native Irish king, Hugh O'Neill, the Spanish sent their forces to

---

riding, music, poetry, and epic. Those of Irish surname were defined as "of servile conditions" and without rights to property or trade. Curtis refers to these laws as "The Outlawry of the Irish Race." The statutes were aimed at halting or reversing the trend of assimilation into the native Irish polity.

Kinsale to aid the Irish attempt to oust the English.[15] The flight of the earls of Tyrone (the Great O'Neill) and Tyrconnell (Red Hugh O'Donnell) and their loyal chiefs marked the end of Gaelic Ulster and the foundation of the first Ulster plantation in 1608. But this was only the beginning of the seventeenth-century wars between the Anglo-Irish lords and the crown. Between 1641 and the Battle of the Boyne in 1690, which marked the victory of William of Orange, there were repeated uprisings. Cromwell's invasion of Ireland in August of 1649 took on the character of a religious war as Cromwell's forces sought to establish the primacy of Parliament and puritanism while the Irish nobles gave their support to the Stuart monarchy and Catholicism. A series of settlement acts followed, which encouraged the plantation of English and Scottish settlers on lands taken from the native Irish, who were excluded from more than half the island. The geographic redistribution of the Irish population played a major role in establishing the east–west division of Ireland into Gaelic and Anglo-Saxon culture zones, respectively.[16] The real division of Ireland has continued on these East/West lines to the present day. Language, culture, and even economic status are thus segregated.

Ironically, King William had the covert support of the Vatican for his claim to the British crown. The Stuart dynasty had, through their alliances with France, presented a threat to the primacy of Rome as the center of the faith. While Irish Protestants commemorate the lifting of the Siege of Derry by the forces of King William (1689) and the victory of the battle of the Boyne (1690), the Battle of Aughrim on July 12, 1691, and the Treaty of Limerick (1692) marked the end of Stuart claims. From 1692 until 1829 Catholics were excluded from Parliament and public office. The Penal Laws, established in 1693, excluded Catholics from owning land, livestock, weapons, or even a horse worth over £5. In 1704, Protestant Dissenters (Presbyterians, Congregationalists, Methodists) were excluded from office by the Test Act. The eighteenth-century Irish populace was demoralized, enslaved, and progressively separated from its native Gaelic culture.[17]

Roman Catholicism became a major influence (in contrast to Irish Catholicism) when, in the eighteenth and early nineteenth centuries, the Penal Laws prevented the training of any priests in Ireland (in fact, attempted to prevent the practice of Catholicism entirely). Irish Catholicism, which had somehow managed to bypass much of that influence in its earlier phases, came increasingly under the influence of Rome and Augustinian Catholicism, which had a major impact.[18] When the State authorized funds for Maynooth College as a seminary for the training of priests in 1792, it was less an act of concession to the religious needs of the majority Catholic population than an attempt to ensure a loyal clergy not "contaminated" by the ideas of republicanism so popular then on the continent. The loyalty of clerics was further assured by making them take an oath to the crown. Meanwhile, the native Irish population had been denied access to education for over a hundred years, and their only learning was achieved through "hedge" schools taught by poets, priests, and laymen in hiding.[19] The population as a whole was thoroughly pauperized and demoralized by forced moves, emigration, evictions, cyclical famines, and religious persecutions. The obliteration of Irish law and custom was thus completed within a couple of generations in the seventeenth century. The Act of Union in 1800, which tied Ireland into the United Kingdom and eliminated any semblance of home rule, marked a final turning point in the imposition of English Common Law and the obliteration of the Gaelic culture. When Catholic Emancipation was enacted in 1829 and the National Education system founded in 1831, even the Gaelic language became a handicap for the Irish in participating in their own society, and it, too, throughout the century became extinct over most of the country.[20]

Under the new laws the education of Catholics and their access to professions and government were severely restricted. Until the late nineteenth century, socioeconomic mobility (ordinarily predicated on education and ownership) was nonexistent. The minor advances during the latter half of the nineteenth century and the early twentieth century only served to reinforce the existing social framework of political and economic power as equivalent with membership and family origins in Church of Ireland.

The rigidity has been further reinforced and made evident by the pattern of heavy emigration caused by job scarcity. It is impossible to understand the social structure and personality of the Irish people without examining the economic condition that exerts the threat which prescribes for them a closed-minded society.[21]

Republicanism, in contrast to the earlier attempts to shake off English rule, was not based on sectarianism, nor did it derive from the grievances of various elements in the aristocracy against the crown or Parliament. Also in contrast with earlier attempts at revolution, eighteenth-century republicanism was an ideology with universal appeal in Europe, and had been realized through the establishment of the new American nation. Ironically, it was developed partly out of the Cromwellian revolution in England.[22] Many young Irishmen, educated in France and having traveled in America, became convinced that in republicanism lay the only salvation from the unequal treatment given them as colonials. In the last decade of the eighteenth century, two political organizations were founded that were to become mortal contenders for the allegiance and direction of the Irish people. The father of Irish republicanism, Theobald Wolfe Tone, son of a Protestant coachmaker of farming background, became secretary to the

Catholic Committee in 1790 and in 1791 founded the Society of the United Irishmen. In 1795, when the Society became revolutionary, the Orange Order was founded.[23] The Order was relatively insignificant and obscure at first, and during its first hundred years was often banned or otherwise discredited as a troublesome, trouble-making, and politically irrelevant group. The United Irishmen, on the other hand, was a nonsectarian, articulate, and popular group, which appealed to Protestants, Catholics, and Dissenters for its membership. They were committed to Catholic emancipation, democracy, abolition of all religious distinctions, and true representation in a national parliament. The Orange Order claimed itself committed "to maintain the laws and peace of the country and the Protestant Constitution, and to defend the King and his heirs as long as they shall maintain the Protestant ascendancy."[24] While the Orange Order pursued, killed, and forced out of Ulster many thousands of Catholics, Presbyterians and militant Catholics enrolled in the United Irishmen in ever increasing numbers. The Insurrection Act of 1796, passed by the Irish Parliament, was an early model for what were later to become known as the Special Powers Acts. These acts allowed the Lord Lieutenant to place any districts under martial law, imposed the death penalty for administering an unlawful oath, and empowered magistrates to *seize suspects** and send them to serve in the fleet. Habeas corpus was suspended for all Ireland, and Ulster, considered the dangerous province, was ordered disarmed in 1797. Belfast, the rebel town, was on the verge of rising even after the failure of an attempted French landing engineered and accompanied by Tone in December, 1796. Cork, Galway, and Limerick were the centers of loyalism to the crown. On May 23, 1798, rebellion broke out in Antrim, Down, Meath, and elsewhere in Leinster. On May 26, a rebellion that broke out in Wexford was not suppressed for a month. When the rebellion was put down in Wexford, it disintegrated into a kind of guerrilla warfare, oftentimes a battle between Orange and Green. The British exacted fierce vengeance. The rebellion continued in fits and starts throughout 1798, and in another attempted landing of French troops to aid the rebels, Wolfe Tone was captured and, along with most of the other leaders of the United Irishmen, was hanged as a common criminal. Although the Irish Parliament had been quite loyal to the crown, it was disbanded by the Act of Union in 1800. This act initiated a new political cause to be undertaken by the still nascent movement of Irish republicanism.[25]

The various uprisings during the nineteenth century strengthened the connection between republicanism and Catholic rights. The islands formally became known as the United Kingdom of Great Britain and Ireland. Ire-

*Suspects were punished without charge or trial.

land was contained in the Union through the efforts of an occupation army numbering up to 200,000 men.

The costs to the crown for maintaining its hegemony in Ireland continued to exceed the crown revenues largely because such a large number of troops was required to maintain public order in a place in which the lands were mostly held by absentee landlords whose utilization of them was far below a productive level. During the time of the Penal Laws, potato cultivation was introduced into Ireland, and by the nineteenth century it had become the primary food supply for the large masses of Irish tenant farmers. The land continued to produce cereals, dairy products, and meat animals, but those who tended these crops seldom had the opportunity to partake of them. They were largely sold and shipped to England. Thus during the famine of the 1840's (not the first but the most extensive famine of that century in Ireland), these products continued to be exported for the profit of the landowners, while the population of Ireland declined from 10,000,000 to 6,000,000 as thousands died by the roadsides from starvation, and thousands more died from diseases connected with the famine.[26] Several million Irish emigrated to the western hemisphere in vessels known as "coffin ships," which sometimes sank with all aboard within sight of the harbor of departure. The average Irish peasant produced the butter and bread for England but could not afford to eat any of it. Landlords seeking to increase their revenues threw peasants off the land to turn it over for grazing herds, while peasant families wandered homeless along the roads and made rude shelters for themselves in ditches from which they were ousted by constables and soldiers.

Daniel O'Connell succeeded in his struggle for Catholic Emancipation with the passage of the Catholic Emancipation Bill in 1829. The Reform Act of 1832, which permitted free entrance of Irish manufactured goods (primarily emanating from Belfast) into England, for the most part satisfied the Protestant northerners' grievances and linked them closer with the Union. O'Connell embarked on a campaign for repeal of the Act of Union and held huge rallies to which thousands of Catholic peasants walked distances of fifty miles or more. Meanwhile, Thomas Davis, Gavin Duffy, and others had formed the Young Ireland movement, which through its newspaper *The Nation* advocated a new brand of militant nationalism. The famine of 1845–1847 and the Young Ireland Movement were an inevitable but unfortunate coincidence. The rising of 1848, coming as it did in the throes of famine, could not but fail. The Young Irelanders who were primarily urban and educated were more successful in stimulating later movements than in bringing to fruition their own separatist objectives.[27] The mid-nineteenth century nevertheless marked the initiation of conflicting strategies for nationalism that have been echoed in later struggles to the present time—constitutionalism versus armed insurrection. The Fenian rising of 1867, with its corresponding development of Irish republicanism among the growing Irish population in the United States, also marked a strategic advance in the struggle for Irish freedom from British rule. Since that time there has been a consistent and articulate overseas support system for Irish republican aspirations. This was to prove decisive in the later Anglo-Irish War of 1918–1921.

In 1879, Michael Davitt founded the Land League, which culminated in 1903 with the Wyndham Land Act and thoroughly repudiated the system of tenancy that had beggared the Irish peasants for two hundred years. Between these events Lord Randolph Churchill, in his bid for leadership of the Conservative Party, played his infamous "Orange card." In 1886, addressing an enthusiastic Orange crowd in Belfast, he urged them to resist home rule. His speeches resulted in the Orange slogans "Ulster will fight and Ulster will be right" and "Home rule is Rome rule," which may still be seen scrawled on the walls of houses in the Shankill of Belfast and Waterside of Derry (Londonderry) in 1976.

During the nineteenth century, Belfast, a relatively new city in the northern county of Antrim, developed as a center for manufacturing linen and for shipbuilding. Meanwhile, Dublin, the only major city in Ireland, once the center for government and culture, languished after the Act of Union, developing little in the way of commerce, manufacturing, or trade. The famine affected the western or most primitive rural areas in Ireland far more than it affected counties Antrim or Dublin. The misery of homeless, starving people was more often evidenced, however, in Dublin, where they sometimes came to embark for foreign refuge or to seek governmental redress. Queen Victoria made several triumphal tours in Ireland, one of which occurred during the height of the famine. Consistent with Dublin's history as the cultural center of the English pale, Victoria integrated her visit into the social life of that city. There was no question of the two cities being antagonistic capitals of separate states, however. Differences were emerging, though, in the kinds of political organizing that began to develop in the two places. Dublin remained the center for intellectual and artistic catalysis. The Young Ireland Movement, Fenians, Land League, Gaelic League, and Sinn Fein (founded at the turn of the century) centered there. Sectarian riots had become regular occurrences in Belfast, and by the last quarter of the nineteenth century these disorders had provoked the development of a dual constabulary system and various governing measures not required in Dublin. From the city's inception, however, Belfast housing and jobs were based on the Acts of Settlement (of the seventeenth century), which had given more favorable terms to non-Catholic settlers in Ulster for land and housing.[28] The bonds of unity that had developed between Dissenters and Catholics in the United Irishmen movement were not allowed to remain or to become re-established in Belfast during the nineteenth century. Although many Protestants had contributed to the construction of the first Roman Catholic Church in Belfast early in the nineteenth century, thirty-five years later, Protestant mobs were attacking that same church, and continued to do so in rioting that broke out at least once in every decade thereafter. In other parts of Ireland, however, repeal of the Act of Union was coupled with Irish republicanism in a common cause shared by Catholics and Protestants.

In 1912, the Third Home Rule Bill was introduced into the United Kingdom parliament. Unionists had organized themselves to oppose home rule and within the year, on September 28, 1912, Lord Edward Carson and his confederates signed the Solemn League and Covenant dedicated to maintaining the Union. The Home Rule Bill was defeated in the House of Lords in January, 1913, and the Ulster Volunteer Force was organized.[29] In that same year, Irish trade unionists declared a general strike and, under the leadership of James Connolly and James Larkin, the Citizen Army for a time successfully impeded the mammoth efforts of military, strikebreakers, and constabulary to force an end to the strike. The Irish Volunteers, launched in effect by the Irish Republican Brotherhood in 1913, came under the sway of John Redmond before taking a more definite stand—with fewer members—in September, 1914. The Irish Republican Brotherhood, a secret military organization, had found common cause with the new Sinn Fein party organized by Arthur Griffith as a nationalist alternative to Redmond's Irish Party.

The Easter Monday Rising of 1916 has been variously interpreted as a confused accident and as a deliberate sacrifice intended to mobilize militant opposition to British rule.[30] In fact, some of the confusions and disasters attendant upon Roger Casement's arms shipment and the call-up of the Irish Volunteers are attributed to the leaders' determination that the rebellion should take place rather than to its military success.[31] During the month between St. Patrick's Day, 1916, and Good Friday, numerous incidents signaled the British leadership that rebellion was close at hand. Nonetheless, after banishing some republican leaders from Ireland at the end of March, they considered the rebellion to be headed off and completely aborted with the sinking of the *AUD*, which carried weapons and ammunition from Germany to the rebel forces, and the arrest of Roger Casement. Not until Easter Monday morning did Augustine Birrell, Chief Secretary for Ireland, issue orders for the arrest of one hundred of the leaders.

The Rising lasted nearly a week in Dublin, while smaller scattered attempts at rebellion took place in various parts of Ireland, confused by the contradictory orders issued by Patrick Pearse, key man of the IRB in the Volunteers, and Eoin MacNeill, commanding officer of the Irish Volunteers. The British army called up reinforcements and the gunship *Helga* pounded away at targets in the center of Dublin city; while the rebels held buildings and positions in factories, mills, and public buildings, the army attacked civilian targets—houses, pedestrians, and shops throughout Dublin.[32] In the rest of the country, wherever a rebellion was put down, the rebels who were caught by the authorities and the military were rounded up and deported to internment camps and jails in England and Wales. The feelings of the majority of people in Dublin and the countryside are reported to have been for the most part against the rebels.

On May 3, 1916, Pearse, McDonagh, and Clarke, three of the signatories to the Proclamation of the Irish Republic were executed by a firing squad and buried in quicklime graves. On May 4, four more executions were carried out and seventeen other court-martial sentences of death were announced. On May 5, John MacBride was executed and William Cosgrave's death sentence was commuted. The next day eighteen death sentences were commuted to penal servitude, including that of Constance Markiewicz, the woman who had founded Na Fianna Eireann and herself held a position of military command during Easter week.

Pearse's theory of the "Blood Sacrifice"[33] echoed in his poetry and, consistent with Irish legend and myth, seemed to be fulfilling its purpose. As the executions continued, the people of Ireland who had opposed or been apathetic to the rising were revolted by the retribution exacted by the British government against these men. Four more leaders were shot on May 7, including two young leaders of Na Fianna Eireann, Con Colbert and Sean Heuston, as well as another signatory of the proclamation, Eamon Ceannt (Kent).

James Connolly, severely wounded in action and hospitalized, was taken by stretcher into the courts martial where he was condemned to death by firing squad. He and Sean MacDermott, on May 12, 1916, were the last executed.

There were 3,000 arrests of which 1,867 persons were interned at a special camp in Wales.

The executions had excited sympathy among Irish Americans and among non-Irish people throughout the western world. To counter this climate, the Home Rule Bill was rushed through Parliament yet again. Ulster unionists conceded the right of home rule for twenty-six of Ireland's counties if Ulster could be excluded; the nationalists accepted exclusion only of four counties—Derry (Londonderry), Antrim, Down, and Armagh —and that for only a temporary period. Predictably, negotiations broke down. On August 3, 1916, Roger Casement, having some years before been knighted by the King, was hanged in an English jail, thus becoming the sixteenth of the Easter Week martyrs. Lloyd George had given Edward Carson, leader of the Ulster Unionists, a secret pledge of exclusion of the six northeastern counties from the Home Rule Bill, but Carson's position was not the popularly held view of Irish unionists, who for the most part may well have accepted the inevitability of home rule and committed themselves to participation in it.[34] But, by the end of 1916, Lloyd George had succeeded Asquith as Prime Minister and Edward Carson, Walter Long, Bonar Law, and others who had urged Ulster resistance to home rule in 1914 became Irish members of the British government.

Political activity in England and Ireland proceeded throughout 1917 but did not really fuse into a single party or objective until April, 1918, when the war cabinet (of which several were Ulster unionists opposing home rule) decided to extend conscription to Ireland. The effect was to strengthen Sinn Fein within a matter of days. The Irish Catholic hierarchy, which had earlier opposed the revolution, came out in opposition to conscription. All political parties declared the right of the Irish people to resist conscription, but Sinn Fein advocated independence, and in the by-elections of that year Sinn Fein won one after another. Arthur Griffith and the other leaders of the Sinn Fein executive were jailed, but the party managed to sweep the general election of 1918, electing into office many of those who were at the time behind bars.

From 1919 until 1921, all of Ireland was a bloody battleground as the Irish Republican Army, organized in small local units, attacked police and army barracks, ambushed patrols, and took over towns. The British government was militarily exhausted by its continental war and had difficulty raising troops to fight again in Ireland. Consequently, it initiated the auxiliaries from among the veteran officer corps, and the infamous Black and Tans were recruited to fill the depleted ranks of the Royal Irish Constabulary. There were eventually about 7,000 of them in addition to the army and auxiliaries. They were allegedly recruited from English jails, but there is considerable disagreement with this popular thesis and one authority points out that up to one-third of the group was recruited from northeast Ulster.[35] There is no question, however, that they left a legacy of terrorism and destruction that drove even the most pacific nationalist inhabitants of that island to identification with the Irish Republican Army.

Lloyd George's Amending Act had allowed the six counties of northeast Ulster to vote themselves out of home rule, and while the war for independence raged, the Unionists of these six counties formed, under the 1920 Act, a parliament that George V opened on June 22, 1921.

Michael Collins and Arthur Griffith were designated by the Dail Eireann (Irish parliament) and its president, Eamon de Valera, to attend the treaty negotiations in London in November, 1921. Some authorities argue that they were deliberately selected in order to cast the onus of the results on two powerful rivals for the allegiance and adulation of the Irish people. From the start, the prospect of their winning an all-Ireland independence agreement was impossible.[36] The northern six counties had already been conceded to the unionists and the only alteration to the prior secret commitment was the agreement to appoint a boundary commission that would negotiate the final partition. Collins and Griffith were faced with the prospect of massive British military and naval retaliation if the IRA continued its campaign.

The signing of the treaty on December 6, 1921, and its ratification by a majority of the Dail on January 7, 1922, marked the end of the campaign against British occupation and the beginning of the Irish civil war. Two tumultuous years of fratricide and destruction followed, during which Collins himself was killed at the height of his popularity,* a short time after Arthur Griffith, who had been acclaimed President of the new Free State, had died of a heart attack. Eamon de Valera led the republican forces against the Free State Army until, in 1923, with his famous address to the "soldiers of the rearguard," he disbanded the Republican Army and sought to continue the struggle on the political level.[37] Ironically, the political party initiated by Arthur Griffith, Sinn Fein, became the rallying point for the anti-Free State forces. In 1923, while standing for election in his home county of Clare, De Valera was arrested and imprisoned for a year in Dublin. Partisan killings continued although, by that year, the Free State government had executed seventy-seven of its opponents and imposed a mandatory death sentence on those who led armed opposition to it. Kevin O'Higgins, who was responsible for ordering the execution of his former secretary and his close friend, Rory O'Connor and Erskine Childers, among others, was himself brutally murdered.

In 1927, the year of the O'Higgins slaying, de Valera recognized the futility of the abstentionist policy of the Sinn Fein, which, although running for office and having had members elected, refused to serve in the government because to take office meant taking an oath to the king. He created a new party, Fianna Fail, and entered the Dail by signing his name in the book without taking the oath. This, of course, split Sinn Fein once again. de Valera's Fianna Fail party was elected to power in 1923 and set about producing a new constitution, which was ratified in 1937 and by virtue of which the Irish Free State declared itself the Republic of Ireland.

The Irish constitution refers to all of Ireland and, upon occasion, the government of the Free State of the Irish Republic has acted as if this whole were its responsibility (as in protesting to the United States government its establishment of bases in the north during the Second World War). The constitution also established and only recently abolished the

---

*The Free Staters, led by Collins, accepted the terms of the treaty. They later organized themselves as the Fine Gael party. Sinn Fein and its military wing, the IRA, refused to accept the treaty.

constitutional prerogative of the Roman Catholic Church as standing in a favored position in *Ireland* (the issue most often argued by unionists against unification of the two Irelands; the second most often argued issue is the economic inferiority of Eire to the United Kingdom). Of course, what is meant by the "south," or the "Irish Republic," or "Eire" are the twenty-six counties that have preponderantly Catholic populations. What is meant by "Ulster," "Northern Ireland," or "Great Britain and Ireland" is the six counties, of which three have a majority of Protestant populations and three others have about equal parts Protestant and Catholic.

Polarization and factionalization of the south have been endemic since the signing of the treaty in 1921. The border fixed by partition had never functioned to separate the two parts of Ireland from each others' troubles.

Ireland has always been a country with strong provincial loyalties and rivalries. It is not uncommon to hear a Dubliner say, "Yes, I want a united Ireland, but leave Belfast out of it!" Or conversely, to hear a Belfast nationalist exclaim, "Ulster's the 'head of the dog' and Dublin's nearer its arse!" (referring to the shape of the island as a somewhat irregularly outlined dog. Turn the map sideways and this shape becomes apparent).

There is a perverse kind of nomenclature that reflects the confusion, conflict, and ambiguity with which people in the Irish Republic look upon events in the north. To begin with, diehard republicans (and this includes Sinn Fein of both wings, officials and provisionals, as well as many who would vote Fianna Fail, Fine Gael, or Labour) consider their war for independence incomplete. Doubt and debate continue about the "real" nature of the treaty that was signed, the nature of the Border Commission and its recommendations, the Government of Ireland Act, and all the constitutional and international law matters attendant upon this confusion.

The nomenclature refers to "Ulster" as a province of Great Britain, but the Province of Ulster also exists in the Irish Republic in the form of three of Ulster's original nine counties—Donegal, Monaghan, and Cavan. The three counties in Eire are referred to as "Northern Ireland" but the northernmost part of the island is Mallinhead, situated securely in Donegal and part of the Irish Republic. The term "Irish Republic" suggests that the state is independent of Britain, yet Britain formally acknowledged its separation from dominion status as declared by de Valera ten years after de Valera declared it, but he recognized it as a "part of Ireland."

The effects of the treaty and the subsequent civil war and new constitution on the government of the six counties in northeast Ulster served to support their parliament's claim to legitimacy. Although the articles of the treaty were intended to supersede the Government of Ireland Act, 1920, the requisite conditions were never enforced. Liam de Paor, a member of the Irish Labour Party and historian, suggests that

The 'Articles of Agreement for a Treaty between Great Britain and Ireland' signed in London on 6 December 1921 related to the whole of Ireland, and, subject to a certain condition, they superceded the Government of Ireland Act, 1920. The condition was that for a month after the passing of the act of parliament for ratifying the articles, they should not apply in Northern Ireland, and that within that month the parliament of Northern Ireland might present an address to the crown the effect of which would be that in the six counties the Government of Ireland would continue to have effect, while the treaty articles would apply only in the remaining twenty-six counties. In other words, Northern Ireland might opt out, which it promptly did. The rest of Ireland was given commonwealth status under the crown, as the 'Irish Free State', whose position 'in relation to the Imperial Parliament and Government and otherwise shall be that of the Dominion of Canada. . . . ' While the war was still going on, the new government negotiated with representatives of the southern unionists, that is the Protestant ascendancy which had held sway in Ireland until now, in a strenuous effort to reassure them as to their own respectability now that the English had left. Rural revolutionary movements—the setting up of soviets in some areas, the burning out of country houses and the taking over of estates by the local tenants—were effectively checked within a few years; the left wing of the republican movement was broken, chiefly by the shooting of prisoners; every effort was made to safeguard property. Institutions of the guerrilla period, such as the Sinn Fein courts, which had functioned as underground rivals of the English courts (sometimes effectively), and the Sinn Fein police, were dismantled, and were where possible replaced by restoring what had preceded them. Most of the apparatus of colonial administration was restored, although some parts of it, such as the Royal Irish Constabulary, must because of the odium in which they had been held, be swept away. A new, unarmed, police force was established—a daring but successful move in time of civil war. In general, the new government made every effort to demonstrate that it was not revolutionary, and in this it was on the whole successful. By the middle 1920's in social terms, counter-revolution was triumphant in Ireland north and south.[38]

The partition of Ireland has remained outside the international arena, although there had been a strong impetus from Ireland to bring the issue to the League of Nations negotiations. Much later, after the 1969 pogroms in Belfast and Derry, the Irish ambassador to the United Nations circuitously inserted the issue in a speech to that body while permitting the abuse of the Catholic minority in the six counties to remain defined as a problem "internal" to the United Kingdom.

In every decade since partition, campaigns have been waged by the Irish Republican Army to eliminate the border, marked by blowing up customs posts along the border, attacking army or police barracks, and breaking into armories to remove the weapons for their own use. In each decade, too, the government of the north has instituted internment and the government in the south has usually tightened its own legislation to allow preventive detention as well. Traditionally, however, the courts of the Irish Republic have been unwilling to try persons accused of criminal offenses in the north (especially when these are usually politically motivated cases) and to honor extradition requests from Stormont castle, home of the parliament of Northern Ireland. During World War II, de Valera extended the trade war of the 1930's with Britain into a policy of neutrality that typified the kind of "aggressive nonviolence" which has characterized so many tactics in Irish history. de Valera not only refused to enter the war with the allies and forbade the use of Irish ports for allied bases, but also maintained relations with Germany throughout the war and interned downed fliers from both sides. But his economic war with the United Kingdom in the end seemed to have hurt Ireland more than England. The postwar era of Irish politics was ushered in by a coalition government headed by Fine Gael (as the pro-treaty party came to be known) and including Clann na Poblachta, a new legal republican party; that government achieved final dissolution of the tie with Britain. In 1948, the Westminster parliament agreed to the condition already announced in the 1938 constitution of Ireland: the twenty-six counties would be known as Eire and would, in fact, be the Republic of Ireland, not a part of the British Commonwealth. The British Government's Ireland Act of 1949 furthermore refused to treat citizens of the Irish Republic as aliens and spelled out the special relationship of Britain to the Northern Ireland parliament (Stormont), which would be the only body empowered to place Northern Ireland outside the crown dominions.

The politics and economies of the two parts of Ireland developed independently of each other, with the consequence of partial disenfranchisement of the Catholic minority in the north and the fierce competition between working-class Protestants and Catholics for the few available jobs.

Northern Ireland has consistently had the highest rate of unemployment in the United Kingdom. Added to that, discrimination in jobs, housing, and education has impelled a high emigration rate, even when there was relatively little sectarian violence as such in Northern Ireland. Since 1911, the rate of unemployment has ranged from 12.5 percent to 30 percent overall, and over 50 percent in some of the areas of highest Catholic population. In terms of housing, health standards, and education, Northern Ireland has been consistently behind the rest of the United Kingdom.[39] Even the level of social mobility—17 percent upward, 5 percent downward —involving a single-stratum movement, is lower than the rest of the United Kingdom and the Irish Republic. There has been a large population shift from rural to urban, reflecting the lopsided development of employment in Belfast with no industrial development in the west. Even at that, the linen industry, which had been responsible for employing mainly women in and around Belfast, declined and terminated, while shipbuilding has been depressed between the two world wars and in the past decade come to a complete standstill. The internal colonialism of the "Celtic Fringe" of the United Kingdom (Ireland, Scotland, and Wales) has been most consistently evidenced in the economic policies. One scholar points out that "because they are limited to a range of subordinate social roles, individuals in the periphery will tend to maintain their cultural institutions and identity. This culture maintenance results from the importance of culture in the system of stratification and the consequent tendencies towards ecological segregation in the work and residential settings."[40]

The postwar era brought major changes in Northern Irish political economy through the Labor government's attempt to bring Britain into a welfare state or social democracy. Nationalized health care and government ownership of major utilities and transportation, opening access to higher education across class strata, unemployment compensation and old age pensions were strongly opposed by the government of Northern Ireland, but they were compelled to comply or face the loss of their governmental subsidies.[41] Of all the benefits of the new system, the most important initiative for social change in Northern Ireland was the expansion of educational opportunities. Catholic working-class students could now anticipate access to the professions. By the mid-1960's Queen's University in Belfast had achieved a social class and religious mixture beyond that of any other educational institution in Northern Ireland. Nonetheless, the institution remained irrelevant to the needs and experiences of this new student group as well as to the larger society of which it was part. This irrelevance, unchanged even by the cataclysmic events of the past decade, was responsible for catalyzing one of the organizations that had an enormous impact on the politics of Northern Ireland—People's Democracy.*

The civil rights marches of the late 1960's mobilized the minority community in a way that the IRA campaigns had never accomplished. Sinn Fein had completely reorganized its strategies and ideology toward the political education of the masses in the expectation that a politicized people would enable the formation of a thirty-two county socialist workers' republic. The IRA laid down their arms and commenced their campaign of education.

---

*Bernadette Devlin recalls the "atmosphere of irrelevance" (at the academic institution) as largely responsible for her own participation in PD and her subsequent withdrawal from the university in favor of pursuing an activist role. In 1969 she had wanted to do her psychology thesis on police methods in minority communities and was met with the objection that she could not do such research in Northern Ireland because it would not be "valid objective research!" (She admitted to having had an opinion about police in Northern Ireland.)

In 1968, civil rights marchers in the north became targets for violent attacks by Protestant extremists associated with the Reverend Ian Paisley and the Orange Order. The sequence of events after that included pogroms in the Catholic communities in Belfast and Derry; a massive troop commitment by the British army (the ratio of which to the civilian population of Northern Ireland was greater than that of United States troops in Vietnam); internment of Catholics and then internment of Protestants; prorogation of the Stormont parliament and a brief attempt at multiparty elections and a power-sharing government, in which for the first time Catholics occupied decision-making positions and republicans had legitimacy.

In 1971, the Catholic population of Northern Ireland refused en masse to pay rents and rates. This civil resistance against the implementation of the Special Powers Act by internment of five hundred men, produced massive problems for the government. It was historically consistent with Irish resistance, and yet another instance of the kind of mobilization that implemented the national liberation objectives of such groups as the PAIGC in Guinea Bissau[42] or rent strikes by tenants associations in Spanish Harlem.

After a year of direct rule of Northern Ireland by the government of the United Kingdom at Westminster and Whitehall, William Whitelaw, who was appointed Secretary of State for Northern Ireland by Prime Minister Edward Heath, issued his plan for the future governance of that place in a white paper.

Whitelaw had earned his reputation for arbitrating disputes between management and labor, government and unions. His white paper outlined a program of power-sharing among the political parties of Northern Ireland, and also recognized the "Irish Dimension" of Northern Ireland's political and economic prospect. The program, for the first time in the fifty-year history of Northern Ireland, recognized republicanism as a legitimate political perspective, proposing a procedure for preferential voting in the election of a Northern Ireland assembly that would, in turn, produce a power-sharing executive.

The proposals, which had resulted from his year-long dialogues with the leaders of various political parties and civic groups, advocated a share in the decision-making process by everybody and for everyone.

There were, however, two notable exceptions to the continuous round table of verbal exchange—the two exceptions that proved in the end fatal to "Camelot": the Provisional Sinn Fein/IRA and the Paisleyites.

These groups had excluded themselves from the charmed circle. True to Yeats's description of Irish politics in an earlier era, the leaders of these crowds cared not what might come so long as their followers provided the music.[43]

The Reverend Ian Paisley's political party, the Democratic Unionist Party (DUP), and William Craig's Vanguard Party (VUPP) stood for election at the polls and won seats in the assembly. They used their mandate to initiate violence in that forum and from there to stimulate further violence in the community at large.

The Provisional Sinn Fein advocated abstentionism at the polls. Although the Republican Clubs campaigned very hard for assembly seats, they managed to elect only local councillors who would not take their seats in any case as long as internment remained in practice.

The Ulster Defence Association (UDA), which by the time of the assembly elections in June, 1973, included nearly the entire Protestant working class, refused to support any party or candidate as such.

By the time of the elections, the unionist monolith that had been the ruling force in Northern Ireland splintered into several separate entities. Former prime minister Brian Faulkner, as the leader of the Unionist Party, had agreed to the power-sharing proposals, but Harry West, John Taylor, John Laird, and others refused to accept the plan and finally split the party into an Unpledged Unionist majority against Faulkner's Official Unionists.

The Executive was scheduled to take office on January 1, 1974, but by October, the elected assembly had not arrived at any agreement about the composition of the executive. After some intensive meetings with Whitelaw at Stormont Castle (the former seat of government), the major issues emerged. The Social Democrat and Labor Party (SDLP) demanded immediate resolution of the "Irish dimension" through the inclusion of representatives of the Irish government at their talks. On December 7, 1973, the Sunningdale talks provided the outline for the shape of the executive and the prospects for a Council of Ireland.

Six months after the inception of the power-sharing executive, the government fell apart when the Ulster Workers' Council called a general strike and the British army, with a troop strength in Northern Ireland of over 20,000 men, failed to confront the UWC and rout them. After that debacle, Northern Ireland came again under direct rule, and once again, elections were held to bring together a constitutional convention and design a new political structure for governing that troubled place. The convention met and, with a majority of politicians committed to majority rule and no consideration of connection with the Irish Republic, was dissolved; in early 1976, Prime Minister Harold Wilson announced that direct rule would continue indefinitely as he dismissed one more futile attempt. Meanwhile, Dublin was bombed several times by extremist Loyalist groups; internment was reinstated there; and the Republic of Ireland joined the EEC, turning its gaze away from the northern six counties and toward immersion in a European future. In 1973, a coalition government of the Irish Labor Party with Fine Gael (an incredible combination of the parties that represent social democracy and free enterprise respectively), deliberately adopting the British and unionist thesis of two Irelands, confirmed de facto the border designed in 1920.

How is it then, that this society—the only Christian European country that never even expelled its Jews—has become the bloody symbol of sectarian assassinations, terrorist bombings, and urban guerrilla warfare? And how furthermore, is it that in Northern Ireland today, the latest devices and strategies for combating insurgency[44] are being tested by the military forces of a government that is proudly hailed as "the mother of parliaments"? The many paradoxes and ironic contradictions that comprise the tight little arena of Irish culture and politics in the latter half of the twentieth century can only be understood through the larger historical panorama of events and in relation to the various social and political forces that characterize twentieth-century Europe and North America.

Ireland has long been the periphery of the European colonial center, and now, being the westernmost European state, a member of neither the NATO nor Warsaw Pact countries, it remains also on the periphery of detente. There seems to be no threat of Ireland joining the Warsaw Pact grouping or allying itself with Third World countries. But it does remain the sociogeographic staging area for Western European experimentation, and therefore its population seems often to be viewed as expendable—not unlike Angola or Namibia. As a kind of final gesture in futile irony, the government of the Irish Republic voted at the United Nations to receive and hear the message of Yassir Arafat, head of the Palestinian Liberation Organization that has daily taken "credit" for the murder of helpless civilians in every part of the world. But they have refused to recognize as legitimate the actions of the Irish Republican Army, which has for nearly sixty years confined its actions to targets within the British Isles, and in the years prior to 1970 had maintained military objectives as their targets for operations.

If these social and political paradoxes appear repetitious after a thorough reading of Irish history, then we must look behind them at the individual psychology and group dynamics of the people themselves. In so doing we must also view the larger sociopolitical arena through which events affect the lives of those individuals and in which they make the effective mark of their own social experience.

While there may be considerable scholarly value in examinig Ireland as a case study by itself—and certainly, its own long tradition of scholarship has earned that treatment—a stronger and unfilled need exists to abstract from the Irish experience in order to relate it to the international one and also to imbue other, similar struggles with their relevance to the contemporary social and political world. At the same time, the particular experiences of the people of Ireland, its geographical containment as an island, its population (4,500,000) and placement, make it necessary to define its circumstances empirically insofar as possible.

The past decade has been in some important ways a replay of nineteenth-century Irish history—even to the level of clerical fulmination of the contemporary Reverend Ian Paisley re-echoing the earlier Reverend Hanna, the violence initiated by Orange Order marches, the unionization of the working class, and the conflict of jurisdictions between the Royal Ulster Constabulary and the British army as the contemporary version of the earlier jurisdictional issues between the constabulary and the reserve force. In a section bordering Lower Falls and Sandy Row in Belfast, rubble is still used as missiles in sectarian disputes as happened over the same ground in the mid-nineteenth century.[45]

Does this suggest in some way that social development has stagnated in Ireland, or that the Irish people have so ritualized their history as to re-enact it as some sort of rite? Such analysis, although frequently articulated in the popular media of the United States and Western Europe, is superficial. The forces of social change that incited nationalist rebellions in this oldest of British colonies during the eighteenth and nineteenth centuries were intrinsic to the surges of republicanism and then nationalism that raged throughout Europe and the western hemisphere and had their Irish enactments as well as their French or American fruitions.[46] Similarly, in the 1960's the winds of civil rights, national liberation movements, and socialism beating hard on the ramparts of political and economic colonialism found climatic conditions in Ireland ripe for a hurricane.

The destruction of the Irish people has proceeded over seven centuries and has been aptly described as the "English Origins of American Racism."[47] As racism often is a precursor to genocide, so it has been for the Irish. For the present troubles in the north have an ominous potential for more permanent destruction than ensued from even Cromwell's "extirpation."

Violence and social prejudice are not unknown in any society. The history of every ethnic and national group is filled with incidents of threatened annihilation, reprieve, victory, and defeat. For some groups, like the Jews, such traumatic events have occurred in almost every country where they have settled and at least once every hundred years. For other groups, national enmities have periodically exploded in warfare and changes in territorial boundaries. The Armenians lost in a single five-year period in this century half their population as the result of a deliberate campaign by the Ottoman Turks to destroy an entire people.[48] In still other societies, there is a long history of suffering under racist laws. The conditions of American Indians, Mexican Americans, and black and Puerto Rican populations in the U.S. are products of a racist and colonial ethos.[49] Such conditions trigger violent flare-ups, a kind of psychopathology, as well as severe disruptions of basic social institutions for these groups. The American Indian was subjected to genocide when, during the nineteenth and early twentieth centuries, whole tribes were massacred and the few survivors were subjected to death marches and other severe privations.[50] The Mexican American was deprived of citizenship and land rights, often too, became the target for explosions of sadistic frenzy by Anglo settlers.[51] In all these cases there has been damage to the survivors up to many generations beyond the generation that experienced the outrage. Many times the damage of attempted total destruction is compounded by the social status occupied by the group after the attempted extermination has actually ceased. Some recent studies indicate that even those concentration-camp survivors from World War II who had never experienced the trauma personally deviated significantly from the personality norms of their age peers.[52]

Life "on the run" has been a common feature of existence for the ordinary person in Ireland during the past one hundred and fifty years. At various periods of Irish history one or another class of people survived as a group by means of this mode of living. Ireland of the 1970's has become a society in which persons of all strata, classes, and conditions are existing this way. Their commonality in this circumstance becomes apparent through the clinical studies of individuals and social psychological studies of groups, particularly in Northern Ireland. Some of the data on individuals and groups in the Irish Republic suggests that this syndrome is not entirely absent from that part of the island. Certainly, those Irish Americans who participate in organizations related to groups in Ireland find themselves under investigation by various U.S. intelligence agencies, and, in numerous instances, under grand jury indictments. They too are often on the run in their adopted land.

Being on the run means, for the individual, that one's own identity is in danger. It means that it is impossible to "be oneself"; impossible to relate in any consistent fashion with those closest to you; impossible to sleep in the same bed more than a couple of nights in a row, or traverse the same streets without dread. It means a constant fear of being "discovered" for what you are and who you are. There is a feeling of guilt, of course—either the guilt of knowing that one has done something for which punishment of one or another sort is customary, or guilt for having wanted to do something punishable, or for being believed by others to have done something against the law. The fear itself is not paralyzing. It is a screen through which everything else is perceived in a skewed perspective, because the constant need for self-protection magnifies or diminishes various details. The fear approaches the circumstances of dread rather than those of anxiety. It is not a formless ambiguity; it is a recognition of the painful prospect of torture and of dishonor as the prospective reality of one's own flesh.

In contrast to other frenetic modern societies often described as being "constantly on the go or on the run," this syndrome in contemporary Northern Ireland does not entail the feeling of having to get too much done in too little time; it is more like running to keep time from running out, while being unable to do anything or see anything being done. One is the hunted, haunted recipient of others' actions and action potentials, reacting with a limited repertoire of responses. Caught up in this ethos, the individual relates to the larger situation by assessing the likelihood of being caught. Those who are on the run are often on the run from former neighbors and even relatives, as well as from the police or military.

Although the names on the military and police wanted lists are most often the names of working-class people and mostly Catholic working-class people, a person in Northern Ireland may also be on the run if Protestant or even if he or she has been a member of the provincial or Westminster government.

Nor is the middle-class person excluded from the syndrome. The man who owned a shop in partnership may find that he can no longer go into the neighborhood in which the shop is located and so sells out to his partner, or to someone else, at a loss and seeks some other way to support his family. He may well be the fellow who is now driving a People's Taxi down the Falls or Shankill roads. Or he may be unemployed for the first time in his adult life. The person on the run may be a Belfast middle-class housewife who spends the summer school holidays driving her children off to the country every week (if she's a Catholic she goes off to Donegal, and if Protestant, perhaps to one of the northern counties of Scotland or England). While thus freed from the daily fear (of being shot or blown up), she worries about her husband's safety and the cost of this escape and runs back home, children and all, thereby increasing the danger a hundredfold. The person on the run may be, and often is, an ex-Unionist cabinet minister who has been during the four out of five years of "the troubles" jobless under direct rule—paid but without his "position." The person may be a leader of the Ulster Defence Association, who has fallen out with former associates and sought refuge under a new name in a new place, perhaps far from Northern Ireland; he cannot escape the haunted hunted feeling even then, because it is part of the fabric of his being. The person on the run is often a child—an adolescent boy who is committed to the myth of identity with young Kevin Barry or the Apprentice Boys of Derry,* depending on whether he is Catholic or Protestant.

*Kevin Barry was an eighteen-year-old student-patriot who was the first person to be hanged by the British in Ireland for treason in the twentieth century. The Appren-

When you are on the run, you cannot go to work or be in school. In a world that identifies the individual by his position in the work force, you are a nonentity. But in a culture that accords reverence to outlaws, a society in which ordinary people are convinced that there is no system of justice out there, in a society in which the act of martyrdom is more revered than the actions of the life which preceded that death, each person is a vigilante and each person is on the run.

Northern Ireland, as distinct from Ireland and from Ireland as a unit in the British Commonwealth, had existed less than fifty years when the polarization that had been the basis of its formulation, in 1922, became a conflagration which spread to neighboring England and the Irish Republic. Its creation as a compromise to a unified, independent Ireland became the formula for resolving minority-majority political or religious rivalries in many countries that had been British colonial territories. The ensuing wars and crises in India, Pakistan, Bangladesh, Cyprus, and Palestine/ Israel have common factors with the Irish case. These are studies more often relegated to historians, political scientists, and economists. While social theorists often extrapolate from case studies to formulate sociological theories, social psychologists more often test individual-group relationships as behavioral samples in their laboratories. Thus, we have simulation experiments from which are extrapolated probabilities for particular phenomena. Or we do surveys or behavioral samplings consequent to some trauma or social change. As clinicians or educational psychologists, we may also utilize standardized samples of behaviors called tests, and after completing such a collection attempt to describe a population in terms of their functioning on a particular behavioral dimension.

When social psychologists emerge from their laboratories having found that they cannot contrive conditions of stress, guilt, confrontation, or prejudice directly replicating those conditions as they exist in the dynamics of the real world, methodological consternation arises. To resolve this frustration partially, some of us walk a methodological tightrope, the strands of which are history, journalism, and sociology. In studies of social conflict, methodological problems and timing usually consign the psychologist to a role as an apologist for history. For those in the profession who want to understand the effects of such social forces as prejudice, political conflict, and institutional violence (as well as for those who are dependent upon social scientists to do this), such studies are less than satisfying. The objective and the achievement of social-psychological study remain the ability to describe these effects through empirical studies of manifest behaviors

---

tice Boys of Derry were lads in their teens who, during the 1689 siege of Derry by the forces of King James, manned the wall cannons and held the city for William of Orange.

and to appraise their effects on the social milieu as well as on individuals with some degree of predictive validity.

Such problems have plagued the efforts of social psychologists throughout the past three decades. Because they are persistent problems in the field, pioneers like Kurt Lewin and Gordon Allport have devised theoretical models for social action research.[53] But social action research is still in its infancy. Social psychologists as such have only just begun to participate in social action and many still question the legitimacy of taking such actions as psychologists.[54]

Psychological Genocide
Patriot Games Children Play

Come all you young rebels and list while I sing
For love of one's land is a dangerous thing
It banishes fear with the speed of a flame
And makes us all part of the Patriot's Game.

My name is O'Hanlon and I've just gone sixteen
My home is in Monaghan and there I was weaned
I was taught all my life to hold England to blame
So I became part of the Patriot Game.

It's barely two years since I wandered away
With the local battalion of the old IRA
I'd read of our heroes and wanted the same
To play up my part in the Patriot Game.

They told me how Connolly was shot in the chair
His wounds from the battle all bleeding and bare
His fine body twisted all battered and lame
They soon made me part of the Patriot Game.

This Ireland of mine has been too long unfree
Six counties are under John Bull's monarchy.
And still there are people who are greatly to blame
For shirking their part in the Patriot Game.

And now as I lie here, my body all holes
I think of those traitors who bartered and sold
I'm sorry my rifle could not do the same
To those quislings who sold out
The Patriot Game.

DOMINIC BEHAN

The children of Belfast and Derry do not so often sing this song, they live it. Whether they are working-class children or middle-class; whether they are boys or girls; whether they are Protestant or Catholic or even Vietnamese war refugees (several families of whom were settled into

Divis Flats, a highrise apartment complex in Belfast's Lower Falls neighborhood), they are caught up in some version of the Patriot Game. All the institutions of their society function as control mechanisms toward socialization into sectarian strife.

Whatever their social or economic circumstances, these children are convinced that there is no system of equal or objective justice and that each of them must act as investigator, judge, jury, and hangman. Yet these children are not psychopaths, nor are they delusional paranoiacs. They are responding rationally to a world gone mad, and conventionally to a society in which respect for symbols is a life-or-death priority.

In July, 1975, Jimmy and Peter seldom had much to say to each other except when I was on a visit in Lower Falls—the housing estate (neighborhood) in Belfast in which they had been neighbors since infancy. From the age of thirteen they had affiliated with the different junior republican organizations with which their respective families had identified. These two organizations had fought each other in the streets and pubs of Lower Falls almost as often as they had shot at British army patrols.

Doug and Sean, also fifteen years old in 1975, had both grown up in Belfast within a few miles of each other, but they would never meet except perhaps across the barrels of automatic weapons pointed at each other. Doug is a Protestant; he is a member of a Tartan gang and has already worn his Sash in Orange parades. Sean had been a member of one of the junior IRA groups, was "lifted" (removed from his home) for interrogation by British soldiers at least eleven times within the previous year, and subsequently turned informer. He was punished by the seniors in his organization by being shot in the kneecaps. Doug also walks with a slight limp. He had belonged to a junior Ulster Defense Association (UDA) group and had been recalcitrant about obeying the orders of a senior member. He was beaten across the legs for this offense. The boys were treated at Royal Victoria Hospital, located almost across the street from Jimmy's house, which also serves as a post for British army regiments that have been occupying Northern Ireland as an armed force of ten to twenty thousand men since 1969.

Patricia, also fifteen years old in the summer of 1975, is extraordinarily thin and pale. She has difficulty sleeping and seldom attends school. Her mother has been hospitalized for nervous breakdown several times during the past five years and her youngest brother, aged six, still does not speak comprehensibly. They live in the Clonnard district of Belfast, but have occupied at least four different houses in the past five years.

Susan lives in an area that was built during the Second World War as temporary housing for the wealthier residents of Belfast who had to evacuate their homes for fear of bombing raids by the Luftwaffe. These temporary buildings then became permanent dwellings for a fortunate few of the

Protestant working class. The area is a stronghold of the UVF (Ulster Volunteer Force), UDA, and, some believe, for the notorious Red Hand (an organization of loyalist sectarian murderers). Susan's seventeen-year-old boy friend was interned in 1974. She was extremely depressed and did poorly in school last year. Then her best friend's father was murdered. She says that she wants her parents to emigrate to Australia or New Zealand.

Susan and Patricia, like Peter, Jimmy, Sean, and Doug, are Irish children residing in Northern Ireland, born in the second half of the twentieth century, who have spent more than one-third of their lives living in a state of siege. They and their peers in Belfast and Derry had originally been the focus of my research in Ireland. In 1971, when I commenced my data collection, the children of Northern Ireland had been living for most of their lives through conditions of social prejudice and violence. The riots and pogroms of 1969 were not their initiation into sectarianism; nor were they the spontaneous product of their parents' animosities toward one another. They were the probable outcome of eight hundred years of British colonial policy in Ireland and fifty years of sectarian fears in six counties of the province of Ulster, which became in 1922 a province of the United Kingdom. These children were the offspring of working-class parents who were themselves of working-class antecedents.

Although many people in Northern Ireland sincerely believe that they can discern from only physiognomy Protestant from Catholic, they actually rely on cues such as speech, dress, housing estate, schools attended, and sometimes, less dependably, on names. In the case of names, it is almost certain that a Gaelic masculine first name—such as Sean, for instance—denotes a Catholic origin; while a girl with a Gaelic first name might be either Protestant or Catholic. As for surnames, these can lead to confusion since there are both Catholic and Protestant Murphys and Snoddys, O'Neills and O'Donnells. In comparison with the task of racists in the U.S., who identify their victims by skin color, or of the Nazis, who identified Jews by surnames, which are simpler tasks, social prejudice and bigotry in Northern Ireland are more complex.

The effects as well as the probable direction of a condition of rapid political change are most readily reflected in the personality dynamics, behaviors, and attitudes of the children within that milieu. The destruction of the psychological integrity of a people is also first evidenced in these dimensions. It is evidenced in the meanings attributed to events and the meanings attributed to their own lives by the children of that population. Earlier studies of the effects of trauma on populations of varied ages indicate that the most dramatic effects are those on the younger age group whose identity and personality are least completely formed.[1]

Serious problems arise in comparing the effects on children of various kinds of social and political conflict. One problem is that research carried out on one such population utilizes different methods and is differently interpreted from research carried out at a different time and place on another population group. Thus, while the work of Coles on black and white children undergoing the crisis of racial integration in the American rural south provides many insights into the personality dynamics, attitudes, and kinds of destruction wrought by these conflicts,[2] it is not directly comparable, for example, with the work done by Anna Freud with the young refugee victims of the Nazi concentration camps.[3] Too often it is the case that even those researching the effects of war and ongoing violence on children of the same geographic place are neither doing empirical nor systematic longitudinal studies not utilizing a broad common methodological base to permit comparison of findings.

Research on the effects of the five years of violence in the lives of children growing up in Northern Ireland serves as an example. It is also exemplary of a broader issue in social research, one described by William Ryan as "blaming the victim" (the kind of circumstance in which the victim being studied is perceived as the source of his or her own misfortune because of either ineptness or reactions in that circumstance).[4] In this fashion, a "culture of poverty" is attributed to the poor, and the Jewish victims of the Nazi Holocaust are presented as "partners with the Nazis in their own extermination."[5] Sophisticated scientists have become so wary of causal relations between events on the one hand and so equally wary of appearing "political" and "subjective" that even those causal relations that are directly traceable become transformed into products of "social history."[6]

Yet if one is to examine the nature of the human struggle for survival and the mechanisms—both constructive and pathological—initiated and developed through that struggle, then it is necessary to examine empirically and longitudinally the developmental processes of many individuals during the period of crisis. And in order to relate the individual and social processes, they must be viewed within the context of the political events. This is not to suggest that political events occur devoid of individual and social group interaction with political forces, but rather that the unit of study must encompass the interaction and the reaction. Since the political events predisposing a violent reaction are usually well under way before the child is of an age to comprehend them, we may suppose that these events are acting on the child long before there is any possibility of his/her interaction with them. Thus, a generation or several generations are processed into a scheme of reacting and coping psychologically, socially, and politically. By studying the children of a society it becomes possible to predict the probable social and political schemata that will emerge from that society within the next twenty years.

Motivation, or, as Arnold defines it, "mode of operation," is a fairly constant personality function.[7] It is also a direct application of an individual's unique interpretation of reality in combination with his/her value system and self-appraisal. Thus, one is "moved toward" action by the appraisal of something as a "good" for action. By analyzing the motivations of children as they proceed through the developmental process from primary-school age through early adolescence, we can see a pattern emerge on which to predict the probable attitudes, beliefs, and behaviors of the children as adults. If, in addition to assessing motivation, we can gain insight into the growing persons' development of moral judgment/political socialization, then we have a sense of where the political direction of a society is oriented.[8] And from these analyses there is evidence of the survival or demise of an entire people. For if the young see no "good" for action other than their own destruction, or see their future as inevitably and invariably beyond their own scope to affect and influence, then we might assume along with them their demise.

Through substituting opinion for lack of empirical evidence, many authorities, even after examining the victims of ongoing violence, suggest that such effects as are evidenced are short-term, and may even be somehow beneficial to the balance of psychic energy. Others, from equal lack of empirical strength, argue that the escalation of violent behavior in children foredooms them to permanent criminality.[9]

One of the first systematic studies of the children of Belfast was conducted by Dr. Morris Fraser, a child psychiatrist affiliated with the Royal Victoria Hospital there. Dr. Fraser correlated the 1969 riots with the effects on mental health and found that there had been significant detrimental effects on both adults and children.[10] In a series of articles and then in a book about the children, Dr. Fraser described these effects in terms of the kinds of clinical cases referred and treated, as well as in case studies and anecdotal materials. He found that although in some cases the effects were similar to those occurring in a condition of full-scale war, their origins made them more debilitating than such a context might have been:

> It might be expected that the effects on mental health would have been more deleterious than those of a war and results seem to bear this out. Riots, in contrast to wars, do not seem to benefit any kind of psychiatric illness; in no area or group was there a significant decline in morbidity. Neurotics, in fact, seemed to deteriorate. Stress is an ambiguous word but it seems justifiable here to conclude that stress productive of psychiatric morbidity appears to be maximal in areas under threat of upheaval or attack, rather than in those areas where there is direct combat or direct risk to life. . . . During the riot months there was a highly significant increase in the prescription rate for tranquillizers in the areas already involved.[11]

After appraising the clinical effects on children, Fraser said: "It is not surprising in this situation that lots of children develop problems . . . they cry, they cannot eat, they wet their beds. And for some, the symptoms continue long after the rioting is over."[12]

In December of 1971, Dr. Joe Cosgrove, a general practitioner, expressed his impressions of the young people who were supporters of the IRA:

> The young boys who were on the IRA and supported it had the need for an ideal, the need to seek the bubble reputation even in the common mouth. He believed that many were quite uncritical as to the nature of their ideal. . . . German nationalism presented to and uncritically adopted by Hitler Youth was a case in point. [He] often was undeveloped in play and lacking in concern for people which he thought could explain some of the savage shootings they hear about. He would believe that when these boys passed twenty their better emotions matured and they would suffer intense remorse for these acts.[13]

But another Belfast psychiatrist, Dr. H. A. Lyons, has repeatedly suggested that violence has not only had no debilitating effect on the population but has actually had a tonic effect on the children:

> These children seem to quite enjoy the excitement of the present troubles but they are being taught a disrespect for law and order, and that violence pays off. By and large the children in troubled areas were not psychologically disturbed by violence in the short term.[14]

As for the effects on adults, Dr. P. P. O'Malley, a psychiatrist at the Mater Hospital, Belfast (a hospital with a mainly Catholic, working-class population), found that actual cases of attempted suicide had increased 73 percent during the troubles and that this statistic might be a better measure for the effects than the data on death by diagnosed suicide on which Dr. Lyons based some of his conclusions.[15]

In another kind of study, James Russell, a sociologist working under the auspices of a government agency in Northern Ireland, found that the influence of history studies in the civic education of secondary school boys had a negative effect on a propensity for violence. Of course, his study, administered through the schools, was a questionnaire survey in which the boys reported their own "violent propensities." But he did find that Protestant youths expressed positive feelings toward the government more homogeneously than did Catholic youth. Among the Protestant youths, aged eleven to fifteen, there were fewer working-class youths included than among Catholic youths. If there is a correlation between attitudes expressed in a survey questionnaire and actual behaviors, then Russell is suggesting that Catholic working-class boys find violence a more appropriate form of behavior because they have not studied history as well as their Protestant and Catholic middle-class peers![16]

Social psychologist S. L. Neilsen of Norway also studied the situation in Northern Ireland (particularly Belfast) from the perspective of the frustration-aggression hypothesis and concluded that the children had developed new moral norms. These norms included successful operation in groups to avoid detection.[17]

Journalists in pursuit of a "story line" have not been at all reluctant to develop their superficial observations of the children into a profound diagnosis. If they cannot find a group of children throwing rocks at a military patrol, they are not above paying the children to do so in order to get a newsphoto.[18]

Several problems are common to all the aforementioned studies. First, none of them utilizes empirical instruments validated on samples of populations in many different societies. In other words, there is no way to compare their data, except in the qualitative clinical sense, with the varieties of normal behaviors evidenced by children in the United States, England, France, or Mexico, for instance. There are no base lines for the behaviors since each study is a self-contained time sample or a series of case histories. While authorities in Northern Ireland have been very eager to promote studies and surveys that will indicate the short-term nature of the effects of the "troubles" or suggest new curricula for schools and community relations groups, nowhere in the literature is there an attempt to come to grips with probable long-term effects of a childhood characterized by ongoing bloodshed and destruction. There seems to be a fondness for pointing to the continuity of history of segregation and prejudice, a lack of focus for political socialization outside the family, an ethos of tribalism, and the conviction that unemployment and poverty are the simple corollaries of violence.[19] (Thus, violence exists everywhere else in the world, too.) Longitudinal, cross-cultural empirical research can explore the nature, extent, and probable long-term effects and also provide the means for effectively breaking the vicious cycle perpetuated through the experience of one generation onto the life circumstances of the next.

Prior to 1969, the 1935 sectarian riots in Belfast had left sufficient effect on their parents to provide the nexus of the pathologies that erupted in the behavior of adults during the summer of 1969. Once again, these studies have, by removing the subjects from the historical-political context, made incomprehensible the behaviors of the subjects. Thus, in the process, it is forgotten that the 1969 riots culminated a five-year nonviolent civil protest movement, which had been repeatedly violently attacked, not by children, but by middle-aged adults, many of whom wore the uniforms of the established forces of law and order. Not only are there ongoing complications to the socialization process of these children, but there are these cumulative effects as well. It is not a matter simply of segregated schooling, periodic rioting, paramilitary organizations seducing the allegiance of the young, anti-authoritarianism, or even a perversity of the Irish cultural milieu. But without the basis of empirical longitudinal study, such events, their context, and effects become blurred and blunted into oblivion. What remains in the public purview is the newsphoto of the angry adolescent throwing rocks and petrol bombs.

Methodology

I initiated this study in December, 1971. At that time the level of violence had reached a new peak. Often as many as fifteen bombings occurred in a single day, and the process of interning adult males out of the Catholic section of the community had been under way for four months. "No-go" areas had been established in the working-class Catholic districts of Belfast, often with the aid of the barbed-wire and brick-wall "peace lines" established by the British army. The government of Northern Ireland was directed by the Stormont—a provisional parliament with a predominantly Protestant unionist majority. Republicanism, the ideology of a united, independent Ireland, was still outlawed as a political party. One fairly new (1970) political party attempted to represent the Catholic minority, the Social Democrat and Labour Party (SDLP), but because of actions taken against the Catholic population, the SDLP was, at that time, taking an abstentionist position in governmental procedures.

The primary target population for this study were the children of Belfast (1972 population 407,000) which had the longest history of periodic sectarian violence in Northern Ireland and the greatest number of Catholic and Protestant housing estates close to one another. The program of testing children aged six through fifteen was carried on at four- to six-month intervals, each time sample including equal numbers of Protestant and Catholic boys and girls, all residing in working-class housing estates. In addition, two other groups were examined for purposes of establishing cultural norms. A group from Dublin (1972 population 537,448) composed of ten working-class Protestant and twelve Catholic boys and girls was examined in December, 1971. Another group of children from the Bogside and Creggan estates of Derry were tested in the summer of 1972. These children had either been themselves present at the January, 1972, civil rights march that had erupted in the massacre of thirteen participants or had relatives killed or injured that day. Rapid population shifts in Belfast made it impossible to plan a longitudinal study that would encompass the identical sample in each subsequent visit. Many of the children in the Catholic sample, however, were retested annually or semi-annually up to three years after the first sampling.

The nature of the testing environment was very unorthodox, since testing was done in schools and homes that were often, at that very moment, racked by sounds of not-too-distant explosions or intruded upon by armed patrols; in one instance, a rubber bullet shot by an armed patrol landed in the hallway just outside the testing room. Because of this, cassette-taped test responses were often inaudible for scoring. Also, problems arose from tapes having been magnetized in their transport from Northern Ireland back to the United States, sometimes by way of three or four stopovers. Thus, the total number of complete test protocols (no repeats) under consideration in this study is 152. Of these, seventy-five are from Protestant and seventy-seven from Catholic children in Belfast. "Completed protocols" included those that had both the Thematic Apperception Test[20] and the Tapp-Kohlberg questions of Legal Socialization.[21] In addition to the tests themselves, extensive interviews were held with the teachers and/or school principals of most of the children and with the parents of those children who were examined at home. These were conducted in order to ascertain that the sample included children whose lives were immediately affected by the violence as well as children whose lives were not. Unfortunately, this differentiation did not apply subsequent to December, 1971, although we continued to do extensive interviews with these adults in the child's life anyway. More often, the sessions became a time to exchange information, suggestions, and appraisals about the child, rather than for gathering information to make greater distinctions within the sample.

The TAT is a well-established projective test used to assess personality dynamics for clinical diagnosis. It has been used more recently in large-scale studies of social and cultural variables in personality dynamics. It has also been used to study political awareness;[22] and through Story Sequence Analysis, it has been used to predict scholastic success and in clinical treatment.[23] Ten cards were used and until winter, 1974, the same ten cards had been repeatedly used. At that time, however, it was decided to change stimulus cards because the pictures had become fairly well known among the children in at least one of the sample communities, and because the change might further indicate whether, as Arnold asserts, the particular stimulus cards are relatively unimportant since it is the stories and their sequencing which provides the raw data for analysis.[24]

The Tapp-Kohlberg questions consist of a series of seven questions regarding rules and laws, which have been standardized on a sample of children from many different countries. They had been used and reported on in studies of the development of moral judgment, legal socialization, and political awareness.[25] I added an eighth question: "If you could change any rule, which rule would you change?"

Coming of Age in Belfast

In 1971, Jimmy, Peter, Susan, Patricia, Doug, and Sean were studying for their "11 plus's"—the examination given throughout the British school system to distinguish those children who would be directed into academic secondary schools from those who would go into vocational preparation, or terminal education. School-leaving age that year was fifteen, and of the children examined in Belfast and Dublin during December, 1971, very few had academic aspirations. When asked what they wanted to be when they grew up, the answers of the boys most often matched their fathers' occupations, and those of the girls indicated wanting to become wives and mothers. Four years later, these children and their peers had not changed their occupational aspiration level, but they had become totally cynical. Peter had witnessed his next eldest brother, David, being dragged off for interrogation when the latter was fourteen years old and was afterward never again able to function in school or in interactions with family members. He was also present on the street when an army patrol opened fire on David, hitting him in the chest. After months in hospital, David had been sentenced to a term in Borstal for alleged possession of weapons. Peter's stories on the TAT changed considerably during those four years. His most immediate ambitions were focused on revenge.

Jimmy's eldest brother had been one of the first men interned in the August 9, 1971, combined Royal Ulster Constabulary and British Army dawn raids on the homes of Northern Ireland Catholics. Jimmy's stories during his first testing session included the following:

He has had an argument with his wife. She keeps narking at him and he kills her. He feels very sorry afterward and he will kill himself.

Mountaineers are climbing on a snow-covered mountain. One falls and pulls the other down with him. They land on a village made of ice and the people that lived there were very-very small—like leprechauns, and were ugly (leprechauns are nice). They had never seen anybody like that before. The mountaineers are never found and nobody knows they're alive except the leprechauns.

A soldier's guarding a concentration camp. Someone jumps on him and kills him. They cut the wire and there is an escape. They find the soldier dead the next morning. The ones who escaped—those left of their nationality in the camp are executed as punishment. There was very little escapes planned since then.

Jimmy was retested at intervals, as were most of the children in the Lower Falls sample. By the time his brother had been released from Long Kesh internment camp, their mother had become quite sickly and depressed. Another older brother and his wife had become so demoralized by months of constant harassment from the paratrooper regiment in Ballymurphy where they lived that their three small children had become physical and emotional cripples before reaching the age of five. Jimmy's stories at that point indicated that he no longer feared retribution for violent actions. He told this story:

> This is a soldier standing guard outside an electric station.
> There's some official IRA terrorists who are going to blow it up. A wee man tries to stop them so they have to shoot him. It ends up there's no electric station left.
> [To the question, "What is a law?" Jimmy answered:] A law is something that someone in the government sets out. Like to have no organizations at all.
> [Why do you follow rules?] I don't follow any rules. I follow the rules in the house—some of the rules outside. Nobody about here follows rules except by their own selves.
> [If you could change any rule, what rule would you change?] Discrimination against Catholics and ordinary working-class people.

While Jimmy seems convinced that killing someone who tries to interfere with the enactment of destruction is not punishable, he is also clearly concerned with right and wrong and with the lack of justice.

Some of his age-mates were not as able to respond to the testing program in 1973 as they had been in 1971. Four of his neighbors had been so severely damaged in the interrogation process that they were unable to produce coherent stories. Their performance on tests of psychomotor coordination indicated that they were suffering from neurological impairments usually associated with brain damage.

If we examine the test protocols and scores of these children over a period of four years, some patterns emerge. These patterns provide an analysis of the various effects of the conditions of ongoing social prejudice and violence. From them we can see that violence and terrorism do not politicize growing children, who turn instead to taking violent actions rather than political measures. They see politics as the spoils of the victor rather than the product of shared participation.

Patricia, at the time she was first tested in 1972, had just been terrorized when a soldier, shot in the doorway of her house, had fallen bleeding on top of her as she opened the door. During the night of horror that followed the incident, a patrol held the family against the wall at gunpoint, threatening all of them with torture and death. Patricia spent a sleepless night sitting in a chair while her mother, who had already been hospitalized once for nervous disability, once again fell apart despite the tranquillizers and sedatives that were ordinarily her only sustenance. By January, 1973, Patricia, because she wore trousers, had short hair, and looked "like a wee lad," had been repeatedly "lifted" by patrols, thrown into the back of a Saracen, and threatened, along with Jimmy and the other "wee lads" of the street. She was no longer afraid of their guns, however—she simply raised her trouser leg to show them her kneesocks and said, "See, I'm a wee lass." But Patricia was no longer going to school regularly, nor was her mother able to encourage her and her sister to keep clean or eat regularly. The children were on the street most of the time scavenging for adult attention and for items from hijacked trucks. The disruption of her family and lack of comfort therein is reflected in one of her stories:

> They were on a ship. The father fell in and sharks bit him in the side. They pulled him out and in the passengers was a doctor. The doctor is operating on him to get the poison out of his side, and the boy is worried. I think he wants his father to die and he lifts the rifle and shoots him in the other side and the wee boy will be locked up in the cabin below. The man will be operated on again but he will die. When they get to the island the mother is waiting. The boy will be sent to Borstal for life and the mother will get married again.

Patricia might well have been telling in parable her expectations for her own homeland or her interpretation of the strife and hatred existing within a family.

Adolescent Provies and Tartans* would never become acquainted with each other and readily deny any kind of commonality. But by January, 1973, these boys were operating in such similar fashions that it would be difficult to distinguish the personality-test protocols of one group from those of the other. Boys from both extremes were equally concerned with law and order. Neither felt there was any system of justice or governance operating "out there," but that because wrongs went unchallenged and the world was chaotic, they had each to act as investigator, judge, and executioner. In short, they espoused a vigilante thesis in combination with a view that any action undertaken in the name of freedom and justice for their groups was intrinsically just. The groups had their own agents to enforce their internal codes, and violators, whether members of the group or not, would be punished for infractions. Kneecap jobs and skin lacerations (by knife or by cigarette burns) were common sentences. Such behavior would ordinarily be attributed to psychopathic delinquents. But not in Belfast, 1973. These actions were taken, not for spontaneous kicks, but for deliberate punitive purposes and by group consensus.

Doug, fourteen, is a member of a Tartan gang. His older brother is also a Tartan. His father left the family some years ago to work in England

---

*Provies or Provo: Local slang for Provisional Irish Republican Army. Tartans: The generic term for Protestant juvenile gangs.

and was never heard from again. Doug's mother is an alcoholic who roams the streets when drunk and confronts people. He is a quiet boy, enthusiastic about football and hopeful of emigrating. His arm and hands are covered with colorful tattoos. On his knuckles, one by one, the word "love" is spelled out:

> What's she crying about? Maybe being hit by her father. Maybe she stole something. She thinks she's being policed on all the time. She's going to leave the house and go to another country and get a job. Get married and not return again.
>
> She loves that fellow. He doesn't love her. She would do anything for him to love her. She would even kill for him. She would like to have a family and a home to rest in.
>
> I don't know how the man has the nerve to do things like this. To kill a person in cold blood. If I had my way I would like to have this man shot and any other like him.
>
> Blank place. I have seen many blank places before which had things in it before it was blown up. How people can do things like this killing innocent people and leaving corners blank!

Eight months younger than Doug, also raised in Belfast, Sean is one of eight children. His father and older brothers were interned. The family has been identified as Provo. Sean's father had been interned several times previously. His eldest brother, reputed to be a top Provisionals' leader, was "on the run" in 1973 and Sean hadn't seen him in several months. His youngest brother suffers a traumatic neurosis: every time he hears an explosion or an approaching patrol he hides behind the TV set in terror. Sean told the following:

> Somebody's hitting her and throwing her out of the house. She's crying because she wants to go back to her mummy and daddy, but she knows she won't be able to get back.
>   The husband's come in drunk. She says things about him that he doesn't like. He wants to leave her. But she's telling him to come back again. But he's still going.

One fifteen-year-old who had been tested in December, 1971, was one of a group of boys who had been lifted and held for interrogation nearly a whole day. At the time he was first tested, he was depressed and confused. He had not been a member of any group and had been trying very hard to keep up with his school work and prepare for an apprenticeship. He was picked up and beaten five more times between December, 1971, and January, 1973. Once he was picked up by drunken soldiers and beaten, other times he was stopped and verbally abused. His home had been raided a number of times. His father and uncles were interned in the 1940's. Seamus himself had not considered joining any group until after the second beating. He wanted some way to retaliate against his oppressors and felt that this was as good as any. He's still not more politically aware than he was prior to the first lifting. He doesn't really care about ideologies or processes, he is only concerned with getting his rights and being left alone. When presented with the blank card, he gave this story:

> The future of Northern Ireland and perhaps the future of the world—blank—a dead end. There's nothing to do in a dead end but go to Vietnam or something like that.
> Seems to be a drunk. A shady kind of character. Looks like an IRA man or an American gangster, more like what you see in films. He's waiting for somebody. He'll have a long wait and do whatever he's intending to do: if he doesn't get picked up for loitering he'll wait there for the rest of the night.

As for rules and laws, Seamus says:

> Why should people follow rules. Shouldn't always follow them but I suppose it's proper for fear if you didn't follow them you get into trouble.
> [Why do you follow rules?] I follow moral rules because I feel obliged to because I'm a Catholic. If I break them I endanger myself or other people.
> [If you could change any rule, what rule would you change?] I'd like to change the rule to have justice in Northern Ireland.

The IRA kids and the Tartan kids are similar but different. It's the difference—an accident of name and religion, the accident of family of origin manipulated by a sectarian political schemata—that makes the difference a mortal offense.

Refugees from the Patriot Game

The children try in many ways to escape the aura of indoctrination to hatred. Few of those tested have managed to escape their part in the Patriot Game. Of those who have, I will mention two girls—twelve-year-old Regina and eleven-year-old Phyllis, tested in 1972. They will probably never meet each other, for although they live in the same city, their neighborhoods are divided by walls and barbed-wire barricades. They will be mortally afraid of wandering into each other's neighborhood, and probably if they continue to be unwilling witnesses to the bloodshed and terrorism they may fall into the pattern of the Patriot Game. Phyllis answered the Tapp questions:

[What if there were no rules?] You'd have to make up your own rules.

[Can rules be changed?] Yes, if they found out it was no good and people were upset about it and said so, they'd have to change it.

[When might it be right to break a rule?] When other people ask you to do something like that and you know it's wrong you have to say you can't do it because it's doing wrong.

[If you could change any rule, what rule would you change?] That you shouldn't be allowed to make rules that are wrong nor allowed to make your own rules.

Regina replied to that last question: "At the moment in Northern Ireland Catholics and Protestants are fighting it out. I would make a sort of division line between them and not let them fight it out together but talk it out together and saying what they don't like about the Catholics and what the Catholics don't like about the Protestants. I would make the law now that people talk it out together." Can you imagine someone making such a law? "No, not really."

Is it really possible that the attitudes of the children toward violence and their participation in it are related only to the amount of history they've studied in their civic education courses? Is it possible that these personality dynamics and the truncation of the development of moral judgment in a whole generation of children are indicative of the tonic effects of riots on the population in the riot area? Or is it perhaps another case of self-fulfilling prophecy? When people—children, in this case—are labeled as "thugs," "revolutionists," "soldiers," "terrorists," or "Patriots," they incorporate that label into their view of themselves and their interpretation of experience. Thus, they become what they are called.

Findings

The first analysis of findings on the 1971 samples indicated a greater difference between the children of Belfast and the children of Dublin than between the Protestant and Catholic children of either city. The sample was relatively small, twenty-four children from Belfast and twenty-two from Dublin; twenty-four Catholic and twenty-two Protestant. This finding is of particular interest since the social conditions of the Catholic working-class area in Belfast at that time would seem to have been dramatically different from Belfast Protestant areas. These differences revealed themselves more in the Tapp-Kohlberg questions than in the TAT stories. However, the content of the TAT stories from Belfast was quite different from that of stories from Dublin. The differences were manifested in two different directions. First, the length and fantasy content of the stories dropped off sharply after age nine for the Belfast sample, but not for the Dublin group. The other differences had to do with the levels of pessimism and fatalism in the Belfast sample. Although there was no statistically significant difference in the dimension of activity/passivity—positive/negative between the two groups, this might be attributable to the fact that the sample was small and that which would appear as a trend would not (unless it was consistent for each individual in the sample) be evidenced as significantly different. For both groups the degree of fatalism in the stories might reflect the relative powerlessness of the child in the Irish society, which is very much dominated by the authority of the adults. The Belfast children from six through eight years old were totally unable to conceive of happy endings for their stories. Since there were only eight children out of the sample in this age category for each city, the trend remains statistically insignificant while clinically very suggestive. The older children in the Belfast sample also exhibited some of the same obsession with death and destruction, but this was not as consistent in their stories as it had been for the younger children. If the stories are analyzed by score per story per child, we do begin to obtain significant results for the younger sample, but for the 1971 sample of older Belfast children in contrast with their Dublin age-mates this does not reach significance (see table 1).

As a group, the characters in the stories told by Belfast children have little or no control over their own fates. They may choose to run away from "troubles" but the troubles pursue them. The characters have incomprehensible drives for destruction and the children in the stories are quite helpless to contravert them.

Table 1   Percentage of Death-Destruction Endings in Stories (1971)

AGE GROUP	6–8.11		9–14	
Religion	Protestant	Catholic	Protestant	Catholic
Belfast (%)	76	83	59	62
Dublin (%)	47	44	50	53

The differences between the Protestant and Catholic children of Belfast were only evidenced in the sources of expected malevolence. The Catholic children attributed it to a "malevolent fate" and the Protestant children saw it as coming from "those close to you." In contrast to the Dublin sample, the Belfast sample saw soldiering and warfare as an undesirable occupation. They also tended to focus their stories more on interpersonal relations, which when disrupted could not be amended by the guilty party making amends.

In responses to the Tapp questions, there were other differences between the Belfast sample and the norms established through the other studies (see table 2). These did not vary much throughout the three years of study. The Dublin sample tended to follow the general pattern of viewing rules and laws as prohibitive (ages 6–9), to seeing them as prescriptive (ages 9–14), and finally, some of the fourteen-year-olds were able to see them as the product of rational considerations in regulating behavior between people. In both cities the children tended not to see any differences between rules and laws. In response to the final question, "If you could change any rule, what rule would you change?" there was a sharp division between Belfast Protestant and Catholic children in 1971. Of the twelve Catholic children, eight responded that they would change "the Special Powers Act" or "the law about Internment." Seven of the Protestant children answered "the rules of all the bombing and killing."

Among the youngest children tested, those aged six and seven, was found some confusion about the word "rules." They were accustomed to a "law of the rule," whereby teachers punish disobedient pupils by spanking with a ruler.

There were some differences in answers to other of the questions on the Tapp-Kohlberg scale between the two groups of Belfast children. These differences were consistent until January, 1973, when, among the older Protestant boys (ages 11–14) there were some shifts that persisted through the January, 1974, test periods. This was in response to the third question, "What is a law?" Besides not seeing any difference between a "rule" and a "law," the Protestant children saw "the law" as being one or another authority figure, such as the Queen or a policeman of "the government." They personified it. The Catholic children viewed rules and laws as anonymous prohibitive forces. This was further evidenced when they responded to the question "Why should people follow rules?" in terms of the negative and punitive consequences of not following rules. In this, the Protestant and Catholic Belfast children were alike and they diverged from the prescriptive nature of responses by middle-school-aged children in the standardization sample.

None of the children in either Belfast or Dublin saw much possibility of rules being changed—at least not by themselves, either now or when they grow up. If rules are to be changed at all, it will be done by people "at the top" who are "in command" and they don't feel themselves likely prospects for that role.

Table 2   **Response Percentages on Questions Relating to Political Socialization: Comparison with U.S. Sample**

EDUCATIONAL GROUPS

LEVELS: CATEGORIES	PRIMARY (6–10)				MIDDLE SCHOOL (11–14)			
	DUB	TK	BEL 71–72	BEL 73–74	DUB	TK	BEL 71–72	BEL 73–74
What would happen if there were no rules?								
I: violence/crime	55	50	89	95	50	57	85	90
II: personal desires, not principles	20	15			25	20		
II: anarchy/disorder/chaos	30	25	11	5	60	57	15	10
II: impossible to imagine					10	7	5	5
III: man as self-regulatory (nothing would happen)					.			
What is a rule?								
I: prohibitive	76	60	92	98	36	30	80	90
II: prescriptive	17	20	7		40	40	12	10
II: enforcement				1	24	10	12	5
III: beneficial/rational		15			15	27		
What is a law?								
I: prohibitive	78	60	92	92	90	43	90	96
II: prescriptive	20	20			10	43	12	5
II: enforcement		10			10	23	8	
III: beneficial/rational					5	13		
Why should people follow rules?								
I: avoid negative consequences	53	50	60	82	25	13	50	90

Table 2   Response Percentages on Questions (Continued)

EDUCATIONAL GROUPS

| LEVELS: CATEGORIES | PRIMARY (6–10) | | | | MIDDLE SCHOOL (11–14) | | | |
	DUB	TK	BEL 71–72	BEL 73–74	DUB	TK	BEL 71–72	BEL 73–74
I: authority	15	5	27	20	30		25	15
II: personal conformity	30	35	6		41	13	14	5
II: social conformity		10	13	5	10	53	12	3
III: rational/beneficial/utilitarian	5					27	4	
III: principled								

Why do you follow rules?

	DUB	TK	BEL 71–72	BEL 73–74	DUB	TK	BEL 71–72	BEL 73–74
I: avoid negative consequences	65	60	94	96	26	47	89	90
I: authority	28	10	12	5	60	10	10	12
II: personal conformity	15	20			15	40	10	
II: social conformity					10	40	10	5
III: rational/beneficial/utilitarian					5	7	2	
III: principled								

Can rules be changed?

	DUB	TK	BEL 71–72	BEL 73–74	DUB	TK	BEL 71–72	BEL 73–74
I: no	40	20	98	98	46		64	70
II & III: yes	60	70	2		54	100	36	30

Are there times when it might be right to break a rule?

	DUB	TK	BEL 71–72	BEL 73–74	DUB	TK	BEL 71–72	BEL 73–74
I: no, unqualified	80	55	95	95	20	7	70	80
I: yes, unspecified		25			10			10
II: morality of circumstances	20	20	5	5	60	73	25	10
III: morality of rule					10	17	30	

Note: All questions except "can rules be changed?" and "Are there times when it might be right to break a rule?" are multiple-coded; therefore, percentages may total over 100 percent. Where answers were idiosyncratic or uncodable, the categories were omitted from the table. Level number indicates increasing cognitive maturity (adapted from Tapp and Kohlberg, 1971, p. 76).

Key: TK = Tapp and Kohlberg
       BEL = Belfast sample
       DUB = Dublin sample

The second field trip was carried out during June, July, and August, 1972. There were several changes in the political and social context by that time. Stormont, as a provincial seat of government, had been dissolved in March, 1972, following fast on the heels of "Bloody Sunday," the consequent demonstrations throughout Ireland, and the lesser known but politically even more significant parliamentary decision that the military be brought out from under the direction of the RUC, and that should go into effect *retroactively*! That decision came after a weekend emergency meeting of the House of Commons, the last weekend in February. William Whitelaw, a leader of the Conservative Party with some reputation for mediating disputes by creative solutions, was named Minister of State for Northern Ireland Affairs in the Home Office (Whitehall), and direct rule from that office was established. This did not negate parliamentary representation from Northern Ireland to Westminister, but it did eliminate the executive and legislative functions of the provincial government. The bombing campaign of the IRA was stepped up, and a new organization emerged on the paramilitary scene, the Ulster Defence Association (UDA). This is an umbrella group for many of the Loyalist (Protestant) paramilitary and community organizations, composed of working-class men, with a women's auxiliary and a youth group. They established "No-go" areas in their enclaves. Whether through that organization or apart from it, a campaign of assassinations had commenced. During the period of testing this sample, several additional major events occurred. First was an IRA-British army cease-fire that lasted approximately two weeks. (The Official IRA had declared a cease-fire in April of that year following their retaliation bombing of the paratroopers headquarters at Aldershot in England.)

One Friday in mid-July, the center of Belfast was racked by a series of explosions that killed nine people and seriously injured many others. The explosions were claimed by the Provisional IRA. (They claimed also to have given adequate warning but that the communication had been deliberately delayed by the British army command.) Next, there was a confrontation between the UDA, massed in strength, and the British army, which had demanded the removal of street barricades in their territory. The UDA with full uniform and equipment marched to a showdown. They won. Finally, in the midst of that period, the end of July, Operation Motorman was effected by the British army, which, with twenty-three thousand troops and heavy equipment, smashed the barricades of the "no-go" areas and commenced heavy and constant patrols in the Catholic estates. They set up headquarters in the schools and when the fall term commenced did not relinquish these posts. Internment activities were stepped up.

Into this scene of extreme and intense ongoing violence, then, testing was carried on in Derry and Belfast. Twenty-six Catholic children were tested in Derry and another twenty-six were tested in Belfast (again, half were Protestant and half, Catholic). The Derry children ranged in age from six through fourteen. As a group, they gave much longer stories with more complexities and fantasy than did the Belfast group. In comparison with the Belfast group examined within the same months, the Derry children told stories considerably more active in their import and, for at least ten of the children, the majority of their stories carried the import, "If something bad happens take action against it, even if you can't win." These ten were in the age group of ten through fourteen. The younger children were less pessimistic and fatalistic than had been the Belfast sample, but not significantly so. They were, however, obsessed with stories in which someone gets shot; or stories about a place at which someone had been killed. Four of the younger children in that sample were siblings whose father was, at that time, interned and who had been one of the fourteen men tortured with the hooding treatment. There had been considerable publicity about those cases, and their mother, who visited her husband regularly, was extremely depressed. These children told stories about orphans and about a mythical Ireland. There were no particular changes in the Belfast Protestant sample from the 1971 group, although different children were tested this time. There were more sectarian themes in their stories, but again, nothing significantly different from the previous six months. The Catholic children tested in Belfast during this period lived in Lower Falls and Ballymurphy, two of the areas most heavily affected by constant military activity. The differences in this group were greater. Even though the older children in this group told longer stories than the ones told the previous time, the stories were characterized even more strongly by helplessness, death, and destruction (see table 3).

Table 3   Derry and Belfast, 1972

AGE	DERRY				BELFAST CATHOLIC				PROTESTANT			
	NO.	M.I.	N/A %	N/P %	NO.	M.I.	N/A %	N/P %	NO.	M.I.	N/A %	N/P %
6– 9.11	16	82	34	10	8	67	30	32	7	74	25	30
10–14	10	80	30	16	5	80	45	36	6	92	32	12
TOTALS	26	81			13	72			13	82		

Key: M.I.   = Motivation Index Scores Average (Mean)
   N/A% = Percentage of Imports of Negative Active Type (10 imports per child)
   N/P% = Percentage of Imports of Negative Passive Type (10 imports per child)

The Interval of Power-Sharing

Winter, 1973, was marked by an increase in sectarian assassinations, which continued unsolved despite massive troop deployments. Several of the killings were proven to have been the work not of sectarian gangs, but rather of military personnel in unmarked cars and plain clothes emulating the weapons and dress of one or another extremist group. The strategy of "divide and conquer" was further evidenced in attempts to maintain factional warfare between the two IRA organizations as well. A study done that winter on intimidation from homes in religiously mixed areas indicated that the army was the major source for intimidation of Catholics, but this study was suppressed "lest the information further inflame the minority group," said the Director of Community Relations.

In early spring, the new plan for a power-sharing provincial government was announced in a white paper. The Diplock Commission Report and the Emergency Measures Provision, which replaced older legislation providing for internment without trial, proved by January 1, 1973, that internment, now called "detention," could be extended to members of the population who had previously been less vulnerable—women and Loyalists (Protestants).*

On January 1, 1973, the first woman was interned, and in the months that followed seven more joined her in the women's prison at Armagh. Attendance fell rapidly at the Finistion School, a primary school in Old Park at which soldiers were garrisoned. Population fluctuations at St. Colman's School across the road reflected the doubling up of families, as those who had been living in mixed or exposed areas pressed back into this small Catholic enclave to stay with relatives. The first UDA scandal had surfaced. A former British army noncom who had drilled and organized the Old Park contingent and then the larger UDA group defected and took his family off to England where he told his story to a team of reporters, and the friction among the leadership of the UDA became public knowledge. By the time the white paper was issued, four thousand people had been lifted, held, and subjected to various degrees of ill-treatment, interrogation, and torture.

A total of fifty-two children were tested in Belfast in 1973. The testing occurred during January, June, July, and December. Of this group, half of them again were Protestant and half Catholic, twenty-six girls and twenty-six boys. Twelve of the Catholic children tested in addition to this group (not included in the overall tallies) had been examined previously.

---

*Detention differs from internment in that detention implies that charges will be entered against the individual. Internment implies that there are no charges pending.

Five boys had been examined originally in December, 1971, a month after they had been lifted and held in jail for the first time. By the time of the second testing, they had each experienced lifting and interrogation another five to eleven times each. Still another boy, aged fourteen, who had been in the summer, 1972, Belfast sample, had died of injuries from a beating by soldiers. One twelve-year-old girl examined in summer of 1972 had been lifted several times but not put through interrogation when she was recognized as a girl. It was clear from the interviews that several of the Protestant boys, aged twelve through fourteen, who were tested at this time were members of Tartan gangs; several of the Catholic boys alluded to their membership in the IRA, although none of the children was ever asked about memberships. There were new problems and opportunities in gathering the sample in 1973. In some areas and among some persons concerned with youth, that which was already known about my research facilitated access to children living in areas not previously included, although they were working-class areas. In other cases, the political opinions expressed in vague allusions verbally and in writing by the Director of the Community Relations Commission and some of his associates closed off access to previous samples in the Protestant community.

Also, in July of 1973, my efforts were severely hampered by my own detention in Crumlin Road jail, Belfast, where I had gone to examine some prisoners at their solicitors' request. Although eventually a letter of apology was sent me by the Home Office, and despite my experience of illegal detention and some of the ill-treatment experienced by others so detained, strangely enough, for the local populace the onus was on me rather than on those who had detained me. Even though, in 1973, loyalists (Protestants) were beginning to be detained and the reaction in that segment of the community was similar to the reaction of the Catholic community— such as, "Our lads were being framed . . . they're not guilty. . . . The army is stepping out of bounds. . . . They're out to demoralize us"—a distinct ambivalence exists toward persons who have been imprisoned and finally released. They are heroes to those with whom they have little or no contact (and are simply a name), and those with whom they are in close contact become frightened lest they be assumed "guilty by virtue of association" —even while proclaiming that those who are thus detained are not guilty! This ambivalence and concern are very prominent in the themes of the stories given by the twelve adolescents who had themselves experienced similar treatment. They crop up in the other protocols too, but not as consistently. The striking characteristic of the TAT stories given in 1973 is the almost total negativism. That is, whether negative active or negative passive, almost all the children examined in both groups were giving stories whose imports suggested that bad things happen and that one must either acquiesce in them or unsuccessfully fight them (see table 4).

Table 4   TAT Imports, Belfast, 1973

	NO.	M.I.	POS/ACT%	POS/PASS%	NEG/ACT%	NEG/PASS%
Protestant	13	74	3%	15%	60%	12%
Catholic	13	70	2%	6%	46%	46%
N = 26						

By the end of 1973, the new Northern Ireland Assembly and executive were sworn in amid threats and demonstrations by both the UDA and the Provisional IRA. Both groups felt disaffected and alienated.

Back to Direct Rule

Some of the children in the 1974 sample of fifty children were examined during January, others during July, and the last group during December. Not included in the totals, but worth mentioning separately, were some middle-class Catholic children examined first in August, and then in December, 1974, in Belfast. Three of them, aged seven, nine, and eleven, are sisters. Their father is a prominent lawyer, a graduate of Queen's University. Their mother is a teacher. The children spent their earlier years living not only in an area predominantly Protestant, but indeed surrounded by Paisleyites. They presently reside in an affluent area in Belfast, predominantly Protestant, but also having some of the more affluent (albeit few) Catholic families. The area is quite cut off, however, from the kinds of organizations and grass-roots institutions that provide a sense of community and security for their working-class coreligionists. The voting pattern of their district indicated that its inhabitants were invested in maintaining this compromise form of government rather than changing to direct rule. These are the people who voted either Alliance Party or Official Unionist Party.* When the Ulster Workers' Council called its massive strike in May, 1974, demanding an end to power-sharing with the minority and a return to Protestant hegemony in Northern Ireland politics, the resulting chaos and violence rocked the security of this part of Belfast to a greater degree than had anything since the start of the troubles. The three girls tested demonstrated this insecurity in their stories. They did exhibit a

*Descriptions of these and other political parties are included in Chapter 6.

greater amount of fantasy and larger vocabulary than did their working-class peers, and they were quite well motivated (by SSA scoring criteria), with Motivation Index Scores of 115, 123, and 118 as of August. In December, their scores remained approximately the same, but they focused on problems in human relationships and adversity almost entirely, whereas their earlier stories were concerned with right and wrong and achievement. Few other children tested during the three years of sampling scored as high on Motivation Index, and few of those who were repeat-tested scored as high the second time as they did the first time (see table 5).

Table 5   M.I. Scores (Averages) Belfast

	WORKING CLASS				MIDDLE CLASS		REPEAT TESTED		
	PROT.	NO.	CATH.	NO.	CATH.	NO.	PROT.	CATH.	NO.
1971	85	12	80	12					
1972	82	13	72	13			68		6
1973	74	26	70	26			64		12
1974	72	24	69	26	4		66		5
TOTALS		75		77	4				23

Again, the 1974 sample included five children who had been examined during previous visits. One of the boys examined in January, 1974, was shot in May and hospitalized during June and July whereupon he was sentenced to Borstal. Many of the others had exceeded the upper age limit of the study, even though this had been stretched to fifteen years of age in order to accommodate the repeats in 1973. The 1974 sample did include children who had been repeatedly lifted and interrogated, shot, beaten and crippled, orphaned, and involved in junior UDA or IRA organizations. The trend that was so strong and obvious in the 1973 sample was again evidenced in the 1974 group. Both groups of children, Protestants and Catholics, manifested a strong concern in their stories for law and order. Neither felt there was any system of justice "out there" for them, and both felt that because wrongs went unchallenged and the world was chaotic, they had each to act as investigator, judge, and executioner. In short, they too expressed a vigilante thesis in combination with a view that any action undertaken in the name of freedom and justice for their group was intrinsically moral. Achievement themes centered on overcoming pain and/or successfully overcoming respect for life and property in order to carry out an action for "the cause." By 1974, another frequently recurring theme was "emigrating"—leaving the place, and often too leaving the people to "tear each other apart, and getting oneself out."

As for rules and laws, the December, 1974, sample of both Protestant and Catholic children, aged ten and over, wanted to have changed the "law of internment." Both groups of children in ages six through eleven continued the earlier pattern of telling stories about being afraid, about death and destruction, about overwhelming events. A child in their stories was always depicted as helpless in a world offering no alternatives and frustrating hope. In 1971, this kind of story-telling was common among the children aged six through eight or nine, but by 1974, these same children were eleven and twelve years old and their age contemporaries reflected the continuity of this view of life into the pre-adolescent years. Meanwhile, children of six had no remembered experience of a time in which there was no violence.

Conclusions

While the data from such extensive empirical testing are rich in hypotheses for additional study and replication research in Northern Ireland —as well as in other places in which minority populations are split off from people of the same religions or ethnic group by partition boundaries and other such internationally created artificial barriers—the data suggest two kinds of immediate conclusions. First, there are immediate negative and long-term pathological effects on individuals growing up in a condition of ongoing violence and social prejudice. Second, the probable survival of the group, the political future of that society, and the social implications of the attitudes, opinions, and beliefs as well as the modes of operation developed by its population are jeopardized. A footnote to both kinds of conclusions is the suggestive data on the middle-class and non-nuclear (Derry and Dublin samples) segments of the population.

As for the individual children, most of the conclusions by local mental health authorities attempt to segregate the effects into immediate and long-term and suggest that the immediate effects may be either dramatically pathological or equally free of pathology (depending on which personality theory the author embraces). They seem to ignore the unity of yesterday with today and tomorrow. The TAT stories and Tapp-Kohlberg questions indicated the incorporation of models of operation with their attendant belief systems and perceptions into the personality dynamics of the Protestant and Catholic and the working-class generation of the coming decade.

The responses of the Belfast children to the questions, as well as their stories, in 1971 indicated their disaffection from the sociopolitical events of which they were unwitting victims. The level of paranoia reflected in the import of these stories was higher for the younger children in the sample. The major difference between Protestant and Catholic children in that sample was on the sources of malevolence. This might be explained in the context of the different value systems of the two religious groups: that is, the Protestant ethic suggests that evil is a personal production and that the individual who is unsuccessful is so because he or she is not blessed. Thus, the evil comes from those persons "near you." This might also be explicable from the feelings of being encircled that were expressed by many of the adults in these areas. They believed that some kind of organized conspiracy existed to isolate the Protestant enclaves from each other by the interjection of Catholic housing schemes. The reaction against the civil rights movement was based on the encroachment of Catholics into the job market, thus making less secure the previously advantaged. In addition the old propaganda line was carried over through Paisleyism— of the Church of Rome subverting the Protestants' independence and freedom through the contemporary ecumenical movement. All these themes play some part in the very consistent views of the children that they are being attacked by those near them. The Catholic children seeing themselves victimized by a "malevolent fate" are expressing both a theological position of human impotence and divine intervention and the very real perception of a minority community's powerlessness. Both groups of children, themselves members of minority groups that are the targets of strong prejudice, and both groups—the entire sample of Northern Ireland children—must indeed be examined from the perspective of disadvantaged minority groups.

It is clear from their responses to the legal socialization questions that these children are developing in a milieu of authoritarianism and hierarchial ordering. They feel no prospect of potential political efficacy. Furthermore, their stories make it clear that this authoritarian regime carries the implication that power is the property of the strongest and that strength comes from possession of the biggest weapon.

In 1971 and early 1972, the Protestant children aged eight through fourteen, feeling themselves helpless to deal with adversity would defer to their elders, according to the TAT imports.* Even during that period, however, they were aware of the likelihood that their elders could not successfully overcome the adversity either. Their imports during 1973 and

---

*The term "import" refers to the psychodynamic theme of the TAT stories, which is derived through story sequence analysis. The import is then scored according to the manual.

1974 contained almost no indications that such problems should even be taken to authority figures for solution. By 1973, they along with their Catholic counterparts became obsessed with a passion for personally attempting to right the wrongs they experienced, and to *do* so meant injuring, killing, or destroying other people and places. This pattern may be a result of aging: the eight-year-olds who in 1971 were obsessed with death and destruction, feeling helpless and afraid, were by 1974 among the older segment of the sample and had grown into adolescence with the conviction that death and destruction and being afraid were constants and as such less meaningful (commonplace). Or, this pattern may have readily developed from the escalation of violence and lawlessness often personally experienced by innocent children, who were lifted and beaten by soldiers, attacked by older members of the extremist groups for minor infractions of discipline, or experienced first hand the death or crippling of a close relative or friend. It is worth noting here that girls were no less inclined to violent solutions than were boys, and that they were less often personally the direct recipients of beatings by authorities, but they were not by any means beyond the possibility of receiving violent punishment from groups within their communities for infractions of their norms.

The longitudinal implications of the erosion of story imports that could be classified as positive/active into a negativistic mode of operation seem to illustrate the theoretical dynamic described in the researches of William James, Karen Horney, Kurt Lewin, and Gordon Allport.[26] When they described the emotion and experience of fear and the effect of it, they pointed out that there are basically two ways to deal with a fearsome condition—that which one perceives as fearsome: to run away or to take action against the feared object, creature, situation, or person (violent, angry action). For the latter course to be chosen, the fear must mobilize into anger and the anger itself must locate an object. That object then becomes the target of hatred. For children who are at the first stage of development of moral judgment, as are the majority of the children in this study, the anger is likely to focus on the symbol quality of the target. Hatred thus becomes directed at the "symbol value" of a person or place rather than at an individual as such or a place as such. Thus, the form taken by the fear-into-hatred-into-violent-expression cycle, on which so much research in social psychology has focused, becomes the rough roadmap of the psychohistory of childhood in Northern Ireland.

The society itself provides the symbols by virtue of which any given individual can be a nonperson for another. The combined circumstances of an authoritarian sociopolitical context with historic attitude of prejudice provide a child-rearing atmosphere of conformity values, a submissive "uncritical" attitude toward idealized authorities of the in group, a tendency to condemn, reject, and punish people who violate conventional values.[27]

Add to this the experience of belonging to a minority group that is the target of strong prejudice—a situation common to both the Protestant and Catholic populations—and the self-influence of that pressure becomes a determinant in developing self-protective schemata and expectations of violence and disaster.

Out of this four-year interval sampling of two hundred children, what might one predict about the future of Northern Ireland? If the United Nations Convention on Genocide[28] were to be applied to the circumstances of Northern Ireland, we would note that the inhabitants of that place are being destroyed both physically and psychologically through the conditions of life that have made the children targets for the fears of conflicting groups. The "mental harm" being inflicted on "members of that group" has seriously decreased the probable survival of the group. Emigration has reached the level of a thousand monthly. As of January, 1976, more than fourteen hundred lives had been lost; more than five thousand persons put through interrogation and internment; uncounted thousands crippled by bullets and explosions; and a generation of children grown into believing that there is no "objective" justice "out there," but that each of them must act to right the wrongs. As the population accustoms itself to the increasingly stringent measures of law enforcement applied to it, the room for divergent thinking, for nonconformity, dwindles. Authoritarianism is further entrenched by the ubiquitous military presence and by frustration of attempts to participate in government. Bettelheim noted a distinct tendency among concentration camp inmates to identify with their guards.[29] The guards in Northern Ireland are military, the children identify with militarism—not necessarily with the British army itself, but with their "own army."

Various voluntary agencies are setting up play schemes for the children of Northern Ireland. Psychiatrists and psychologists there are engaging in more extensive clinical practice with children than ever before. The published theories and conclusions, however, of most of the indigenous professionals betray a kind of piecemeal wishful thinking. There is no solution to the effects on children of ongoing violence and political repression within that context. Once the military and political context is resolved, there will remain the need for massive rehabilitation efforts. Without them, the children of Northern Ireland—those who survive physically, those who do not emigrate—will be militaristic automatons, incapable of participating in their own destiny.

3 Psychotechnology
Its Effects

The British Society for Social Responsibility in Science, with a relatively small membership of psychologists, has been actively looking into the problems that result from the practices of the military and police in Northern Ireland. In response to the Compton Report's admission (1971) of "physical ill-treatment" of detainees, the BSSRS issued a lengthy statement, which included the following delineation of issues:

> The hooding and the noise appear to have been developed from a line of research initiated in the early 1960's—sensory deprivation. This research began partially in an attempt to understand brainwashing, but was also being used by the Canadian psychologist Hebb in the development of a theory that there exists an optimum level of arousal for cognition. The first sensory deprivation experiments were conducted in Hobbs' laboratory in Montreal. They involved student volunteers who lay on a comfortable bed. . . . Despite being paid twenty dollars a day, few were willing to remain more than two or three days, even though they slept for a considerable portion of the time. . . . What was generally accepted to be a handsomely paid rest turned out to be extremely unpleasant.[1]

BSSRS researchers found, as I did, that much of the vast and rapidly increasing literature on sensory-deprivation experiments emanates from studies done in the United States funded by the Department of Defense or through other military contracts.

After having examined several men who had been subjected to these treatments during interrogation in Northern Ireland, I expressed in a press interview a strong conviction that the use of such experimental techniques should be condemned by the profession. In response to the publication of my statements, Suedfield, an eminent American psychologist, wrote to me on January 10, 1972:

The American Psychological Association does not have the authority to outlaw research techniques. The 1971 indices of *Psychological Abstracts* published by the APA list over thirty publications under the heading "Deprivation/Sensory" in which human subjects were used. . . . Extensive research on sensory deprivation has shown that while it can indeed have deleterious effects, these are temporary except when deprivation occurs during early life or for extremely long periods; and, in fact, there are beneficial effects as well. For example, the technique is being used as a tool in psychotherapy.[2]

Psychological literature increasingly abounds in descriptions of experimental techniques that effect "coercive persuasion." Much of the experimentation in the United States has been carried out on prisoners. Classic experiments of this type have been performed at Vacaville Medical Facility, a part of the State of California prison system, and at Patuxent, a Maryland prison for young offenders. The techniques include massive ego threat through encounter techniques, isolation, sensory deprivation, aversive conditioning with chemical agents (Anectine is one example) or electric shock. Such technology is also utilized in regular programs for inducing behavior change among inmates of prisons, mental hospitals, and similar institutions. Psychosurgery is also being used for these purposes. The range of techniques has come to be popularly referred to as "brainwashing," because the individual subjected to them manifests entirely new behaviors, attitudes, and even beliefs, or so it is conceived.

Studies indicate that sensory-deprivation experience breaks down resistance to suggestion, and that sensory deprivation under conditions of severe physical restriction results in an intensification of the psycho-neurological effects. The BSSRS report and an in-depth study written by a physiological psychologist describe in detail the history and application of these techniques by the British military on various colonial populations.[3]

The ethics and social responsibility of the scientist (in this case, the psychologist) must be examined from three basic perspectives. First, the value of the research itself. What are the social institutional forces from which a particular project acquires its values? This is often answered by the nature and source of its funding. Second, the ethics of the research procedure. Does the experiment or study involve risk to the subject; is the subject provided complete information about his/her alternatives or are deception and compulsion part of the method of study? Third, dissemination of the information. Who will use it and for what purpose? For American psychologists there is a stated ethical criterion by which to measure these prospects. It is often ignored and/or twisted into obscure rationalizations, but as stated in the APA ethical code, the goal of psychology is "to promote Human Welfare."[4]

That the techniques of coercive persuasion are an intrinsic part of British army intelligence procedure is verified through the words of General Frank Kitson in his book;[5] and the charge is provided further legitimacy through the majority reports of the Compton and Parker commissions.[6] Perhaps the legitimacy of sensory deprivation and stress as experimental variables contributes to the acceptance of these techniques as legitimate military procedures.

Techniques of Interrogation

The abuse of psychological research and treatment is glaringly revealed by the entire interrogation and internment process that has taken place in Northern Ireland since 1971. The contributions of psychology to military science are cited in the Parker Commission Report: "Some or all of these techniques have played an important part in counter-insurgency operations in Palestine, Malaya, and Cyprus and more recently in the British Cameroons (1960–61), Brunei (1963), British Guyana (1964), Aden (1964–67), Borneo/Malaysia (1965–66), the Persian Gulf (1970–71)."[7] Furthermore, the report states that these techniques were taught by members of the English Intelligence Centre, a unit of the British army, to members of the Royal Ulster Constabulary in April, 1971. The report attempts to legitimize the use of these procedures by defining their effects in the same terms as used for such techniques in experimental procedures with voluntary subjects within a subject-limited time sequence.

The object of all the techniques is to make the detainee from whom information is required feel that he is in a hostile atmosphere, subject to strict discipline, and completely isolated so that he fears what might happen next. A further object of some of the techniques, varying according to local conditions, is one of security and safety: "Evidence we have received is to the effect that, while the techniques may produce some mental disorientation this is expected to disappear within a matter of hours at the end of the interrogation. It is true that in a small minority of cases some mental effects may persist for up to two months."[8]

The process of interrogation and internment was earlier described in the report of the Compton investigatory commission.[9] While it did not consider these techniques "torture," the inquiry acknowledged the use of psychological techniques to break resistance and obtain information. The Compton Report accepts the allegations that twelve of the men initially arrested under the Special Powers Act on August 9, 1971 were subjected to harsh treatment of the following description:

After being held for two days at Regional Holding Centres they were transferred to an interrogation centre at 6:30 A.M. on August 11th, held there until 15.45, transferred again to Crumlin Road Gaol for "service of detention and removal orders" and then returned to the interrogation centre by 19.00 all on the same day. While the prisoner was held at the interrogation centre he was subjected to these procedures while not actually being interrogated:

1. Hooding—his head was hooded in a black bag of tightly woven or hessian cloth.

2. Noise—the room in which he was held was filled with a noise described as "like the escaping of compressed air" or the "whir of helicopter blades" —presumably white noise of 85–87 decibel (Parker Report, p. 16).

3. Wall-standing—the internee was made to face a wall with hands high above his head on the wall and legs apart. If he moved or collapsed he was forced or lifted to regain position. Periods of wall-standing up to sixteen hours at a stretch (Parker Report, p. 10).

4. Sleep—none allowed for the first two or three days.

5. Inadequate diet—diet was severely restricted to occasional administration of dry bread and a cup of water.[10]

Several further points were strenuously emphasized by the Parker Report. It was apparent, first, that more than twelve internees had been subjected to one or more of the depth-interrogation procedures, and second, that such interrogation processes resulted in dysfunctions over a prolonged period of time for some internees. Finally, the minority report required the termination of use of such techniques whether on a few prisoners or on all of them. The British government claimed to have stopped the use of these "brutalities" when direct rule became the political format. Ample evidence has been given in sworn depositions and case interviews that these techniques were employed against a majority of the several thousand men who were interned or jailed under the Special Powers Act, and that they have been used against persons arrested under the Detention of Terrorists Act, which succeeded it. Second, all or some of these techniques have been used against thousands more, who were lifted for interrogation in any period since August 9, 1971, whether or not they were finally jailed, interned, or detained. Third, the techniques have undergone refinement since they became institutionalized as ordinary procedure. And finally, having performed psychological tests on the psychomotor and personality functions of over two hundred such men and boys at intervals ranging from twenty-four hours to a year following the application of these methods, I contend that the effects are long lasting, widespread, and disabling. When these techniques and their psychoneurological consequences are examined either in the abstract or in case studies of individuals who have experienced them, the behavioral consequences combine to create a society on the run.

The Effects of Interrogation

It is quite impossible to separate psychological from physical torture in terms of both infliction and effect. Much of the effect of hooding and wall-standing, for example, interrelated with the constant threat of and repeated physical beatings inflicted if the position was changed or if the detainee fell. Hooding restricts the supply of oxygen to the brain. The extreme fatigue induced by sleeplessness, impaired nutrition, and sudden weight loss combined with the physiological effects of anxiety extend the probability of impairment to the brain and central nervous system. When case histories of interrogated men are investigated in detail, it becomes apparent that none has been treated exclusively to a particular method of physical or psychological torture. Instead, there is what is called in experimental methods "contamination effect"—multiple treatments that impede the calculation of specific cause-effect relationships. There is every indication that the probable effects as projected from laboratory experiments will be multiplied and exacerbated in this application of psychotechnology.

The number of methods has been augmented during nearly four years of practice. They can be categorized according to three basic kinds of experimental psychology. First, sensory deprivation: this includes special white, soundproof, perforated-tile cubicles with special-position seats in which anything but a rigid position (sometimes sustained for hours) is met with physical abuse. In conjunction with this are blindfolding, masking noise, hooding, and isolation cells. Second, aversive conditioning treatments: these include a variety of kicks, punches, beatings, and electroshock with cattle prods to various parts of the body and finally to the genitals, burning with matches and candles, beating with instruments, and squeezing of the testicles. Third, the array of chemotherapies or altered states of consciousness: these include treatment with injections and force-feeding tablets (later chemical analyses reveal that these were amphetamines, and later effects suggest that LSD was also administered in this fashion).[11] Some variations of the treatments included forcing internees to run a gauntlet barefoot over broken glass, playing Russian roulette with prisoners, and the "helicopter treatment," in which blindfolded men were taken aboard a helicopter (or believed they were) and threatened or thrown out of it.

Surveying the experimental literature, Shallice points out the probable physical and behavioral consequences of such treatment singly or in combination: "A patient exhibiting this syndrome can no longer carry on his usual complex activities, assume his daily responsibilities or cope with interpersonal relations. As its symptoms develop he may become restless, talkative and delirious: ultimately he becomes totally confused and lapses into unconsciousness."[12] This refers to the syndrome associated with brain dysfunction, which has been found by prior researchers to result from experiencing these circumstances. From the earlier experimental findings, Shallice goes on to project the probable expected effects on the internees' perceptual functioning:

> The internees had a thick black bag over their heads, were subject to a loud masking noise, had to remain in a fatiguing and painful fixed position while dressed in a boiler suit. Thus there was virtually no variation in visual, auditory, or tactile input—a clear PD (perceptual deprivation) situation. Moreover they were strongly physically restrained, a situation that one knows exaggerates PD effects from the results of tank-type respirator experiments, such as that of Mendelsohn in which only one subject lasted for longer than 11 hours. In Ulster subjects were "at the wall" for durations of 43, 40, 30, 29, 20, 15, 14, 13, and 9 hours.
>
> Sleep was prevented and food was inadequate. Thus cognitive functioning would be impaired. Pain would be present both from beatings, and from the use of the "stoika" position at the wall. Finally, anxiety must have been at a high level for the internees even before sensory deprivation began, especially as no one knew that internment without trial was to be introduced. . . . One would expect the positive feedback process . . . to operate starting from an initially high level of stress with no need, because of objective danger, for chance "id" factors to initiate it (what could reasonably be considered a paranoid delusion under such objective circumstances?) and with cognitive functioning much impaired so that rational defences would be impossible. Clearly very high levels of stress would be reached rapidly.[13]

At the level of speculation over probable effects, Shallice, Storr, and others have raised the ethical issue of carrying forward and publishing such research, its value in promoting human welfare versus its obvious utility in subduing dissenting individuals and groups.[14]

Psychologists have to face the problem of how their research work is to be used, but practitioners (psychotherapists) are confronted by a different ethical issue—whether to cooperate with military authorities whose objective and actions are destructive to the bodies and minds of human beings. Are psychotherapists, like medical practitioners, bound by the International Code of Medical Ethics, according to which "under no circumstances is a doctor permitted to do anything that would weaken the physical or mental resistance of a human being"? There is direct evidence of the involvement of psychiatrists along with other medical personnel in assessing and prescribing for persons during the period of interrogation and internment, in compliance with the objectives of the interrogators.

The following statements have implications vis-a-vis the ethics of a physician's functioning toward his prisoner patients:

> The doctor in charge requested the patient (George Burt) to give an undertaking that he would not make any further attempts to escape, but this was refused. Mr. Burt was then given a suitable sedative and transferred at 6:30 A.M. under military guard to a side ward of a surgical unit. Ward records clearly show that during the time he was in this ward he was under continual medical and nursing supervision. Before discharge at 10:30 A.M. he was examined by a consultant Surgeon, who decided that further hospital treatment was unnecessary. [Northern Ireland Hospitals Authority]

> Should the role of a physician, in a manifest civilian hospital, demand that he prevent a political detainee from escaping? Should he use drugs if necessary to accomplish that end? We are not told whether Mr. Burt refused the sedative. Since he already indicated his desire to leave, presumably he did refuse.

> Obviously, for a doctor to retreat from a politically neutral position when acting in a professional capacity is a perversion of medical practice. Violence is even more dehumanizing if subtly meted out, particularly from the hands of a physician [Letter from doctor].[15]*

The medical personnel involved in various steps of the proceedings included psychiatrists. Internees later reported to a psychiatrist and psychologist who examined them at their own request that they had been visited, while in Crumlin Road jail, by one or the other of the staff psychiatrists then employed at Purdysburn Mental Hospital, located just outside of Belfast. In addition, at Long Kesh, there was a psychiatrist in attendance. According to several internees who had been hospitalized in the infirmary at Long Kesh, "this psychiatrist attempted to encourage internees' confidence. However, in no case did the reports of these medical and psychiatric personnel go to the patients or their patients' families." Only Dr. P. P. O'Malley, a psychiatrist employed at Mater Hospital, Belfast, who was called in to see three of the men who had been administered the hooding treatment along with other most intensive forms of interrogation, described his find-

---

*See also the case of the Catholic ex-serviceman, Thomas Maguire, 6 Bunbeg Park, Andersontown, Belfast, reported in the *Irish News*, February 12, 1972: "While in the hospital—the Royal Victoria Hospital—he had been told that the nursing staff were fed up with the army 'running the place.' They were not allowed to treat some patients until the soldiers had questioned them" (Faul and Murray).

ings to the patients and to relatives of the patients (internees). It is all too evident that the primary responsibility of psychiatrists employed by the military was to their employers. Of those patients seen and treated by Dr. O'Malley, all demonstrated severe psychoneurotic disturbances, and one patient appeared to have permanent damage.[16]

After release, many of the former internees described behavior of their own and their comrades that clearly indicated psychiatric syndromes. When questioned further about their psychotherapy, they described having been given large amounts of pills, Roche 5 and 10 (Librium and Valium), whose use became so endemic among the inmates as to have finally aroused the concern of some of the inmate commanding officers, some of whom began to commandeer such supplies and forcibly ration individual dosages.

Meanwhile, no call from within or from outside came for and by psychologists to lend their skills to ameliorating the effects of those techniques their colleagues had devised. The British Society for Social Responsibility in Science attempted to obtain access to the camp for three of their member psychotherapists. This was finally denied by the Stormont government. So far as can be discerned, local psychologists and those in the neighboring Republic of Ireland maintained their distance. A psychologist in Dublin researching cognitive processes volunteered his services for released internees. He wanted to evaluate them on cognitive functioning in his laboratory. Dr. G. Plunkett of Armagh courageously testified on behalf of some internees who had been variously tortured. He directed his testimony to the effects of such treatment. No psychologists or psychiatrists, however, offered their services directly to families, agencies, or others. In Ireland it may be considered unprofessional to make such overtures, but through their professional associations concerned psychologists and psychiatrists of any country may make such offers, as did the BSSRS. Of course, a government or government agency may *choose* not to accept the services (as might an individual if he/she is *not* imprisoned or hospitalized).

Destruction of Identity

Given the sociopolitical circumstances of Ireland, some moral issues remain undefined concerning the role of the psychologist and more broadly, the role of the medical and social scientist. These issues, related to the context of the political and military practices in Northern Ireland, demand attention and resolution. As psychology has advanced within the past two or three decades it has come ever closer to the goal of "predicting and controlling human behavior." This aim stands in potential conflict with the ethics of "promoting human welfare." Ethical considerations arise both from the prospective ends for which behavior control may be used and from the fact that psychologists and medical people are using it. If there was ever any doubt that the scientist exists and functions within a political milieu, subject to the ideologies and purposes of a partisan power system, these have been rapidly dispelled in the United States by the McCarthy era; by the involvement of social scientists in the Vietnamese pacification program; by the use of psychological research in brainwashing, first by the KGB and then by the Chinese against prisoners of war in Korea; by the American army in Vietnam; by the British counterinsurgency campaigns; and by the Russian policy of committing political dissenters to mental hospitals. Herbert Kelman describes this ethical dilemma:

> The social scientist today—particularly the practitioner and investigator of behavior change—finds himself in a situation that has many parallels to that of the nuclear physicist. The knowledge about the control and manipulation of human behavior that he is producing or supplying is beset with enormous ambiguities and he must accept responsibility for its social consequences. Even the pure researcher cannot withdraw into the comforting assurance that knowledge is ethically neutral. While this is true as far as it goes, he must concern himself with the question of how this knowledge is *likely* to be used, given the particular historical context of the society in which it is produced. Nor can the practitioner find ultimate comfort in the assurance that he is helping others and doing good. For not only is the goodness of doing in itself a matter of ethical ambiguity . . . but he also confronts the question of the earlier social context in which a given action is taken. The production of change may meet the momentary needs of the client—whether it is an individual, or organization, or a community—yet the long-range consequences and its effects on the units of the system of which this client is a part may be less clearly constructive. . . . Our knowledge about the control of human behavior is increasing steadily and systematically. Relevant information is being developed in various areas within psychology—clinical, social, and experimental—as well as in sociology and anthropology. . . . There is an increasing readiness to use whatever systematic information (or mis-information) about the control of human behavior can be made available. . . . Social scientists are becoming increasingly responsible and many agencies within government, industry and the military . . . are becoming interested in our potential contributions. An interest in controlling the behavior of its population is . . . a characteristic of every society and by no means unique to our age. It behooves us therefore to be concerned with . . . the social process to which we are contributing.[17]

Kelman saw the possibilities of a politically produced, massive "experiment in social psychology." At the time of his writing, in 1968, American scientists were reacting to the proposed Operation Camelot venture. This was a proposal to utilize social-science knowledge, techniques, and personnel on a CIA-sponsored counterinsurgency project in Latin America.

If one were to conceive of the troubles in Northern Ireland in terms of a huge experiment, the variables of which are manipulable exclusively by the military and political powers in Westminster and Whitehall, with a Dr. Strangelove psychologist utilizing established experimental procedure, design, and the eagerness of these governmental agencies, then the research report might read as follows: The program of "psychological genocide" has more potential than the actions of the Tudors, Cromwellians, Williamites, and Hanoverians, and more than the Poynings Law, the Penal Laws, and the Corn Laws. These earlier attempts to change the nature of the native Irish population were ultimately defeated through armed rebellions or civil resistance. The repeated attempts to plant new settlements in order to assure a loyal ascendancy followed, in various ways, the pattern set by the original Norman settlements—they were assimilated into the native culture. There are even indications that the Ulster plantation of Protestants failed equally and that instead of Anglicizing Ireland, they were themselves Irishized.[18]

The intent of any program of genocide is to eliminate the unique characteristics of a population group. It is not considered sufficient to eradicate only a particular religious practice or a particular family line. As demonstrated in Nazi Germany and Soviet Russia, the goal of such a program is to obtain homogeneity through eliminating any indices of differential cultural identity. To be completely successful, such a program must ensure that no capacity for future ascendancy in succeeding generations remains. It must ensure that the unborn will be unable to re-engage the struggle. This can be biologically engineered through chromosomal damage produced environmentally by chemical or mechanical stimuli.

An experimental social psychologist utilizing the literature of the science and the cooperation of civil and military authorities might begin to be effective where there has already been a manipulation of the political economy of the society (or by arranging for that). Endemic unemployment, inadequate housing, rigidification of social-class mobility, and a system of limited education based on an authoritarian model,[19] and incorporation of a rigid pattern of sex-role dichotomization, all might be requisite preconditions. In such a society, masculinity is prized and equated with physical aggression and dominance. If economic strivings in gratification of this role model are frustrated, and restrictions of access to power is added to the other preconditions, rebellion would occur. Such an outcome, however, would not necessarily provide a climate for continuance of this kind of experiment, so another variable must be introduced—the population must be maintained in a condition that would preclude a successful overthrow of the existing system.

The next logical step might be to utilize existing divisions in this society to foment intergroup competition for artificially scarcified products.

Since these "scarce commodities" are actually basic human needs such as food, safety, and shelter, aggressive competition is ensured through long-term aversive conditioning. Besides the strong reliance on corporal punishment in the socialization process, the recurring theme of heroism through martyred subjugation to overwhelming physical force (the rape myth) is inherent in the ethos of each of the competing groups.

Physical punishment leads to greater aggression, and severe punishment gives rise to patterns of behavior that are even more undesirable than the experimental behavior. Furthermore, use of physical punishment provides an aggressive model for imitation, which counters the effectiveness of the aversive stimuli and tends to increase the frequency and amplitude of aggressive behavior.[20]

Within a generation or even less time, the modus operandi in this "experimental society" becomes aggression. This provides the necessary empirical evidence for providing an even stronger system of controls to "prevent murder and pillage." Such a control system maintains itself on the support of those individuals and groups who are thus convinced that their survival (the security of their human needs) is predicated upon the survival of the control system. Meanwhile, the psychosomatic concomitants of the "fear into hatred cycle" generates a variety of pathologies which act in two ways to destroy the population: through the maladies themselves—ulcers (called "Ulsters" in Northern Ireland), paranoia, heart disease, malnutrition, alcoholism, birth defects, psychoses, suicidal depressions, nervous disabilities, and through the enactment of sectarian murders and riots. At this stage the exercise has been relatively inexpensive and if consistent control of the variables is maintained, the long-term effect will be debilitation and demoralization. The subjects have been left with few ways of countering the system if they are to be able to meet their basic needs. Those who have not lost their self-confidence recognize the overwhelming odds and quietly emigrate; these no longer present any threat. They will maintain only the stereotypic vestiges of their origins in their propensity to meet adversity with physical aggression and their commitment to the ethos of martyrdom. They thus demonstrate and dramatize their peoples' "self-destructive nature."

When, on August 9, 1971, a portion of the Catholic male population was abruptly and violently removed from their habitations on the basis of arbitrary selection, the action provided the authorities with their vehicle for social definition. Labeling this diverse group "IRA terrorists" told the populace that "terrorists" comprised a broad spectrum of the Catholic population. It demonstrated the efficacy of the government control system, which had been questioned by the majority of the population and threatened by an increasingly vocal minority. The method of picking up the men was itself aversive conditioning, in that it was physically aggressive, arbitrary, and fixed.

Estimates indicate that in one or another fashion at least twenty thousand Catholics were subjected to one or more of the following experimental treatment conditions: sensory deprivation, sleep deprivation, extreme fatigue, sensory overstimulation, crowding, gross physical abuse, hallucinogenic and emetic drugs, incarceration, electroshock conditioning, intermittent threats, and intimidation. Treatment time ranged from four hours to fourteen months, with no apparent rationale for the differences. The very arbitrariness of the treatment program succeeded in demoralizing, defusing, and distorting the functioning of the subjects thus treated. There was never an assurance of continued detention or release. Periodically, brief supervised visits between the incarcerated group and those close to them allowed each to witness the other's deterioration. This maximized the effects throughout the broadest possible segment of the community. Disputes that served to create factions among the internees could be thus extended into the community and vice versa.

By maintaining controls over the release of scholarly study—exemplified by the confiscation of an incarcerated social scientist's collection of empirical data*—and by denying independent scholars' requests for access to the subject,† hegemony was maintained over the subject population. This is not uncommon in experimental social psychology, since the subjects are often "locked up" for the duration of the experiment.‡

Near the end of the third year of crisis (September, 1972) the appearances and behavior of women and children indicated dazedness and apathy; the suicide rate increased; consideration of alternatives was severely limited; people were dying from untreated curable diseases; cumulative effects of prolonged chemotherapy and overdose had produced bizarre symptoms and organic damage.[21] P. O'Malley's data on suicide rates sharply controverts Lyon's claim for the ameliorative value of riot behavior. Statistics on

---

*Des O'Hagen, Lecturer in Sociology, Stanmillis University, had attempted, with my help, to document the psychological effects of internment on ten inmates of Long Kesh. His careful compilation of objective test data was confiscated when he was released and before it could be shared with the larger scientific community.

†Anthony Storr and other British psychiatrists and psychologists requested permission of the Stormont and Whitehall governments, through the British Society for Social Responsibility in Science, to evaluate the effects of the internment and interrogation processes. Their request was denied.

‡A Yale University team, headed by Edward Klein, Leonard Doob, and J. Miller, and financed by a private source, removed fifty-six inhabitants of Belfast to Stirling in Scotland for a laboratory experiment in social-conflict resolution. None of the subjects was allowed to communicate with the outside world for the two-week duration of the experiment.

drug use were requested in Parliament by B. Devlin, MP: these statistics were published for England, Scotland, and Wales, but not for Northern Ireland. Devlin was told that such data were "not essential and too expensive to compile." Thus, statements here are based on estimates derived from discussions with physicians in Belfast, pharmacists, nurses, and clergy.

Not alone among the applied scientists, the busy general physician collaborated in the larger program. Aware of the escalating stresses and psychosomatic complaints, the general doctor prescribed tranquillizers and sedatives, and, by limiting referrals to specialists, relieved them of the overstrain. Finally, without denouncing the causes for the vast increase in the use of medical services, the doctors attempted to cope with it by avoiding time-consuming physical examinations whenever possible. These efforts did much to mask individual and social maladies.

Intermittent aversive conditioning continued through the natural behavioral sequelae to the police and military in the form of prolonged fear of reprisals and a combination of severe restrictions with limited rewards. (Soldiers on duty in Northern Ireland are not accorded combat pay, yet they are constantly reminded that they are in hostile territory—more than four hundred men had been killed by 1975 and there are no figures on the number wounded.) Since it is quite impossible for these agents to vent their hostility on the political controllers they can only react against the subjects whom they perceive as the source of their discomfort. Thus, the soldiers and the subjects act on one another as intermittent aversive conditioners.

The male population, released from the internment camps, had been routinely placed on sedatives and tranquillizers. The men rapidly increase their own dosage as they emerge into the added stress of a disrupted family life. Many have suffered damage to the brain and central nervous system, which, through the indifference of professional personnel and inadequacies in the medical referral system, go either untreated or are masked by palliative prescriptions. The consequences of polarization, produced within the "cages," have been greatly intensified upon the return to joblessness, marital discord, and escalating anxiety.

When they were initially selected, it was clear that many of the men had no political commitment or partisan preferences within the loosely labeled "nationalist" spectrum. The intense crowding and competition, the arousal of hatred and physical aggression, resulted in the polarization of the internees into two groups—those sympathetic to and committed to the Official IRA and those committed to the Provisionals. In the name of such divisions, acts against individuals took on a significance that reaches into every aspect and segment of the community and ultimately has a countereffect on the Protestant working class. The larger number has become committed to the terrorist tactics of the Provisionals, an easier alternative for persons who have been socialized into equating the positive value of masculinity with the capacity for physical aggression. This choice is abetted by the aversive conditioning received during interrogation and internment. When loyalists (Protestants) were also interned during 1974–1975, in smaller numbers, they experienced separate but similar treatment.*

Polarization has been simultaneously effected in two directions—in major subgroups, Protestant and Catholic; and within each, in the divisions between those whose program is violent retribution and those who, either out of apathy or real commitment, cling to peaceful preferences. Sectarian assassinations and kidnappings are matched in number and grisly quality only by the partisan assassinations and kidnappings.

Although this sophisticated experiment in psychological genocide has not yet reached completion, it is possible to assess its efficacy. In a more primitive and obvious fashion Hitler's scientific disposal teams managed in eight years to reduce the world's Jewish population by more than half. They were, however, dealing with (1) larger geographic distribution and (2) a war of aggression against a number of other national powers. Though they could afford to be more obvious in designing an efficient system, they could not put as much effort into carrying it out. In assessing the difference, one should note that the experiment in Northern Ireland is being carried out on a smaller budget and that other nations are aiding, with materials and supplies. Through the NATO commitment, for example, CS gas and rubber bullets manufactured in the United States are part of the standard experimental equipment. This experiment is now in its fifth year and more accessible to viewing by the rest of the world. It is furthermore not contaminated by the exigencies of an external armed conflict. In fact, it cannot be properly raised as an issue of human rights within the assembly of nations because the United Kingdom claims it to be an "internal matter."

The final effects must be assessed in terms of the ultimate demise of any ethnic identity and the permanent subordination of the inhabitants of that territory to whatever ruling power is finally imposed.

*In 1974–1975 I examined loyalists who had been interned and found that they had been subjected less often to psychological torture in interrogation but had been severely beaten and incarcerated under the same debilitating conditions.

4 Social Control Mechanisms
Putting a Society on the Run

Is it possible to make a whole society accomplice in its own destruction, without the use of massive cattle-car transports, gas chambers, and ovens? In the age of the ultimate weapon—nuclear bombs—limited warfare, massive social and political upheavals, and massive international cooperation, it has been possible to destroy most of the arable land in southeast Asia, for millions of people to die of famine in Africa, and for "limited wars" to result in big power confrontations, and yet we congratulate ourselves that the gas chambers and guillotine have receded into history in Western Europe.

Internment, a feature of life in Northern Ireland since the founding of that province, serves as the specific instrument for the destruction of the Irish people. It provides the institutional framework through which the victims are depersonalized and dehumanized in preparation for the deadly acts of the aggressors. Internment without charge or trial, or preventive detention as it is now euphemistically referred to, is a particular heritage of the British colonial legal system.* This machinery was not used in their home island until the enactment of the Prevention of Terrorism Act in November, 1974. In the main, this act has again been applied against Irish people who are either attempting to enter England or who already reside in England and maintain any republican or loyalist contacts. Through preventive detention for indeterminate periods, persons who are not guilty of any crime, but who are suspect by reason of their "being," may be subjected to physical and psychological brutalities in interrogation, and their families and friends stamped, too, with the guilt of their association.

---

*Internment was the term used throughout the British colonial system to describe preventive detention of persons who might engage in anti-government activity. The Emergency Provisions Act of 1973 and the earlier Detention of Terrorists Order, 1972. See Appendix on Detention Orders.

This process is the specific instrument for the ultimate destruction of the captive society's capacity to participate in determining its own destiny. My own studies of the effects of internment in Northern Ireland from 1971 through 1975 provide an empirical assessment of them on the individuals incarcerated, their families, and their communities. On August 9, 1971, between three and five in the morning, hundreds of men were rousted out of their beds and brutally dragged off, first for interrogation and then for internment. In the years since that date, thousands more have endured this experience, whose consequences have proved far-reaching.

Careful phychological examination of persons who have been put through depth interrogation and/or internment in Northern Ireland indicates extensive personality damage to all internees; and that at least 60 percent of the persons interned suffer consequent psychomotor dysfunction —an indication of organic brain damage.[1] The specific processes applied in interrogation and internment since 1971 were first tested in experimental laboratories of psychologists during the preceding three decades and were derived from the earlier application of such scientific work by the Gestapo and the NKVD.

Internees in Northern Ireland and those who have since been incarcerated as "detainees" have been subjected to sensory deprivation, sensory overstimulation, de-oxygenation, massive ego threat, extreme stress resulting from enforced sleep deprivation and dietary insufficiencies, as well as constant threats of total physical annihilation. These techniques, sometimes referred to as "brainwashings," are oriented toward the destruction of individual identity, increased suggestibility, deterioration of cognitive capacities, and "conversion phenomena." While they were incarcerated, internees (a group which by 1975 included men, women, and adolescent children, Catholics and Protestants) were subjected to overcrowding (to the point of total deprivation of privacy), beatings, gassings, treatment with massive doses of tranquillizers and barbiturates; they were housed and fed at a level below the minimum International Red Cross requirements for prisoner of war camps. Yet these were not prisoners captured from a foreign army. These were Irish people who had been brutally removed from their homes and carted off to concentration camps within less than one hundred miles of where they and their forebears had lived out their lives.

The initial internment sweep of August 9, 1971, was carried out by the British army ostensibly in conjunction with the Royal Ulster Constabulary and at the request of Brian Faulkner, then Prime Minister of the Northern Ireland government. As of July it had been fairly clear that Faulkner would call for internment, an action that had been taken by Northern Ireland prime ministers at least once every decade since the Civil Authorities (Special Powers) Act of Northern Ireland had been enacted in 1922. But never before in the history of this fragment of a province (which made itself into a full province of the United Kingdom) had so many people been incarcerated under its provisions. During the first six-month period, 2,157 were arrested under the Special Powers Act, 598 interned, 159 detained, and 1,600 released after interrogation.[2] But the figures on internees have never added up. One citation during 1971 and early 1972 indicated that there were well over nine hundred internees[3] and detainees in Long Kesh alone. Later, of course, there were many more detainees, fewer internees, and more sentenced prisoners. Many individuals experienced all three catgories. The special courts set up to administer the Emergency Provisions Detention of Terrorists Act of 1973 were able with very little help to turn an internee or detainee into a sentenced prisoner. If there was any basis on which RUC or military officers could charge a defendant with illegal activities, they did not even have to testify in front of the accused or present their evidence in advance to the defense solicitor. Hence, seldom was there any way to prepare a defense except through presentation of character witnesses—usually parents or spouses. The Commissioner(s) hearing the cases would then decide whether there was sufficient evidence on which to base charges. If the evidence was insufficient, but provided reason to continue the defendant under suspicion, then the latter was returned to custody anyway and provided with a new detention order. If, however, there was evidence of specific incidents, the defendant could be charged, tried, and sentenced in relatively rapid order. Thus, often an individual was simply shifted from one compound to another rather than released. Sometimes a few days would elapse during which a released internee would begin to readjust at home or even set foot outside the detention facility, only to be returned with a new internment or, later, a new detention order. According to some published figures as of June, 1973, seven months after the initiation of commissions recommended by the Diplock Report, a maximum of 120 out of approximately 600 detainees were released after coming before the commission.[4] On Sunday, June 3, of that year, Patrick Crawford, a young detainee, committed suicide. He was not the first inmate to attempt this desperate action, nor was he the last. Others slashed their wrists, took overdoses of barbiturates, some banged their heads against waterpipes during interrogation, and still others initiated fights with other inmates or guards. There is no statistical record of the number of men and women who had to be removed to mental hospitals or other institutions for treatment of mental or physical breakdown.

In Long Kesh

In December, 1971, I made my first visit to Long Kesh. The camp itself, still in use as a detention center, although renamed "The Maze Prison," was then made up of six compounds, referred to as "cages." They were indeed cages, enclosed by wire. Each compound held approximately ninety men who were totally confined to their compound and one another's company, with the exception of the weekly half-hour visit with close relatives. With some slight variations, the cages contained four galvanized, nissen-type huts with doors at both ends. The walls were porous and on wet days the rain soaked through the insides. It was necessary to move the bunks into the centers of the huts to keep the bedding from becoming soaked. Part of one hut in the complex was reserved for use as a chapel, canteen, and meeting hall, another was used as a washroom and toilet, half of which became a workroom. The remainder of the space was divided to allow between thirty and forty men to the larger two huts and twenty more to the remaining half of the other one. The huts containing forty (and sometimes more) men measured approximately seventeen meters long, eight meters wide, and five meters high at the apex of the arc. The permitted 136 square meters of floor space was considerably less than that provided in a housing development project intended for a couple with one child! Experiments conducted with rats and macaques indicate that there is an increase in cannibalism and incidents of hostile aggression respectively, commensurate with decrease in space.[5] Forty chimpanzees, for instance, would never be successfully maintained in a zoo enclosure of this dimension.

Long Kesh had been an airfield during the Second World War, and the cages were placed on parts of the former runway. The enclosures consist of a wire fence three-and-a-half meters high, meshed with coiled barbed wire on top and measuring seventy meters by thirty meters. The entrance is formed into a small wire cage on which are two heavy doors, both locked on the outside. In this way, among ninety men or more, many remaining a year, the geographic perimeters of life encompass a total of 585 square meters, of which approximately 460 are outdoors, an outdoor space of muck and mire. Rats were so common that cages were often issued cats to act as control agent. Other vermin contributed to the spread of repeated epidemics of gastric and skin diseases.

On the outer perimeter of the camp is another fence with several inner barbed wire fences, which are patrolled by armed soldiers and dogs. There are five watchtowers with continuous lights. At the time of my first visit, the camp had not received its full complement of inmates, nor had they received the full measure of restrictions and brutality that followed conflicts over camp conditions which erupted periodically. Through the winter the numbers increased, as did the cumulative effects of the earlier interrogation methods and limitations of diet, exercise, and distractions.

To the physical miseries of everyday existence, the lack of privacy and diversions, one must add the psychophysical effects of the interrogation process these men had experienced. It is impossible to parcel out the cause and effect relations among these variables. It is, however, apparent that the men who undergo this process suffer some combination of the effects characteristic of each separate circumstance. Further, of course, there is the polarizing effect produced by the social dynamics of an internment camp society. In this case, potential antagonisms were enhanced by the particular fashion in which the men had been selected. In some instances arresting patrols had gone to a house or flat asking for a particular individual and, finding him absent, had simply taken whatever man or men were present. In one instance, a mother, employed as a night nurse, had returned home to find that her husband and four-year-old daughter had been lifted together. During some point in the processing, the child was separated from her father and then held in several different places through the next six hours. In other instances, with an apparent lack of understanding in discriminating among similar Gaelic first names, brothers and/ or fathers and sons were taken together, to have it later become evident that only one or another of them had been listed for internment.

The only common characteristic among the internees was their Catholic parentage. Those who were either members or supporters of the Provisional wing of the IRA were, in most instances, men with a strong nationalist ideology. During the period of internment and subsequent detention, those held at Long Kesh ranged in age from fourteen to sixty-eight. The majority were working-class men, a proportion bound to occur in any random sampling of the Catholic population in Northern Ireland. The complement did, however, also include six school teachers, one college professor, an accountant, several journalists, a lawyer (he passed his examinations while interned), university students, a couple of social workers (youth leaders), and a number of entrepreneurs. The implication for people in Northern Ireland was patently clear (albeit erroneous): "IRA criminals are to be found in every echelon of the Catholic population. All Catholics are violent and dangerous men."

In these circumstances, so like an enlarged, elaborate experiment in social and physiological psychology, the techniques and findings of psychologists remained the possessions and tools of the military authorities. An effective technique (borrowed from the psychological laboratory) is the pedagogical and military tactic of "making examples of cases." This tactic requires a kind of partially open program, which was provided by limited visits and the publication of various reports (unofficial, of course) regarding the conditions of interrogation and internment. As relatives and friends anxiously noted the deterioration of the interned men, the existing prison facilities were expanded to include increasing numbers, and conditions within the camps worsened. Teams of outside observers from various agencies were denied official access, thus relegating their reports to a realm of ambiguity sufficient to arouse general anxiety, but insufficient to be authoritative.

Within the camps military doctors were the only possible source of help. Doctors examined the prisoners at various stages of the interrogation process and a military psychiatrist offered the men tranquillizers and sedatives during their imprisonment.

The Hooding Cases

During the first two months of internment, at least fourteen men were subjected to a depth interrogation treatment which became infamous as "the hooding treatment," so called because throughout their days and nights of interrogation torture, their heads were kept covered by thick, coarse cloth bags. Among the fourteen were nineteen-year-olds and men in their mid-forties. Several of them were members of the Provisional IRA, several were members of the Official IRA, several were committed to nonviolent civil protests as members of Northern Ireland Civil Rights Association (NICRA). Some of the fourteen were republicans, politically, but were not members of any particular organization.*

Of the original fourteen hooding victims, I did depth interviews and clinical testing of nine during the summer of 1973. At that time, four others were still incarcerated in Long Kesh, and one other after his release had been hospitalized for mental illness in the south. These were not the only internees who underwent the hooding treatment. They were, however, the subject of a case brought by the government of the Irish Republic against the United Kingdom in the European Commission of Human Rights, which, in August, 1976, found the British government guilty of violating human rights by torturing political dissidents. But the use of hooding in interrogation did not cease entirely when direct rule was initiated in March, 1972. Nor did torture during depth interrogation end with the issuance of the Emergency Provisions Act. Neither of the reports of the United Kingdom investigatory commissions (with the exception of the minority report of the Parker Commission, entered by Lord Gardiner)[6] described the processes of hooding, sensory deprivation, overstimulation, isolation, beatings, extreme prolonged stress, or even the use of drugs as torture or brutality. In late 1972, the European Court of Human Rights accepted a second case brought against the United Kingdom for such treatment of political prisoners. This second case was sponsored by the Association for Legal Justice and Northern Ireland Civil Rights Association in

*Republican politics—the antimonarchy ideology that incorporates a thirty-two-county united Ireland—were illegal in the six counties of Ulster from 1922, when Ireland was partitioned, until spring, 1973, when the Whitelaw white paper outlined a plan for a power-sharing government in whose elections republican political parties could take part.

behalf of prisoners tortured after the initiation of direct rule. When I, at the request of the solicitor, sought to examine two of the prisoners in that case, I was detained in Crumlin Road jail.*

The "hooded men," with the exception of two who were lifted in October, 1971, included four men from Belfast—Jim Auld, Joe Clarke, Kevin Hannaway, and Francis McGuigan. Two of these men were subsequently detained for nearly four years. Sean McKenna and Gerry McKerr were from County Down, and Brian Turley and Pat McNally from County Armagh. Mickey Montgomery and Mickey Donnelly were lifted from their homes in Derry and Paddy Joe McClean and Pat Shivers from small towns in County Tyrone. Of the 342 men arrested in the initial internment sweep, these twelve from diverse parts of Northern Ireland were collected at Ballykinlar and Magilligan detention centers. After their first forty-eight hours of being physically mistreated and deprived of food and sleep, they were separated from the others at the two camps. They were already exhausted and confused by sleeplessness, forced exercises (which were referred to as "positions of discomfort"), being made to do standing runs, urinate while running, frog-marched, handcuffed, and forced to run a gauntlet between two rows of MPs wielding batons.

These twelve, either individually or together, were put into a helicopter after being hooded and handcuffed. What followed afterward might have been done differently with individuals or pairs; or was possibly an experience of the twelve in common. There was sufficient difference among their recollections of specifics to suggest that the torture program was "individually tailored." Paddy McClean, a teacher of mentally retarded children, seemed least affected by his ordeal. He expressed a hypothesis, however, that their experience was a kind of "experiment" and that for some inexplicable reason twelve other men of similar geographic and age distribution had been placed in a separate section of Crumlin Road jail and had not been allowed out in the yard and had had "only" the ordinary physical brutality during lifting. He believed that they were scheduled to be dispatched to the same treatment as his group but that the plan had been changed. In his interview with me he said:

Here's something I've never made known before to anybody. . . . During that time we were in the interrogation place, another twelve men were kept inside Crumlin Road jail and not let out at all except to be put through the exercises. Whenever we came off the thing they were let off into the

*By that time I had already conducted many examinations of prisoners within a few months of their interrogation ordeals. In other instances, where persons had been put through interrogation and subsequently released rather than being charged or detained, I had conducted examinations within hours of their release.

yard. I thought if they had gotten any great information from us they would have taken this other group and put them through the same thing. But they never did that. . . . I knew some of them that was in that group . . . one had been a paratrooper in the British army . . . They were kept in isolation . . . each of us were numbered on the soles of our feet.

Two of the other men named by McClean were also examined by me after their release. One of them had mentioned the peculiarity of his first ten days in Crumlin Road, which contrasted sharply with the physical brutality he was accorded afterward when he was imprisoned on the *Maidstone* (a prison ship that afforded the least humane treatment of the three internment facilities).

If indeed this was a planned experiment in torture, there are some differential results to be reported. Among the hooding victims, for no more than three could a clinical prognostication be made about any likelihood of a return to normalcy. The other eleven evidenced some kinds of permanent debilitation.

The statements by McClean and Shivers describing their treatment provide an account of these experiences:

Report on Arrest, Interrogation and Treatment of Frank McGuigan, Belfast; Kevin Hannaway, Belfast; Michael Donnelly, Derry; Joe Clark, Belfast; Jim Auld, Belfast; Michael Montgomery, Derry; Gerry McKerr, Lurgan; Brian Turley, Armagh; Patrick McNally, Armagh; John McKenna, Newry; **by J. P. McClean**

During the first 48-hour period of detention I was subject to the same treatment and conditions experienced by the majority of my fellow detainees.

At the end of these initial 48 hours a hood was pulled over my head and I was handcuffed and subjected to verbal and personal abuse, which included the threat of being dropped from a helicopter while it was in the air. I was then dragged out to the helicopter, being kicked and struck about the body with batons on the way.

After what seemed about one hour in the helicopter I was thrown from it and kicked and batoned into what I took to be a lorry. The lorry was driven only a couple of hundred of yards to a building. On arriving there I was given a thorough examination by a doctor. After this all my clothes were taken from me and I was given a boiler suit to wear which had no buttons and which was several sizes too big for me.

During all this time the hood was still over my head and the handcuffs were removed only at the time of the "medical examination."

I was then taken into what I can only guess was another room and was made to stand with my feet wide apart and my hands pressed against a wall. During all this time I could hear a low droning noise, which sounded to me like an electric saw or something of that nature. This continued for what I can only describe as an indefinite period of time. I stood there, arms against the wall, feet wide apart. My arms, legs, back, and head began to ache. I perspired freely, the noise and the heat were terrible. My brain seemed ready to burst. What was going to happen to me? Was I alone? Are they coming to kill me? I wished to God they would end it. My circulation had stopped. I flexed my arms to start the blood moving. They struck me several times on the hands, ribs, kidneys, and my kneecaps were kicked. My hood-covered head was banged against the wall.

As I have said, this particular method of torture lasted for an indefinite period, but having consulted other men who suffered the same experiences I believe the period to have been about two days and nights.

During this time certain periods are blank—fatigue, mental and physical, overwhelmed me; I collapsed several times, only to be beaten and pulled to my feet again and once more pushed, spreadeagled against the wall. Food, water, and the opportunity to relieve my bowels were denied me. I collapsed again.

I came to in what I believed to be Crumlin Road Jail, having been pushed into a chair. The hood was removed and I was handed what I was told was a detention form. I was told to read it. My eyes burnt and were filled with pain; they would not focus and I couldn't read the form. I was thanking God that my ordeal was over. No more pain, now I could sleep. But no! The hood was pulled over my bursting head. I was roughly jerked to my feet and half-pulled, half-kicked, and beaten for about 400 yards. This was the worst and most sustained beating to date. Fists, boots, and batons crashed into my numbed body, someone else's—not mine. Hands behind my back, handcuffs biting into my wrists. Pain! Someone pulling and jerking my arms. Thrown headlong into a vehicle—soft seats, beating continued, boots, batons, fists. Then the noise, that dreaded helicopter again. Dragged out of the vehicle by the hair, thrown onto the floor of the helicopter. Blacked out.

Conscious again. Hands manacled in front of me. Pushed against a wall, legs wide apart. I dug my fingernails into the wall. Pain all over me.

Now that I can relax and think about it I can't find words to describe the pain. Without attempting to be melodramatic I think I can best describe it by saying I was enveloped in stretching cramping pain.

My mind began to drift. I tried to sing to myself. I was going mad. I must already be mad to stick this.

Still standing rigid against the wall, someone takes my pulse, sounds my bruised chest over my heart. Must be a doctor.

Dragged along. Pushed into a chair, hood pulled off. Screaming blinding light, questions fast and hard, couldn't speak. "Spell your name." —tried to find the letters, swimming in my brain—couldn't spell my name. I must be insane. More questions—blows, hair pulled. Still can't see well. A table—three men at it—all writing—blinding light.

I was told I would be given half an hour to rest and think. Then I would be asked more questions and if I didn't answer them I would be taken back to the "music room"—the room with the noise—pain.

Sleep—deep, black sleep. Pulled to my feet. Back to the questions again, would not give answers. Back to "music room."

Feet wide apart, hands handcuffed—against the wall. Droning noise fills my head. By this time I could feel no pain. Just numb. Dragged away from the wall, legs buckled under me, fell to the floor. Dragged by the ankles up and down shallow steps. Didn't care—past feeling pain.

Didn't have a body.

From now on it was interrogation—back to the "music room"—some sleep. Then the first taste of water in—how many days? Some dry bread and more water.

We were given our first "meal." This consisted of a cup of watery stew, which I had to eat using my fingers as utensils. The hood was lifted just enough to leave my mouth free. We were then allowed to the toilet for the first time since we arrived.

Punishment now eased off. Interrogation continued. Strict questioning —no beatings—just threats and personal insults. Food of a more substantial nature, still badly cooked and served, but at least it was regular.

The hood was taken off and I was allowed my first wash.

Now I was allowed to sleep, but the room was so cold that sleep was hard to come by. The fear of more beatings was still with me. I was terribly alone! They gave me one blanket—to keep me warm they said.

I was then told it was "all over" and that I was going to be interned in Crumlin Road Jail. I didn't believe them—another trick, I thought. Still uneasy—still worried—still alone.

Hood still over my head, but treated better now. No questions, no beatings.

Journey to Crumlin Road Jail by lorry, helicopter, and Land Rover. I was still sane, still alive—thank God!

Patrick Shivers was a plasterer by trade, born and educated in Scotland. He was interned for republican activities during 1958–1959. Shivers is a nonviolent man whose activities have been directed toward fund-raising for memorials to such patriots as Henry Joy McCracken, the Protestant leader of Belfast republicanism of an earlier era. Shortly before he was interned, his sister died of toxemia in pregnancy and his wife gave birth to a sickly infant, seven weeks premature. Of his five children, one died shortly after Shivers's own ordeal, and others have been diagnosed as suffering from a chronic, usually fatal deteriorative disease. Pat's wife, Mary Elizabeth, is epileptic. The Shivers family was awarded compensatory damages of £15,000 ($37,000). Considering that both husband and wife suffer from chronic nervous anxiety, that neither will ever work steadily again, and that no one in their family can expect to overcome the effects of this debilitation, there is little comfort to be taken in his financial compensation. In Pat Shivers's words, this was a very hard-earned sum.

In July, 1973, I examined Ann Walsh, nineteen years old, who had been detained in Armagh Women's Prison since January of that year. Ann's case was scheduled to be brought before the Commission at Long Kesh the following day. She was accused of IRA leadership and participation in armed robbery. Despite the use of secret witnesses, allegations rather than documented facts, and her subjection to repeated and brutal depth interrogation over the previous year, however, the Commission was unable to establish charges against Ann Walsh and she was continued in detention. Ann was, at the time of examination, suffering from incipient schizophrenic breakdown. She also appeared suicidal and unable to maintain contact with reality for the period of one and a half hours required for testing. Ann's productions on the tests of psychomotor coordination indicated that she was functionally impaired and possibly suffering from organic central nervous system damage. Her stories on the projective test of personality, Thematic Apperception Test, revealed morbid fantasies and despair. My report to the Commission hearing, where I was the sole defense witness other than Ann's father, was a recommendation that Ann be placed in medical and psychiatric treatment. My expectations were that if she was continued in her present situation she would either attempt suicide or deteriorate into a schizoid condition. Ann was returned to Armagh prison, where she was kept incarcerated for nearly a year afterward. My report was incorporated into an affidavit subsequently published by the Northern Ireland Civil Rights Association (see Appendix).

Ann was one of six young women detained without charge or trial from the beginning of 1973 until late in 1974. They were not the only female political prisoners during that period. Most of the other women who were already in Armagh women's facility, however, or who had been there earlier (Bernadette Devlin, former member of Parliament, had also served a term there for riotous behavior), were either on remand or sentenced. There's a long history of hard-fought struggles for differentiation between criminals and political prisoners in all the British former colonies as well as in this last colony. The six young women who were first interned at the beginning of 1973 persisted in demanding that their rights as political prisoners be respected and that they not be treated as persons charged or convicted of an offense. Ann Walsh, despite her mounting depression and growing perceptual impediments, engaged in petitioning for these rights. The women described being locked up four times a day, being denied the extra food parcels and extra visiting periods granted to internees as distinct from charged or convicted prisoners. This brought further retaliation on them from the prison authorities.

In October, 1974, when rioting broke out in Long Kesh (by then re-named "The Maze" prison), the women at Armagh, republican and loyalist political prisoners together, took over the prison, holding the wardens hostage and demanding amnesty for their Long Kesh compatriots. The prison was surrounded and besieged. They gave in only after the men at Long Kesh surrendered.

The Men behind the Wire

The psychological-test and clinical-interview data collected by 1975 on a sample of more than two hundred reveals that every man and boy who has undergone interrogation—whether or not internment has fol-lowed—has suffered a damaging personality change. There is no way a person (male or female) can undergo the anxiety characteristic of the interrogation situation and not suffer severe stress reactions. Depending on the subject's physical and mental condition at the time of interrogation and, to a lesser extent, age, the effects vary in degree and permanence.

It might be argued that the effects of these particular kinds of stress (interrogation and internment) are difficult to differentiate from the effects of harassment and the ongoing intermittent violence experienced by all the inhabitants of Northern Ireland during the past five years. Since similar testing programs have been carried on with various segments of the com-munity, showing some differences (to be discussed in other chapters), this description is limited to the effects peculiar to (a) interrogation and (b) interrogation and internment.

The psychological test battery consisted of the Bender-Gestalt, Mem-ory for Designs, and Thematic Apperception tests. The testing procedures, as well as collecting the sampling, were not performed under ideal clinical or research conditions.

It was apparent to me that the most scientifically valuable data would accrue from a longitudinal study on a cross-section of the internees. For this reason one internee, a sociologist, was briefed on the administration of the tests and a specimen set was smuggled in to him. He completed a number of sets but the data, as well as the tests themselves, were taken from him when he was discharged. Testing was then attempted at the ear-liest possible date following the release of internees. This varied, however, between a few days and several months. Lists of internees and their ex-pected release dates did not become available until June, 1973.

Problems in data collection resulted from the hostilities among the factions within the republican population. Alternative agencies were labeled by many as "front groups" for either the Provos or the Officials, so that no single agency elicited sufficient confidence from all the former internees to allow adequate sampling through one organization. Testing was done under the auspices of the Northern Ireland Civil Rights Association, the Association for Legal Justice, and the republican clubs. It was conducted either in the offices of the ALJ, in my temporary residence, or in the homes of former internees. Of the three kinds of settings it was found that, despite the distractions, testing in the men's own homes provided the optimal clinical conditions. The ages of men in the sample extended from fourteen to fifty-six, and their experience ranged from involvement to noninvolvement in the republican movement. This differential political involvement has proved an interesting variable against which to measure the final psychological effects of interrogation-internment on individuals.

Of the 125 clinical cases analyzed and tabulated during the first two years, 1971–1973, the time in internment or detention varied from six weeks to more than a year. The internees had been in a variety of interrogation centers and camps; many of them had run the gamut of the various barracks, Crumlin Road jail, Magilligan internment camp, Long Kesh internment camp, and the *Maidstone* internment ship. After the Compton Report determined that the interrogation methods had provided valuable and necessary information and produced no definite permanent injuries to the subjects, in April, 1972, the Secretary of State for Northern Ireland declared that under direct rule no further brutalities would occur.[7] From the tests and interviews on men whose interrogation experiences occurred after this declaration, it is apparent that some procedures were continuing in use up to the time of this writing. The subject has now often been given a medical examination at various points during the interrogation process. He has not, of course, been given the information accruing from these medical findings, but presumably these have been provided to the authorities. It would seem that one of the Compton majority Report's recommendations has been followed, namely that "a doctor with some psychiatric training should be present at the interrogation centre at all times . . . he should warn the controller if he thinks the questioning is being pushed too far." The varieties of internment experience and locations are recorded in table 6.

Test Findings

All but twenty-four of the men reported ongoing ill effects either of a mental or a physical nature. Effects described as "mental" include: recurring headaches—apparently migraine type—with accompanying nausea; nightmares, occasional hallucinations; irritability; sleeplessness; sexual disturbances—impotence or premature ejaculation are common; dizziness;

disturbed memory function; "nervous tremors"; disabling fears (of going to work, of falling asleep, of passing or being stopped by the army or RUC); vague anxiety states and depressions.

Physical symptoms were reported by 32 percent of the men (with no particular relation to age or length of time interned). The physical disorders ranged from ulcers and exacerbated asthma to back pains, recurrent or constant chest pains, disabling of one or more limbs, facial pains, diges-

Table 6   1973 Internment Experience of 125 Men

Detention	More than one	30
facilities	Magiligan	9
experienced	Maidstone	226
	Long Kesh	85
	Goal	35
Interrogation	One barracks	111
experience	More than one	14
in barracks		
Amount of time	1–6 months	50
in detention	7–12 months	70
	Over 12 months	5
Ages	Under 20	25
	21–30	52
	31–40	28
	41–50	14
	Over 50	5
Reported	Mental	97
	Physical	40
	Both	36
	None	24
	N = 125 men	

tive dysfunctions, lack of energy, visual problems, hearing disorders, rheumatic-type pains, and poorly healed or unhealed wounds (that is, broken cartilage in nose, fingers that were not set when broken, facial scars and other apparently permanent cosmetic damages).

Of the men tested by 1975, 60 percent evidence either transitory or permanent brain damage or borderline brain damage. In functional terms, these men have difficulty in eye-hand coordination tasks, memory, spatial orientation, left-right coordination (necessary for reading and many verbal skills), speech impediments, and truncated attention span. Again there is little relation to age, but there is some relation between this kind of damage and the length of estimated interrogation time. This would also, of course, be as much a direct product of beatings on and around the head as it could be a product of the sensory deprivation and hooding treatments. There is absolutely no way to differentiate.* In two instances, however, I was able to test brothers who were close in age, one of each pair having been interned and the other having been beaten up in interrogation(s) but not interned. In other instances, I was able to obtain test protocols on fathers who had been interned and their sons who had been harassed but not interned. There is also a pair of protocols belonging to brothers, one of whom was "on the run" and the other of whom had been interned. These combinations, although not sufficient for any strong generalizations (both from insufficient sample size and reasons of genetic differences in fraternal and paternal relationships), indicate some possibility for eventually differentiating effects specific to being interned, such as degree of nervous disability or impaired sexual potency.

Out of eighty-three former internees from Belfast who answered a questionnaire through the post, 58 percent assessed themselves as having suffered some "mental disability," 34 percent assessed themselves as having

---

*After I had conducted clinical interviews with and tests on six of these cases, several important facts emerged. Strictly speaking, these were not sensory-deprivation cases, since they were continually subjected to noise treatment. This treatment provided a variety of irritating auditory stimuli, which contributed to the fatigue effect on these subjects. The treatment included sounds of screaming, which were variously interpreted by the subjects as their friends' distress, and which intensified their own anxieties and forebodings. Auditory overstimulation, whatever its nature—whether high intensity, "white noise," or simply intermittent dissonance—can result in an overcrowding of sensory intake channels, thus inducing fatigue. Auditory hallucinations were common for those who experienced the treatment.

The hooding itself resulted in a decreased supply of oxygen to the brain and central nervous system. It stimulated claustrophobic reactions which, combined with the effects of de-oxygenization—dizziness, fatigue, confusion—exacerbated the condition. It also resulted in extremely limited sensory input—in fact by virtue of hooding and the stretch position, all sensation was ultimately reduced to the auditory input of the noise treatment.

some physical disability, and 25 percent assessed themselves as having both mental and physical disability (table 7). These figures differed little between the group who had been interned from one to six months and the group interned six to twelve months. Of those who appraised themselves as

Table 7   Self-assessed Disabilities
in Eighty-three Released
Internees/Detainees

a   Released after 1–6 months' detention (N = 36)

	17–20 YEARS (N=9)	20–29 YEARS (N=17)	30–39 YEARS (N=5)	40–49 YEARS (N=2)	50+ YEARS (N=3)	TOTAL
SAMD	4	11	3	1	2 = 21	21
SAPD	2	6	2	1	0 = 11	11
MD–PD	2	5	1	1	0 = 9	9
NONE	5	4	1	2	1 = 13	13

b   Released after 6–12 months' detention N = 47

	(N=7)	(N=19)	(N=14)	(N=6)	(N=1)	TOTAL
SAMD	3	12	7	5	0 = 27	27
SAPD	2	9	4	2	1 = 18	18
MD–PD	2	6	2	2	0 = 12	12
NONE	5	2	6	0	0 = 14	14

c   Through-group percentage choices

PERIOD OF DETENTION	SAMD	SAPD	MD–PD	NONE
1–6 months	58	30	25	36
6–12 months	57	38	25	29

SAMD   = self assessed mental disability
MD–PD = self assessed both mental and physical disability
NONE   = self assessed neither disability

having no disability, there was some difference—by duration: 36 percent of those interned less than six months claimed no disability, but only 29 percent of those interned over six months said that.

Men who were more than fifty years old in this sample of former internees reported themselves as having suffered mental disabilities and physical disabilities in higher percentage than other age groups. This age group is, however, one of the smaller categories in the total sample, and that fact alone might account for the difference. The age groups were not evenly distributed. The bulk of the internees were between the ages of twenty and forty-nine, with sixteen respondents under twenty, and four of them aged fifty or more. Although it was impossible to secure psychological-test data on all the men reporting no disability, five of them were tested, and the analysis indicates that all were, at the time of testing, undergoing anxiety states and depression.

Self-assessment has great disadvantages in this kind of population. Many of the men hold to their conviction that to bring damage charges into court would be *de facto* recognition of a government to which they granted no legitimacy. Further, Northern Ireland (indeed all of Ireland) places a very negative meaning on the implications of mental or nervous disability. It simply is not "manly," and evidences of such disability are willed away.

Among the men given the test battery, the only marked differentiation was between those who had symptoms of brain damage and those who had insignificant psychomotor anomalies but demonstrated personality disturbances. Further differentiation might be made on the basis of the kind of personality disturbance, whether gross or minimal. These are distinctions that would have no functional value, because the plain fact is that these men were, at the time they were tested, unable to relate to themselves or other people or situations in such a manner as to establish positive human relationships or goal orientation and achievement, or to deal with adversity. Whatever their previous capacities, after interrogation and internment they had no way of effectively carrying on their day-to-day functions unimpeded. There are apparent differences in degree of impediment. This ranges from cases of diagnosed brain damage to those whose dysfunction would be manifest either temporarily or permanently through disrupted family relationships.

There was a further complication in assessing the empirical test data. While testing the men, I became aware that most, if not all, were taking tranquillizers and sedatives. These had been issued in quantity by the medical officers in Long Kesh. Because of combined pain and anxiety, they had been increasing their dosage and thus initiated what threatened to become the most vicious of the vicious cycles into which they had been thrust.

In addition, these men were realistically anxious about their sexuality and sexual competence. Most of them had been beaten with batons or kicked repeatedly in the genitals or had electrodes attached to their testicles and electroshocked when they failed to answer questions to their interrogators' satisfaction. Those who did not receive this specialized treatment had been subjected to various emasculating humiliations throughout their interrogation and treatment. Further, they suspected that the camp food (which many refused to eat) was treated with saltpetre to depress and finally extinguish sexual response. Since prolonged heavy usage of tranquillizers has precisely this effect and it is impossible to determine whether in fact saltpetre was employed, for some of them, their conviction of having been chemically "treated" to induce impotence had the effect of producing sexual anxiety. Thus anticipation of release carried emotional ambivalence, as much for the relatives awaiting the reunion as for internees themselves.

From my initial interview with an internee while at Long Kesh until the last former internee in this sample was tested in July, 1975, the one consistent complaint about the internment experience was the overcrowding. The effects were exacerbated by the placement in these close quarters of men whose group allegiances were in violent contention for legitimacy and adherence. The Provisionals had at this point acquired a larger following than the Officials, and viewed the latter as a "Commie threat," "atheists," and "Brit lovers." For those who were initially uncommitted, there was no chance to remain unaffiliated, since cage organization proceeded along partisan lines. Where Provisionals dominated (as they did in most cages), there were delays for Officials and uncommitted cage-mates in receiving their parcels from home. For a long time the only diversion was a TV set, and choice of programs became an issue determined by relative strength of numbers. Fights occurred and wardens reportedly watched with amusement rather than intervene.

Following the brutal repression of the inmates' October, 1971, protest, they felt there were "informers" among them. Several successful escapes were made both from Long Kesh and from *Maidstone*, the prison ship, and information to the authorities on planned escapes could result in death or torture for the planners. In each cage some level of equilibrium would be reached, only for several men to be removed temporarily or permanently, and others put in. There never appeared to be a system to trace changes, the effect was to increase tension.

By January, 1972, Des O'Hagan (originally a lecturer in sociology at Stranmillis University) had put together something of an education program, and the men had developed a camp council. The social worker for the camp had secured materials and tools for woodworking and leathercraft as well as material for making decorated handkerchiefs.* These activities provided only a minimal diversion, but were sufficient partially to alleviate the tedium.

When epidemics spread through the camp, and crowding, along with poor sanitary facilities, contributed to the malaise, the medical staff was augmented by regular clinic hours with a civilian doctor (a Catholic who had a record of loyal service during years in the British army). Various psychiatric conditions—both acute and chronic—emerged. One man "had a pet rabbit, black and white, who walked on ceilings and required regular helpings of lettuce." Another man had "a budgie bird who follows on a leash." These conditions, apart from being a source of amusement for their fellows, became so intense as to have confused the guards and attending physicians.

Meanwhile the men grew gaunt, listless, and debilitated from their scanty diets. There was no privacy and the constant bright lights sweeping through their huts from the guard towers thwarted sleep even when bunkmates and other immediate bed neighbors were not undergoing loud nightmares or experiencing vomiting, diarrhea, or persistent cough. Yet some men seem to have sustained and even enhanced their ideological commitments. Others, frustrated and thwarted by being deprived of the only kind of expression of anger to which they were accustomed, often deteriorated and submitted to massive doses of tranquillizers.

The various physical and psychological torture techniques have been well documented in several small books.[8] For several cases there is medical evidence from Dr. P. Lane, of Mater Hospital, Belfast, substantiating the effects of the physical brutalities.† Several of the men described in these books were given the full battery of psychological tests, and an effort was made to compare the results with the test performance of men whose cases were less well known and/or who had undergone various of the processes after these had supposedly been stopped. I found their conditions to be similar. The only conclusions to be extracted from these findings are that the majority of those interrogated and interned were probably damaged permanently (more than 1,500 had admittedly been through interrogation by December, 1971).[9]

Let's look at the clinical data of two very different cases—the torture process of one of whom has been documented in all of the aforementioned texts. The other is documented by his own witnessed deposition.

---

*Traditionally, republican internees have made wallets and purses with their political mottoes carved into the leather. They have also carved wooden harps, crosses, and Thompson submachine guns. Long Kesh handkerchiefs have on them symbols, portraits, and other stencil-painted designs.

†Cited in a conversation I had with Dr. Lane in July, 1972.

The Case of "John Higgins"

John Higgins (pseudonym), a thirty-seven-year-old father of five young children, had been a republican all his life. Being a republican in the six counties was for fifty years an illegal political affiliation, sufficiently illegal to warrant rejection of job applications, rejection of housing needs, and finally, rejection of the right to freedom. John has experienced imprisonment before for his political activity. The night of 9 August 1971 he was one of the first in Derry to be lifted. He was subjected to all of the tortures and by the time he was cast into Long Kesh was so severely injured as to require admission to the camp hospital.

John was released after a year, returned to his family, and about four months after his release (in January, 1973), I interviewed and examined him in his home. Although rapport had been established through prior visits, John remained quite agitated both initially and throughout the testing session. He chain smokes, shifts continually in his chair, and turns about in the direction of any kind of noise. His reactions clearly indicate a chronic hypertensive condition. He is highly irritable about any kind of interruption. He and his wife (separately) complained that he alternately becomes distracted and irritable over the ordinary noises of his children at play and completely loses track of their presence, questions, and expressed needs. The interviews and examinations took place over a series of two visits. His behavior was no different if people were present or absent or at different times of the day. It would appear that his extreme nervousness is constant, rather than sporadic or induced by new company.

John described his experiences during interrogation and internment. During his recounting of them, it was apparent that his overriding condition was one of humiliation and shame. He reported hallucinations—both visual and auditory—during various points in the week-long process. He experienced spatial disorientation as well as temporal confusions and extreme physical pain. His statements were highly emotionally charged, as though he is still reliving these experiences. Indeed, he mentioned recurrent nightmares in which parts of the experiences reappear with vivid detail. He frequently awakened from these nightmares unable to return to sleep. He reported having been taking tranquillizers but that he was not using them at the time of examination. He was not, in fact, using any medication.

The tests administered to him were the Thematic Apperception Test, Draw-A-Person, Memory for Designs, and Bender-Gestalt.

Thematic Apperception Test (TAT)

The Thematic Apperception Test is a long-established projective test most often used to assess personality dynamics for purposes of clinical diagnosis and treatment.[10] The same test and method of analysis was used in the psychological assessment of the children (see Chapter 2).[11] The test consists of a total of twenty ambiguous pictures. Of the set, usually ten cards are used for a single test. As Arnold asserts, the particular stimulus cards are relatively unimportant; it is stories and their sequence that provide the raw data for analysis. The pictures range in clarity and specifically in detail from a card that is totally blank to several pictures that are sufficiently well defined to allow the viewer a clear image of pictures "hanging on a wall within the larger scene." Using Story Sequence Analysis, attitudes and modes of operation expressed by the viewer are revealed through the import of his stories.[12] Each import is a summary of each story. Taken in sequence, they reveal the subject's overall model of operation, consequent behavior, and underlying belief systems.

John Higgins—TAT imports

1. If you stick with something you want to do, you eventually master it, and when you die it lives on.

2. You seem to be moving away from one thing, but it's another you're really trying to get away from. You leave the domineering person and unpleasant situation, but when someone else overcomes it you will return.

3. You are saddened by a quarrel with one close to you and you think about it and make up your mind to settle it. Even though you do settle it and are happy, it comes up a few more times in life.

4. You get angry and want to do something, but one close to you is more passive and less involved, and because of that they have control and you end up dominated the rest of your life.

5. And if you are left alone to raise a child, you think about how life goes on and that the child will some day be doing to her children as you are doing with her, but she will know how hard it was for you and do everything possible to avoid the same fate.

6. Because you are impressed with the struggles of those who came before you and with how hard it was for them to carry out their work without pain killers and gear for their task, and when you have your turn to do that work you will not forget those who helped you get where you are.

7. A place begins changing and getting built up, and you go along unconcerned until the places in which you resided are changed, and, although you've been there for a very long time, when other things come along you have to leave.

8. You have sexual relations with someone—or want to, but feel angry and guilty about it because you are a timid man with somebody else domineering over you. If you are a beaten man, you'll be beaten the whole way through life and unable to stand up before the world at all.

9. When you are young you experience the difference money makes in the way you and your family are treated and in the person doing the

treating, and it makes you determined that when you grow up you'll fight for equality so the poor can have equal chances.

10. And you may have a split personality—one part of you is good. And you could be a working man searching for a better way of life or a policeman, but if you're a worker and start to work with shady characters, and if you've been in gaol and try to make a new life, it's hard because you fall into your old habits. You have to get away from your old environment, or maybe you've been thrown out from a job and feel hopeless and sorry for whatever you've done, or maybe you're a guard at a penitentiary seeing the same things over and over, but whoever you are can make a go of it if you don't fall back on your old ways, and you can pay back what you owe and make it all right.

John's feelings of helplessness, shame, and rage are manifest in his TAT stories. He has great concern about right and wrong reflected in anxiety about "doing the right things." There is ample evidence of feelings of shame and humiliation; he feels himself to have somehow been a failure in comparison to some ego-ideal. Generally, he makes a negative comparison of himself with others and sees himself as not being in control, but overwhelmed and paralyzed by the powerful hostility of others. In consequences, he feels small, helpless, and childish. He sees himself and his progress through life as being determined to a large extent by the behavior of others toward himself rather than by his own action and decisions. He has difficulty in establishing a consistent identity for himself (this is evidenced in the shifting and reorientation of the persons in his TAT stories, indicative, also, of overwhelming uncertainty and ambivalence). He sees close relationships as being more frequently points of conflict and domination by others rather than sources of comfort. In situations of adversity, he feels there is little for him to do but wait and hope for a better future— which, in the long run, he feels is decided by others. He is terrified of authority figures and has no confidence in himself at all. He seems unable to re-establish his identity and fears further torture and humiliation. He wants to work hard and succeed, but is afraid that he is somehow unfit or will not be acceptable.

Draw-a-Person*

The sketchiness of Higgins's drawings corroborates the other test data, indicating grave insecurity and regressive tendencies: most notable are

*The Draw-a-Person test is used for estimating intellectual maturity and/or personality syndrome. It has been used with children and adults in a variety of studies. The subject is usually asked first to draw any person, then draw a person of the opposite sex on a separate sheet, and, in this case, to draw a picture of himself on a third piece of paper.

feelings of helplessness and impotence. He is desperately afraid of something and looking for some escape from it. He is quite dependent. Most striking is the evidence of incomplete or "blurred identity." In depicting a female he depicted a person with greater strength and sturdiness than himself or the other male he drew. There is a notable lack of "affect potential" in all his drawings, as well as immobility and physical deterioration.

Memory for Designs (MFD)*

There is considerable evidence of neurotic dysfunction, which is manifested in some memory impairment and visual-motor dysfunction. He demonstrates some difficulty in organizing sequential stimuli. The evidence of immaturity in his perceptual-motor performance is indicative of regressive behavior derivative of insecurity. There is some evidence of borderline organic damage, but it is not sufficient to account for some of the symptoms by itself.

Bender-Gestalt (B-G)†[13]

There are indications of pent-up aggression as well as possible cortical damage. He displays some of the symptoms of paranoia (feelings of persecution and inconsistent contact with reality). This test confirms some psychomotor dysfunction, as shown on the MFD. The kinds of dysfunction herein demonstrated are most frequently discovered in patients who have suffered from recent cortical trauma (blows to the head or brain surgery). The findings, however, are not conclusive since this test evaluates only impaired cortical functioning as it relates to the occipital section, and is not known for demonstrating other kinds of brain damage. According to the B-G, Higgins may be suffering a psychogenic disturbance without necessarily having suffered permanent traumatically induced brain damage.

Summary of Findings

There is every indication that John Higgins is still experiencing the effects—both in personality function and psychomotor function—of a se-

*The MFD test serves a purpose similar to the Bender-Gestalt test (see below). It is also effective in distinguishing between some of the symptoms of neurological and personality dysfunction.
†The B-G test is used to evaluate disturbances in psychomotor eye-hand, visual dominance, and maturational development. It requires the reproduction of increasingly complex designs—the gestalt function, a product of the central nervous system process, is distinguished by injury to the brain either through trauma or chemical effects.

vere, prolonged traumatic experience, apparently that of his treatment during interrogation and internment (9 August 1971–August 1972). The psychomotor dysfunction may stem from impaired brain tissue and central nervous tissue produced by oxygen insufficiencies from the combined effects of hooding and fatigue. It may also originate in the effects of repeated blows to his head. There is no doubt that the combination of experiences has resulted in a severe personality problem, further evidenced in difficulties in relationships within his family and impaired ability to relate to others. He would be unlikely to be able to carry on any work activity requiring motor coordination, concentration, or memorization. There is some likelihood that the effects will respond to psychotherapy in regard to personality function, but little reason to expect that either time or treatment can ameliorate his impaired psychomotor and memory function.

Some may argue that John Higgins was neurotic or had been suffering a personality disturbance prior to his internment. They may point to the record of his known association and standing with the official republican movement as a clear indication of aberration. After all, he had, in 1966, been on remand and has, in previous periods of internment, been on the run. In answer, one would have to examine his record of accomplishments as a member of the republican movement. He was highly esteemed by people in Derry for his geniality and competence in organizing clubs and programs. He enjoyed the respect of his community even when his abode was the crudest available and his record of joblessness would have suggested incompetence. His standing in the community was such that when he was interned and the nature of his interrogation was realized, offers of help poured in to his family, and on his release and apparent recovery there was widespread celebration. Perhaps another indication of the regard in which he was held is that when better housing became available, John Hume, MP, arranged for his family to be moved into a decent home. Hume is an astute politician and recognizes focal points of popular esteem. Hume is also affiliated with a rival political party and quite well realized that the Higginses themselves were not going to swell his vote, but that his actions on their behalf could contribute to that effect.

It is crucial to understanding John Higgins and the effects of interrogation and internment on him to know that he recognized internment as a political strategy and the period of internment as a time for politicizing men who otherwise saw the situation as a matter of Catholic versus Protestant and nationalist versus unionist. He felt that there were some men who benefited from internment by having developed an ideology of socialism. For John is shaken in neither his ideological commitment nor his conviction of eventual victory. He is free from hatred toward "the Provies" and quite unbiased toward Protestants as a group. He returned to his organization and to a position of respect within it.

The Case of "Sean"

John's case may be in sharp contrast with that of a forty-eight-year-old Belfast man who was reputedly a former leader in the Provisional IRA. Since he and his family are already too frequently harassed and imprisoned, I've chosen a pseudonym for him. Sean lives in the Ballymurphy estate and has been an IRA man, as he put it, "all my life." He had been interned in the 1940's and again in the 1950's, but had somewhat dropped out of the organization during the 1960's. By then, his eldest son had become a member, carrying on the family tradition. His children ranged in age from six to twenty-three at the time of his internment, and his regular occupation as an electronics technician had required fine eye-hand coordination. Sean is a devout Catholic.

Sean and his two eldest sons were taken in together on 9 August, 1971. They were all subjected to depth interrogation, including extensive physical abuse. At one point, during the time in Long Kesh, Sean and one of his sons were housed in the same cage. No reason was ever given for their having been joined, and no reason given for their later separation. Although his eldest son had some ideological commitment to socialism, had he not been under court martial for disobeying an order at the time of the Provisional split, the son might have maintained a commitment to the Officials. Not so the father. He shared the Church's attitude toward "communism" and "godlessness," and saw the value of the IRA as an army of the people to wreak such economic havoc on Britain as to make it impossible for them to remain in Ireland. He maintained a position of leadership even while interned. Sean was respected and admired even by men who found it impossible to "like" him and who abhorred his politics. He suffered numerous head injuries in the course of beatings prior to internment and while interned. Following his release in July, 1972, he and his eldest son were again severely beaten by an army patrol. The family had suffered extreme harassment. The youngest son hides behind the TV set at any loud noise outside. The fourteen-year-old son is stopped daily by the army and alternately insulted and beaten.

When Sean was tested in his home, it was within the week following his post-internment beating. The tests administered to him were the Memory for Designs, Bender-Gestalt, the Word Association Test, and Thematic Apperception Test. He was disoriented and his speech slurred. He was hesitant to speak to more than one person at a time and had some difficulty in concentrating and maintaining continuity. He is depressed, shows little affect, seems sleepy. He is of stocky build, has graying hair and a deeply lined face, with several scars on and around his face and head. He was deferential toward the examiner and quite willing to speak about his experiences.

Memory for Designs

Sean's score on the MFD indicates borderline brain damage. He is likely to be erratic in psychomotor functions and has difficulty remembering concrete impressions. He tries hard to be precise and "correct," indicating a very compulsive behavioral syndrome, which probably aids in offsetting the full effects of his disability.

Bender-Gestalt

The erratic relationships of the designs to one another in Seàn's placement suggest that he is having great difficulty orienting himself and probably is continually searching for conventions or guidelines. He is worried about his coordination and is more likely to make a herculean effort than to seek help. His tremor (evident when he is engaged in any other tasks) is not evidenced in the lines of his drawings.

Word Association Test

Sean's score on the MFD indicates borderline brain damage. He is likely to be erratic in psychomotor functions and has difficulty remember-severe associational dysfunction, probably ordinarily evidenced in poor recall, and great difficulty in problem-solving behavior.

Thematic Apperception Test

Sean's stories have a single repetitive theme: "You are in distress and alone with it and there doesn't seem to be anything you can do about it, because if one close to you doesn't offer their help or actively rejects you, there's not much to be done. A reconciliation is possible if there is love, but it isn't necessarily present on a basis of relatedness."

The testing session was interrupted by a caller with an urgent message. Two teenagers who lived in the estate and were Provos had been blown up when a bomb they'd been carrying accidentally went off. One of the young people was a nephew of the caller.

Afterward, Sean confided that he no longer had any position in his organization, he was useless to them and to everyone else since he'd been released. There seemed to him nothing he could do for the cause any longer. To add to his discouragement the Church had taken a very strong position against the Provos and condemned them from the pulpit. This double alienation—from the Church and his organization—seemed too much for Sean. He could neither understand nor cope with it. Shortly afterward, his eldest son had to go on the run again and Sean began to live vicariously through his son's actions. This has lessened his disillusionment, and although he remains a very sick man, he is no longer despondent.

These case studies are not atypical. They were selected as examples of the more typical identity problems characteristic of the men who have been interned. Both men suffer from recurrent nightmares, occasional hallucinations, irritability, anxiety, and depression. Both men are committed to republicanism, albeit different wings of it. The alleviating factor for Higgins has been the feeling of continued value and respect he holds within his organization; and, of course, his "God" has not "forsaken" him. His place in his world has not slipped away from him nor has be been disillusioned in lessened esteem from his comrades. Although both men live at home, they remain emotionally "on the run." They admit feeling terror when confronted by the army or RUC, are hesitant to attempt to find and hold regular jobs, cannot maintain a comfortable relationship with their wives and children, are reluctant to assert themselves within their communities, and are uncomfortable within their own homes. (Sean has since moved his family to another house within the same estate, hoping for at least a temporary respite in their harassment.)

The Case of Seamus C.

It is not clear—and perhaps will never be known—how many victims of interrogation and internment have gone so far on the run as to have left Ireland altogether, and how many others have "gone south." There is steady one-way traffic across the border, bringing to the south former internees who have been threatened by the RUC or the military with a second round of the "treatment." Some men return weekly to visit mothers and girlfriends. Others are afraid to disclose their whereabouts, return sporadically at first, and then not at all.

Some of these cases are surprising. They seem to be making great strides toward overcoming the effects of their internment and then suddenly, they're gone, and it's told that "so-and-so went on the run—he had been stopped by a patrol one night and was so upset he couldn't sleep again. So he just took off." It would be valuable to have such specific information about these men as the personality variables differentiating those who have gone off and those who have remained. In the process of three separate expeditions, some individuals were tested shortly after their release and found to have later gone on the run out of Northern Ireland, but many released men could not be reached for testing at all because they had immediately departed. Married men with young children appear to have been less likely to go south.

One of the men who went west rather than south is Seamus C. (pseudonym). He is a crane-driver, aged twenty-eight, married, with four children.

Here is his story as he told it to me verbatim in July 1972, shortly after his release.

Picked up at my home [Shantallow, Derry]. I was in bed asleep, and was awoke by banging on front door by soldiers. I got up and went to the front window and opened it and looked out. I saw three soldiers standing at my door; they jumped back and pointed their rifles at me. One of them said, "Are you Seamus C?" I said, "Yes," and then he said, "Come on, boy we are taking you." I said to him, "You had better wait until I get dressed." He started to scream, "No, no, no," and started to bang the door. I then walked back from the window into the back room and started to get dressed. In the meantime my wife went down and opened the door letting them in. I heard one of them shouting to my wife. "Where is he? Where is he?" I shouted down to them, "I'm up here." One of them came up to the room where I was and got me by the hair and dragged me down the stairs behind him. He stood me up in front of the sergeant. The sergeant said to me, "I'm arresting you under the Special Powers Act. I am obliged to say nothing more to you. You can come easy if you wish." A soldier put a blanket over my head and told me to keep quiet. Then I felt more soldiers jumping into the jeep crawling over and trampling me as they took their seats. Then the jeep drove off, I heard one of them say, "The little bastard has got a whacking great picture of Che Guevara in his bedroom." This man held my neck down through the journey to Abrenton Barracks. Halfway through the journey of ten minutes I felt what I thought to be warm water on my bare feet and legs. I later realized they had urinated on me. The blanket was taken off me and I was tossed out of the jeep at Abrenton Barracks. I was then handed my boots and told not to put them on or look back. I was marched in between two soldiers up behind a line of prisoners. I stood there between an hour and an hour and a half. Eventually I was taken in for identification by sight. I was then taken into a large hall with the rest of the prisoners. After a three-hour wait there we were loaded into a furniture wagon and driven into Magiligan Camp where I was held until the second day when I was moved to the *Maidstone*. I was held there approximately five weeks at which point I was flown by helicopter to Long Kesh.

The 25 October brought a destructive protest to the deplorable food, frequently nothing more than a greasy piece of mince meat and starch. . . . The frustration had built up during this period as no satisfactory changes were being made. Some of the internees protested by throwing their tin plates over the cage fence in the direction of the cook house at about four o'clock. The army was immediately called into the perimeter of the cage and surrounded it. The canteen was, perhaps foolishly, set afire by certain internees as an expression of protest. The army waited about two hours outside the cage laughing and joking, and then fired a quite a large amount of tear gas into the cage. Practically everyone was gassed to the ground semiconscious. The army, about two hundred men, armed with pickaxe handles, full riot gear, and Alsatian dogs then entered the cages. I personally witnessed them beating a man who had already been unconscious about the head, smashing his skull. Anyone on the ground was kicked or beaten with the pickaxe handle when approached by the army. Other people had taken to hiding in their huts, hiding under beds, or doing as I did, hiding in the lockers. Soldiers then came into the huts. Anyone taken in the huts was given a severe beating about the head, face, arms, and legs and thrown out the door into a group of ten to twelve soldiers with heavy batons for further beatings. I noticed that an internee who could stand once he was thrown to this group would receive a lesser beating than the unconscious or semiconscious men. At this point there was a call, "Is anyone here?" Out of fear I did not answer. I then heard them counting the internees outside and realized I couldn't stay where I was. I was afraid I'd be killed. I started staggering towards the door where the soldiers were, and I was grabbed from behind by an officer with shoulder markings and a beret. This man turned me around and said to me, "You sneaky bastard!" and he caught me around the neck with his hands, butting me in the face with his head, causing my nose to bleed. He attempted to knee my genitals, but I had pulled in too close to him. Just then a prison warden pulled me by the hair and says, "Out you bastard!" I was then flung into the group of waiting soldiers, ten to twelve, forming a circle. I was beaten about the shoulders, my arms, and my legs. I was saved a truly severe beating because I'd my arms over my head and they were so excited they actually hit one another. I dived from the middle of them to my right and landed on top of a pile of internees who'd been beaten and lacerated. All I could hear was moaning and crying. An internee said to me, "Will you get off Frank [McGlade], he's had a heart attack and I think he's dying." I slid over and looked at McGlade and I saw blood from the back of his skull and he was as white as paper. I really thought he was dying or dead. I asked a boy who was nearer Frank's head to whisper an act of contrition into his ear and, sobbing, the boy did so. I then shouted to a soldier who was passing by. I said, "This man is dead or dying. Can you get him a stretcher." Frank is in the sixties. The soldier told me to shut my mouth. I could get no pulse on Frank and gave up, thinking he was dead.

We were left there for about half an hour. We were then told to get up and form into three lines. As we got up Frank was left lying and another boy who was severely injured could not get beyond his hands and knees. Two soldiers began to beat the boy again. I pulled the boy away from them and stood him up, semiconscious, and held him in the rank ahead of mine, by the collar. Another man helped hold me up. I took out a handkerchief and put it over his eyebrow which had a great slash in it. I held the handkerchief as tightly as I could to stop the bleeding, as blood poured down his lacerated neck and down my hand. I must have stood there ten minutes as internees were picked out for beatings around the back of the huts. The boy was too heavy for me and he began to slide down as I could no longer hold him up. I shouted again as another soldier I believe to be an officer passed, "Can you help this man? He's severely hurt." The officer came over and forcibly pulled my hand from the boy's eye, observed the wound, put my hand over it again, and walked away. After a few minutes a prison warden came and took the boy away. I then witnessed another internee collapse and fall to the ground to be dragged away by the feet by a soldier. We were then taken in groups of six from the formation. We were violently thrown against a wire fence, hands against the fence and legs kicked apart. We were then searched.

After being searched we were again put in three lines. We were made to turn around to face lines of soldiers six deep. An officer came between us and the soldiers and proceeded to lecture us. He said, "Anytime you bastards want trouble my boys will sort you out. You have one hour to clean up your huts which you wrecked. We didn't." We went into the huts and they were a shambles. Beds were wrecked, clothes torn, valuables stolen. We cleaned up the mess as best we could, although no internee had wrecked anything. Most of the internees then collapsed on beds or the floor to sleep. The chemical toilets had been dumped over the room and beds. I noticed quite a large number of internees with bumps, lacerations, cuts, and sprained joints which were often found to be fractured later. I then went to the medical officer and told him of the injuries. He said, "Pick out the most severely injured and bring them here," to the gate where he stood with some soldiers and several warders. I asked why he wouldn't come himself and he replied that the army was in charge here. Between stages I went back to the hut and brought back injured men to get bandaged wrists and receive surgical spirits over the bandages. He said, "They're too many and I haven't time. Take these bandages and surgical spirits, plaster and scissors. Don't lose the scissors, they're the army's." He was a human being and was scared himself as he slipped these to me.

I went back into the hut that I slept in and bandaged and cleaned wounds with a solution the DMD had given me. Then I went to two other huts and did the same. We were then locked in for the night at about 10 P.M. More fell asleep but further wounds became noticed and I treated them.

The next morning at eight o'clock the troops came into the cage and ordered us out and we were searched again. We were again put in three lines, this time where the canteen had been, with our backs to the huts. We were ordered not to turn around and compelled to urinate where we stood, should the need arise. We were held standing until about ten o'clock through periodic rain. The soldiers then left the cage and we returned to our huts to find they had been wrecked again and any valuables stolen.

This is my sworn and true account of my stay up to and through 26 October. One hundred and nineteen men can verify this statement [Seamus was in the most overcrowded cage at that time].

The tests administered to Seamus were Bender-Gestalt, the Word Association Test, and the Thematic Apperception Test.

Bender-Gestalt

Seamus arranged his drawings in a very unorthodox fashion. He asked at the beginning whether he could start the first design in the middle of the page, and after a couple of minutes (having been told that he should draw them however he chose), he decided that he wanted to do it that way and did. Although there is no inaccuracy in the designs themselves—they are near perfect—they are bizarrely arranged. They are equidistant from one another but follow in an erratic progression. It was an indication of Seamus's need to test the limits of reality and arrange it, so far as possible, to his own needs. Apart from the B-G performance, Seamus demonstrated good coordination and no perceptual problems. I decided to use the Word Association Test rather than the MFD at this point.

Word Association Test

Seamus did not respond with spontaneity. His responses were quite deliberate and therefore averaged five seconds with three seconds minimum time and eighteen seconds maximum time. He blocked on associations with the following words: light, slow, cold, woman, war, wish, spider, high, memory, and love. In response to "memory," he complained that that was his biggest problem.* In response to "slow," Seamus gave, after eighteen seconds' pause, the word "symptom." He is intensely aware of his diminished cognitive capacities.

Thematic Apperception Test—Imports

1. If someone is in trouble with the law and seems to be ordinary looking —no radical—perhaps he is let go, but will be resentful.
2. But if there is panic and no one is able to help, they may argue about it, but because of the panic there is nothing that can be done to save someone.
3. Because if you've done something wrong and then take someone else's advice to escape the ill effects, you are still left with a mental burden.
4. Or if someone is a politician, when a violent incident happens, getting people angry and concerned, you can't offer them any explanation; no one will be satisfied with your answers and more violence will come.
5. But a criminal who uses violence to hurt and rob workers goes along thinking that he is right.
6. Young people end up going along their own way because when they are looking for something, older people are suspicious and resentful and don't offer any advice.

*All former internees seem to suffer memory problems. They frequently mentioned this problem in the course of testing.

7. And if there are only a few left and most are defeatists, then even one who is serious and trying to find a solution dies with them in the end.

8. But even if someone advises you against doing something dangerous they are rejected because you are determined, so they go away and worry a lot about it.

9. Because greed and inhumanity cause a clash between rich and poor through unconcern, and this gives rise to violence.

10. And when young people find out about such things as concentration camps they seek information and try to destroy such an institution or system that implements and maintains such places.

Seamus did not use the pictures as a stimulus except to incorporate some details into his own ideas. He examined the pictures thoroughly and seemed to glean all the information possible, but after a careful study, focused on some details. His TAT protocol indicates that Seamus is not "field dependent," as are most of the others who were tested.[14] He is pessimistic about the eventual success of right over wrong and views injustice and evil as bad, but unavoidable—at least their practitioners do not suffer immediate and personal disadvantage. He believes that younger people are more apt to correct injustice and make a meaningful change; that perhaps older people have already been too corrupted to see the light. He is bitter and depressed rather than anxious. He seems quite convinced that his future is not good, but he doesn't seem to be concerned with escape—in fact he doesn't mention any escape possibilities.

Seamus is "on the run" from the violence and evil he perceives. He totally lacks confidence that as an individual he can be positively effective in stopping the destruction around him.

Imbedded in his test responses were some clues to the choices Seamus demonstrated some six weeks later when he went "on the run" over the border. His Thematic Apperception Test stories demonstrate his conviction that there is nothing he can do about things himself. It may be that he is more able to leave his familiar surroundings because he is less dependent upon his environment to meet his need for stability, and is instead seeking feelings of individual personal efficacy (best achieved where there is little environmental restraint on personally determined action: less structure and fewer associations with prior experience). Seamus's prior commitment to live, work, and take action in the community of his birth would indicate that he did prefer a familiar environment and operated comfortably in the context of environmental and experiential associations. If he is the "independent" now, it is probably symptomatic of the vast personality upheaval attendant upon his interrogation and internment experiences.

It would seem, from the cases studied, that the interrogation and internment experience effects changes in a man's cognitive processes and in his concept of self that render his anomic and alienated—conditions characterized by feeling alone in a normless society and without a consistent positive identity.[15] The modes of behavior evolved under extreme conditions become emotional habits that persist beyond their period of utility into postinternment life. This syndrome is inappropriate to forming and maintaining close relationships, to decision-making, or to taking responsibility for anything beyond one's own immediate safety. It is the syndrome and limited perspective of the man on the run.

Women of Ireland

Slaves of Slaves

5

I was coming home from the store with bags full of groceries and saw the gate in front of my house. I made for the gate and suddenly there were two soldiers sprang up on either side of me. They'd been hiding in the bush and jumped up at me with their guns and demanding to know my name and what I was doing. . . . I dropped my groceries and started to scream, and then I just fell down in a faint. . . . My little girl came running out and shouting "mummy, mummy, they killed you, mummy, mummy," and she started beating at them with her little fists. . . . I saw it but I couldn't move or speak . . . and then I saw them grab her . . . and then I screamed again and jumped at them and fell dead away in a swoon. (Alice H., Derry, July 1972)

Alice, pallid and emaciated, trembled as she told the five people in the tiny Creggan parlor about her fear of the soldiers. She was one of a group of six Derry people who had gathered for an intensive three-day workshop on counseling and drug education. Alice had been hospitalized and given electric shock treatments several times. She was escalating her dosage of tranquillizers and sedatives so much that she was ordinarily too drugged to be able to carry out alone even the simplest housework task. On a bright and relatively hot July day she was dressed in a coat, slacks, a sweater, and a headscarf. She remained dressed that way indoors as well as out, and yet, periodically, she would begin trembling with "chills." Alice epitomized the destruction of the ordinary working-class people of Derry. But like them also, she was determined to do something about it and so had come to learn to do crisis counseling. She was convinced that she would learn to help herself and help her neighbors, who were, if less dramatically, suffering from the same syndrome.

In the summer of 1972, when people like Alice in Belfast and Derry were learning how to do crisis-intervention counseling, desensitization therapy, and drug education, it was part of my action research. The program was an effort to bring to the people of Northern Ireland an antidote for the poisoning evidenced in my earlier studies of that place. Training local people in self-help projects is a way of mobilizing them to combat their own victimization. Helping others is a direct way of helping oneself; and in so doing comes the realization of one's own ultimate freedom—the power to create oneself.

Through this and other such projects initiated during the years 1971–1975, I became especially close to the women of Northern Ireland. My involvement with them proceeded from living in their homes, sharing problems and joys, and working directly in training and therapy programs with them. I met with university women who were struggling to organize a women's liberation movement despite the growing sectarian divide in Belfast and Derry; working-class women in Dublin whose estimate of their northern counterparts was "if they'd stay home and mind their children instead of being out banging dustbin lids, there wouldn't be so much trouble for their menfolk up there"; and members of the Dublin founding group of the Irish Women's Liberation Movement. I also discovered that some of the most well-informed and intellectual women in Ireland were a group of nuns in the Dublin convent of a teaching order, whose intellectual vigor denoted a degree of liberation lacking in their housewife sisters. But for all of them, in a society that had been characterized by James Connolly, seventy years earlier, as a "slave society," the women of Ireland were "slaves of slaves."[1]

Violence and internment in Northern Ireland have driven the women of that place—Protestant as well as Catholic—to despair, like Alice's. Their situation points up the particular degradation of the status of women in any society that is at war or that is under the imperial heel of a foreign power.

Until the seventeenth century, the women of Ireland, and particularly the women of Ulster, enjoyed equal status with the men of their society at a level unknown in any other European culture. Under ancient Brehon law, the law that had survived in Ulster even after the rest of Ireland had been yoked into the English common law system, women enjoyed the rights of independent property ownership, had access to divorce and remarriage, and could be respected practitioners of the arts and sciences if they chose to do so.[2]

The change in women's status in Ireland directly parallels the conquest of the Irish people and the extinction of their native culture. Ironically, some critics of Irish society equate the pre-eminence of the Catholic Church with the puritanical segregation of the sexes and hence the stereotyping into rigid sex roles.[3] To view the relationship thus is not only simplistic but also ignores the fact that Catholicism in Ireland had proceeded along very "un-Romish," unconventional lines, as did sex-role stereotyping, until the final conquest of Ireland by Cromwell in the mid-seventeenth century, which accelerated the land-ownership transfer begun with the earlier Ulster plantation.[4]

The puritanism afflicting women's status among Protestant and Catholics in Ireland was not and is not a consequence of Catholicism, but rather the infusion into secular life of the archaic domestic code imposed by the Cromwellian invasion. It was further enforced by the nonconformist sects, which have been the dominant force in shaping the mores and morals of the majority of the Northern Irish working class of all denominations, and it was fused into indigenous institutions.

In this last quarter of the twentieth century the sex-role dichotomization and the subordination of women are no less remarkable in that part of the United Kingdom that is Northern Ireland than it is in the predominantly Roman Catholic Irish Republic. As part of the United Kingdom, women in the six counties enjoy access to contraception, but they cannot obtain abortion in their home counties; they, like their sisters in the south, must go to England for that service.

Not unlike the imposition of potato cultivation, of the English language, and of Anglo-Saxon customs, the system of marriage and family, with its consequences for the role of women, was imposed by the British rulers to facilitate their dominance. Prior to the seventeenth century, Irish social and cultural affairs were guided by the ancient Brehon law and Celtic tradition, which permitted a far more egalitarian relationship between the sexes than was found among their British and European contemporaries.[5] Indeed, the Irish language itself reflected and still reflects the equipotentiality of male and female to the executive position. The sexist overtones of the word "chairman" are entirely missing from the Irish equivalent, *carhadirleach*, which approximates the neuter "occupant of the chair." The word for God is likewise neuter, and the word for the Holy Ghost is of feminine gender!

Language is a reflection and determinant of thought. Through it, behaviors and attitudes are shaped and conceptualized. The values of a society are spoken in its words, the ordering of those words, their variety and idiom. Thus, despite the destruction of Gaelic Ireland, as the language has persisted, so also have some variances in the status and role of women.

The very name *Eire* is taken from Queen Eire who held out against the queen of the invading Milesians, Queen Scota. In regard to women's status in war, it would appear that there was little difference between the older and the invading Celtic groups. And from that time forward, kings in Ireland, upon being installed, were "married" to the great goddess for legitimation of their reign. And Cuchulain, the great warrior, we are told, learned his martial arts from women, Ailbe and Aife in Alba (Scotland).[6]

Saint Brigid epitomizes the evolution of the Irish womanly ideal of the earlier Christian epoch. Unlike many of her continental sisters elevated to sainthood, Brigid was neither a Magdalene nor an insipid virgin clinging to her chastity. Saint Brigid was renowned for her brilliance in the law and classical learning. She was in the tradition of the Celtic woman, wise, strong, and active.[7]

There are indications that she was an abbess, which in the historical context suggests that she was director of a community of scholars, not contemplatives or ascetics, and possibly a member of a professional clan devoted to the healing arts. Of such, there were two divisions—the lower division, which applied herbs and medication, and the higher division, which through mysticism and psychic powers would "will away" ailments or ill fortune. Since women as well as men performed the professional tasks of their class, it is conceivable that Saint Brigid, or whoever served as the model for her in popular folk culture, was such a a mystic.

The myths and legends, by their reference to matrilineal descent and the consequent assumption of land, title, rights, loyalties, obligations, or even character traits resulting from maternal descent, sharply contrast with the patriarchal Roman, Greek, and Teutonic legends. Scholars researching Brehon law have repeatedly commented on the superior position of women in Irish society when compared with their contemporaries up to the seventeenth century.[8]

There is every indication that Brehon law prevailed over Christian orthodoxy throughout the Middle Ages, especially as regarded marriage, divorce, child-rearing, and of course, the status of women. Diocesan organization was not even attempted until the twelfth-century Synod of Kells, and afterward there was a brief establishment of fiefdoms. The clergy, many of whom were married and frequently had concubines (multiple marriages), and political as well as familial relationships with secular chieftains, functioned more as a learned class in continuity with the ancient Brehon system than as leaders of the religious domain. While royalty on the continent and in Britain were constrained to monogamy by church law, and even at the time that Henry VIII required an ungranted papal dispensation to dissolve his first marriage, Irish chiefs and chieftains, clergy and free peasants were not prevented from having multiple and serial marriages to close kin![9]

Women were able to enter into any of a dozen different kinds of relationships, with the attendant property and personal rights attached to the form of the relationship, their own familial status, property status, and the status of their paramours. Women until the seventeenth century could, by "naming," declare the paternity of their children for paternal and filial responsibility in accordance with the law. The education and care of a child was the sole responsibility of the mother only if she had knowingly conceived the child with a slave or a clergyman bound by vows of chastity. Women who were poets, satirists, or otherwise professionals and women who were physically or mentally unfit were not held responsible at all for the rearing of their children.[10]

The level of promiscuity among the Irish scandalized Cromwell and his Puritans. In various correspondence from him and his appointed civil authorities (as well as that of his predecessors from England) there is frequent mention of the need to reform these "wild pagan customs."[11] An illustrative case is the sixteenth-century courtship and marriage of Hugh O'Neill, Earl of Tyrone, with Mabel Bagenal, daughter of the Queen's Marshal, Sir Nicholas Bagenal. O'Neill, brought up among the English aristocracy, had spent twenty-five years as a native Irish chief when he met Mabel Bagenal. He well understood English custom, and even religion, sufficiently to have been married to his abducted financee by an Anglican bishop! It would appear, however, that his bride had little understanding of and much repugnance for the lifestyle into which she entered:

> How can she have understood what it really meant to live according to Gaelic ways, and may he not have begun to forget how rude they were? . . . The girl was . . . numbed at first, and then horrified and then furious. . . . She must have realized her isolation in the foreign world of Gaelic Dungannon; seen the slighting looks of the hardy fighting men; pined in the routine of a life that became more and more uncouth as she became mistress only in the kitchen and had to prove herself by qualities that she apparently did not possess. . . . He could hardly be expected to give up his highborn women living in the same house as his wife, manners old as the lovers of Queen Maeve and the courtesans of Brian Boru, . . . and he saw the contemptuous looks of his own full-blooded women and heard the sniffs of neighboring amazons like the O'Donnell's Ineen Duv—she whom the Four Masters describe as a woman like the mother of Maccobees who *joined a man's heart to a woman's thought.* . . . (Italics mine)[12]

After the defeat of O'Neill and his allies at Kinsale, the plantation, military, and political occupation of all Ireland, and, finally, a series of enactments and military victories during the seventeenth century, the institutions of Gaelic society—the legal system, class system, and literary/professional tradition—were all but annihilated. With the imposition of laws against the existence and training of Catholic clergy, this group, which had become the primary agent for transmission of Gaelic culture, lost its function.

But the language itself, purveyor of the forbidden value system, survived throughout this period. And along with it, the manuscripts that detailed the laws governing the status of women in Gaelic society also survived. Looking at these, we find that women could and did hold property in their own name.

There is evidence that in earlier Pict society, a matriarchy existed and women could contract independently, regardless of marital status, but since contract law is a relatively later development than laws of inheritance or marriage rights, there is some confusion and contradiction about the early condition of Gaelic women in regard to contract right. The earlier laws describing the categories of marriage and rights accruing to each category suggest, nevertheless, that in at least two categories the wife had absolute veto rights over their husband's contracts, and that other categories of wives and unmarried women could conclude "good" contracts in their own or their spouse's behalf, which, although subject to veto by him, could on their own be held legitimate. If the woman was an heiress or if her properties exceeded those of her husband or lover,* his honor price was derivative of hers.[13]

The mother of a child could declare the child's paternity regardless of her marital status or the brevity or nature of her relationship to the child's father. Likewise, her "portion," both assets and liabilities, devolved first on her sons and then on her family of origin. If she inherited property or received it through gift, her right to it could be limited to her lifetime if she *relinquished the obligation for military service*, which accompanied the property right. It is apparent, however, that in the seventh century, and perhaps later, women and clergy maintained their obligation for military service, and it was only through the *Cain Adomnain* of about 697 A.D. that killing or harming a woman or cleric became *such a major criminal offense as to negate their participation in warfare*. On the other hand, it may be that these laws were intended to provide greater protection for their non-combatant status, since also "innocent children" were included. "If a woman dies a violent death which can in any way be attributed to malice or the neglect of man, full fines are to be paid. Visitation of God and lawful childbed are expressly excluded; death caused by cattle, pigs, dogs, tame beasts in general and everything that is made by human agency . . . expressly included."[14] Prior to this law, it is probable that the two sexes had been on equal footing in regard to military service and criminal law. The fine for the offender was to be paid to the religious community, in cases of violation of women. This stands in contrast to earlier law in which the honor price of the woman was to be paid to her sons (if she was a mother), or to her *fine* (clan), or to her husband (depending on her

---

*Actually there was no distinction between "husband" and "lover"; there were only different categories of "husband." There was no such thing as an illicit relationship or illegitimate child.

status, such honor price could be split among all the aforementioned). In fact, a woman's inheritance was most often expected to be from her father, while the son inherited from his mother, and the liabilities for the parents' debts were first assumed by sons and then by the *fine*, but not, in any case, by daughters.[15] A woman's status in marriage derived in part from her family of origin and from her *fine*'s consent to or disapproval of the match. She did not, however, need their consent in order to form the alliance and she did not require her husband's consent in certain instances to form a legitimate relationship with another man. The responsibility of her family of origin or her former husband for her assets, liabilities, and children from the informal alliance was accordingly decreased, albeit not eliminated! Further, her husband was required to return her dowry or other property to her family or to her sons if she died or divorced him.[16] If the woman's familial status was higher than that of her husband—if he was a foreigner or without property and clan—he assumed membership in her family and derived his status from hers. Their children were to be considered of her family.[17] If a woman remained single, she could during her lifetime have property and make contracts in her own name, the property reverting to the *gelfine* upon her death. In all cases, she could own in her own name property given her as a gift or earned through her business dealings. This she could bequeath as she determined.

A distinction was made between the kind of marriage connection and the category of wife. As women were defined in terms of property relationships and through their relationships with men, men were defined in relation to women and in relation to one another through property and familial bonds. It is clear that while a woman lost her rights vis-a-vis honor price if she left her husband for another partner without her husband's permission, a husband had also to arrive at some sort of agreement with his wife in order to form a secure relationship with his second wife and/or his concubines.[18] It is hard to imagine from the vantage point of the twentieth century what must have been the feelings of a woman who entered in a relationship as a second wife, or as one of the classifications of concubine; and it would be erroneous to assume that the chief wife would feel betrayed by her husband's acquisition of other wives. Extensive consideration was given, however, to the legitimacy of actions taken by the chief wife (*cetmineter*) in hostility toward the second wife (*adaltrach*), and vice versa:

> Both minor assaults and major assaults, even such as involve life and death are permitted to a *cetmineter* during a period of three nights, and (only) half fine (is payable in respect to such assaults) committed from the end of three nights. The *adaltrach* is free from liabilities during the first three nights but full fine is payable by her for all other deeds (i.e., after that period). . . . The *cetmineter* is completely free from liability for anything

she may do during the first three nights short of killing, and retribution is due from her for killing. Half fine is due from her after the first three nights for a month or *until she goes to a man*. . . . The *adaltrach* has the right to inflict damage with her finger nails and to utter insults and screechings and hair pulling and small injuries in general, i.e., to her belong three meals from the man's food, up to three days apart from the great hardship she suffers, full fine from then out; or full fine at once from an *adaltrach* for every injury she does . . . among the seven bloodsheds which might be inflicted with impunity was blood shed by a *cetmineter* through rightful jealousy of the *adaltrach* who took her place.[19]

The kinds of marriage connection refer to the relationships of property, not to the kinds of wife. These connections were: (1) a union with joint property; (2) a woman with a man of property; (3) a man with a woman of property with service; (4) a woman received on inducement; (5) a man who frequents without service, without inducement, without performance, and without bringing property; (6) a union with abduction; (7) a union of wandering mercenaries; (8) a clandestine union; (9) a union brought about by force.[20]

A *cetmineter* could be involved in any of the first three kinds of connections. She held a position of prestige and honor and was able to nullify contracts made by her husband without her consent. If she was invalided or bore no sons, her husband could take a temporary, second *cetmineter* or, if he took a wife of lower station, an *adaltrach*:

> Very elaborate details regarding the relative positions of adaltrach and cetmineter and their mutual relationship are to be found in the commentaries. . . . An adaltrach's admission to the *mna digtheacha* group depended on her having sons, unlike the cetmineter who enjoyed that status whether she had sons or not . . . a contracted woman (adaltrach) had no control over her husband's contracts unless these had to do with the sale of clothes, food, cattle or sheep.[21]

Two kinds of concubine relationships existed as well. Although these were recognized relationships and property rights were specified for them, they were not referred to as "lawful relationships," as were those of the *cetmineter* and *adaltrach*.[22]

The Irish custom of "fosterage" (giving one's children to another couple to rear and educate) was the major provision for child care and education. It was also a basic political interchange through which families and clans might be brought into alliance. Fosterage fees were arranged by rank and, depending on rank, a child might have several foster parents. Some authors have suggested that fosterage also served to avoid the conflicts attendant upon having numerous sons, by different wives, growing up in the same household. It well could be that fosterage for the Irish served a purpose not dissimilar to the kibbutz system initiated by the early settlers of Israel, that is, to provide for children an environment that would eliminate the kind of parent-child conflict they themselves had experienced; to ensure that the child would be focused on the community rather than narrowly on the family; to minimize sibling rivalry and provide a wider variety of adult role models for the children. Given the communal organization of Gaelic Ireland, it is not inconceivable that fosterage was similarly motivated. Furthermore, fosterage arrangements devolved equally on males and females or was to be shared between them. That is, the arrangement could be made by and to either or both parents.

Fosterage for a boy lasted until he reached seventeen, and for a girl, until fourteen. These were considered the respective "ages of choice." The fee for fostering a girl, despite the relative brevity of her stay, was greater than that for fostering a boy, perhaps because the boy would later be more able to protect, maintain, and support the foster father. The gift given the foster-child upon leaving was equal for male and female, and in both cases, the education provided, while dependent upon social class, was not necessarily defined in terms of sex-role stereotyped skills until the later commentaries.[23]

It would be very difficult, if not impossible, to find any kind of direct link between such women as Grainne O'Malley and Ineen Duv of the sixteenth-century Celtic breed, and Constance Gore-Booth (Markiewicz) and Maud Gonne MacBride of the twentieth century; although they stand together as heroic Irish women who totally disregarded English notions of appropriate sex-role behavior. Even at the height of Maud Gonne's passionate campaign to free her country from the oppressive British rule, she became celebrated for her performance in W. B. Yeats's play as Kathleen Ni Houlihan, the female symbol of Ireland—a beautiful woman in chains.[24]

James Connolly and Constance Markiewicz considered Irishwomen north and south as being in chains. The chains they described in their frequent speeches to women factory workers were the chains of capitalism:

> The Irish peasant in too many cases, treated his daughters in much the same way as he regarded a plough or a spade—as tools with which to work the farm. . . . Growing up in this atmosphere, the women of Ireland accepted their position of social inferiority. . . . Fidelity to duty was the only ideal to be striven after, consciously or unconsciously, fashioning a slave mentality. . . .
> Just as the present system in Ireland has made cheap slaves or untrained emigrants of the flower of our peasant women, so it has darkened the lives and starved the intellect of the female operatives in mills, shops and factories. Wherever there is a great demand for female labour, as in

Belfast, we find that the women tend to become the chief support of the house. Driven out to work at the earliest possible age, she remains fettered to her wage-earning—a slave for life. Marriage does not mean for her a rest from outside labour, it usually means that, to the outside labour she has added the duty of a double domestic toil. . . . Overworked, underpaid, and scantily nourished because underpaid, she falls easy prey to all the diseases that infect the badly-constructed "warrens of the poor." . . . None so fitted to break the chains as they who wear them.[25]

During the late nineteenth and early twentieth centuries in Ireland, the women who banded together in the Citizen Army, and in Cumann Na mBan (the Women's Organization for the Irish Republican Army), were often the same women who were activists in the suffragist movement in Ireland. Later, the Gifford sisters—Muriel and Grace—Doctor Kathleen Lynn, the O'Rahilly sisters, Anne Higgins, and others totaling 79, were arrested for republican activity.[26] Hanna Sheehy Skeffington, Mary Mc-Swiney, and many other women became the nucleus of leadership for the republican movement after the mass arrests and deportations that followed the Easter Rising. They raised funds in Ireland, England, and America, carried on correspondence, and organized services for their male and female colleagues who were on the run.[27] None of this would be particularly remarkable except for the fact that these women had been born and reared within a system that provided them no role models for their unconventional behavior as females.

Their rhetoric did not challenge the existing sex-role stereotypes, but their behavior was totally inconsistent with the code imposed by Victorian England. The Cumann Na mBan organizational history and handbook describes the tasks deemed appropriate for these auxiliaries, who were organized into areas corresponding to IRA battalion areas. They were to learn and teach Irish language and history, do public relations work for the republican cause, promote women candidates. Military activities included first-aid practice, cleaning and unloading rifles, scouting, and signaling. They were to set up dressing stations in safe houses, and equip food and rest stations. Some were trained to carry despatches and perform intelligence work.[28]

After the revolution and the civil war that followed and the establishment of the six counties in Ulster as a separate entity, the status of women in both parts of Ireland seems to have not merely reverted to its nineteenth-century condition, but actually to have regressed. Once again it is clear that Catholicism was not the only influence compelling this subordinate status, which seems to have been as much a part of Irish Protestantism. It is not necessarily so much an inherent feature of the religion as a carry-over from eighteenth- and nineteenth-century Victorian values that trickled down to the working class through their major social institution, religious organizations. Historical evidence suggests that Northern Irish Protestant women took the leading role during the nineteenth century in violently protesting the imposition of religious leaders on the Northern Irish congregations by the government in England. The Orange Order—the fraternal institution through which nineteenth- and twentieth-century Irish Protestants have been unified to support the political institutions of the Anglo-Irish ascendancy—does not, however, include women. The Orange Order, a somewhat secret society organized in part on the style of and using many symbols of Freemasonry, which through its mystic rites has incorporated much of the unconscious ideology of male supremacy and its underlying fear of femaleness: "Religious fervour has organized itself in the proverbially anticlerical form of masonic lodges. . . . The prejudices and obscurantism which feeds these fears seem to many to be sustained and perpetuated by the Orange Order."[29] It is indicative of the mystery maintained in regard to human and biological functions that the Orange Order maintains strict sex-role dichotomization in membership, ceremonials, and rhetoric. Not unlike more primitive societies, this ethos mystifies the power of the female by virtue of her capacity to both mother and seduce (contradictory but equally "emasculating" functions, of which men are incapable and from which males are forbidden understanding). The ambivalence is characterized through one Orange song that grants Mary of Orange the initiating idea of the order: "Why should Orange men, our sex one and all/ Shut out from their secrets, when Mary was founder?"[30] Yet there are many indications that Ulster Protestants "regard the emphasis upon the Virgin and the female imagery of the Catholic Church as amongst the most striking and fearful aspects of Catholicism."[31] The imagery of Eire as the Mother further alienates and fascinates the Ulster Protestant. His religion and society are so strongly male-oriented no equivalent symbolism can be readily available without incorporating and inverting the fear-evoking symbolism of the hated Church of Rome. Thus, as a female, "She" (Eire) has the potential to "possess" a man and somehow influence him away from his masculine objectives. The psychoanalytic theorist Ernest Jones found the ambiguities of masculine/feminine characterizations in Ireland so dramatic that they inspired his volume of essays in which psychoanalytic theory is applied to political psychology.[32] Commenting on this, the classicist (himself an Ulsterman) H. D. Rankin says that even the names for Ireland are often female—Eire, Banba, Fodla:

> Many of the most important Irish patriot leaders were Irish only on the maternal side. We must recall that some of the most formidable deities of the ancient Celts were female: the war deities of the Irish—Babh, Morrigan, were goddesses, and women have played a prominent part in the

leadership of war or revolution in Celtic culture from the time of Boadaecia in Roman Britain, to Constance Markiewicz and Maud Gonne MacBride in this century. . . . Older country people in Ulster have a superstitious dread of the power of Catholic women to influence their sons away from their religion and to swallow up the family's future in Catholic assimilation. Also, it is perhaps significant that Ulster Protestants have always been willing to give their daughters distinctively Irish names, but have on the whole been hesitant to give Irish names to their sons, preferring to give those which have a Scottish or an Old Testament flavour. The USC [unconscious symbolism] 'logic' underlying this custom is possibly as follows: "Ireland is female and you can ratify your possession of her by naming women in her honour, but if you name your sons in this way she will thereby in some sense possess them."

The prejudice still persists, though it is declining at present amongst the more urbanized Ulster Protestants.[33]

This kind of fear of femaleness translates into or possibly derives from an attitude that "God, in creating desire for women in men, had been guilty of a lapse of taste."[34] For the Catholic, the Church is male-dominated, if not male-oriented, and family life tends likewise. Ignorance of facts about sex and the guilt emanating from engaging in it have conspired to produce a strained relationship even between those spouses who enjoy each other. In both segments of the population it is expected that males will prefer the company of other males and have a right to it. So much so, in fact, that pub bars are for men only, and if they invite mixed company, pubs provide a "lounge" for that purpose.

The subordination of Irish women has been exacerbated during the past decade of escalating violence. Of course the most obvious effects have been in Northern Ireland, although women in the Irish Republic have not been unaffected, nor has their status advanced even at a period of history when the Irish Republic has been urged by its colleagues in EEC to bring the economic status of women into conformity with their standards.

The status of women in any society is not only a kind of barometer of democracy and equality, but also a measure of the economic basis of that political system. The status of women in Irish society is particularly exemplary of the progression from a system of clan socialism to advanced capitalism. In fact, without having thoroughly explored the legal history of Ireland, Engels, writing in the nineteenth century, saw the history of the family, and particularly the status of women, in Ireland as a prime example of the relationships between the family, private property, and the state.[35]

The following criteria, when applied to the women of Ireland now and through the recent past, serve to illustrate their condition as the apotheosis of denigration: (1) The status of women is adversely affected by wars and an ethos of violence. (2) Sexism, like racism, is, in most societies, an excuse for the economic exploitation of women. (3) The subordination of women is exacerbated within groups that are oppressed groups in the context of the larger society. In such groups the male is forced into a subordinate, subservient role to his masculine counterparts in the majority group. Since power and masculinity are generally equated, his only recourse for expressing his "masculine potency" is through sexual domination of the women in his group.

Adverse Effects of Violence

The Official Republican Movement has focused attention on the issue of women's equal status. The *ArdFheis* of 1972 proclaimed not only the policy of the movement within itself, but also a political program of equal rights for women in the thirty-two counties to which the party stands committed. Nonetheless, a woman member remarked, "When we stand shoulder to shoulder with our guns, we're equal, but when the shooting is over, the men go off to the pub to talk of strategy and the women go off to the kitchen to cook their supper."[36]

Neither the UDA nor the Provisional IRA seems to have broken down the tradition of separation. The former have their "ladies auxiliary," which marches and issues statements periodically. The latter has maintained the Cumann Na mBan, the women's club with its own skirted uniform, tradition, and functions. There is something almost pagan about the participation of the youth section of this group, scrubbed and uniformed, carrying wreaths and, symbolically, performing the contemporary equivalent of the "Chorus of Virgins" in Provisional IRA funeral processions. In fact, the quickest way to spot the difference between an Official and Provisional funeral is to check the position of women in the procession. In the former, they are interspersed, although the wreath-carrying is still allocated to the women!

Sectarian murder in late 1972–1973 often seemed to be the fate of those who crossed sectarian lines to "date." There have been numerous reports of intimidation threats against those who violate sectarian lines in courtship. Yet, in the mid-1960's, this barrier had seemed to be disintegrating. When Des O'Hagan, sociologist and NICRA leader, was interned in 1971, his wife, Marie (Protestant-born), was forced out of their home in a mixed neighborhood by the intimidation of her Protestant neighbors. She and her infant son were finally compelled to take up residence with her parents, which afforded some minimal protection and comfort. Similarly, a young woman whose efforts as a recreation leader in the Shankill had evoked my admiration confided that she would have to leave her position in six months. She was Protestant, but, she said, "I'll be marrying a Catholic in May."

Sectarian barriers to romance loom even within the nationalist community. A young woman, a member of the Official Republican Movement, going to a pub one evening to collect for the Prisoners' Dependents' Fund, was flung down the stairs by her boyfriend and his friends, who were members of the Provisionals. He was later interned, and while she remains a loyal "Official," she is torn by her continued attachment to her republican (but Provie) boyfriend.

Bluntly, a woman's value in a paramilitary or military organization is the degree to which she is a pseudo-man. Violence, terrorism, and strife glorify the combatant, the militarist, the aggressive, the unafraid. Masculinity itself is prized for the physical power subsumed by its traditional definition. Sexuality other than rape of the conquered—the assertion of supremacy by physical force—is viewed as weakness and vulnerability.

Torture of women in interrogation in many places features rape and threats of rape while torture of men emphasizes emasculation. The former clearly emphasizes woman's stereotypical weakness, and the latter is a destruction of male "prowess." Body searches carried out on both males and females typically feature genital humiliations. In Northern Ireland women are ostensibly not to be subjected to body search by males, but rather by female warders or policewomen. Many cases are reported, however, in which suspects have been ordered to strip down to their brassieres for photographing when they have been brought into army barracks for interrogation, and have been beaten and threatened when they have refused.

The Provisional Sinn Fein has not committed itself to any policy that might imply a contradiction with Church authority on the status of women. But when three of the leaders of their Army Council were interned in the south, Maire Drumm was named to the top post in Sinn Fein (Provisional) formerly occupied by Sean MacStiofain. While the latter previously held all the leadership positions himself, Ms. Drumm was established as one of a troika (with two men). By virtue of being a woman she was less likely to be interned and therefore her position assures continuity of leadership. Furthermore, it is recognized that as a female she could not be a member of the outlawed IRA. (The Provisionals retain the "men only" policy. The women are members of Cumann Na mBan.) In summer, 1976, she was again imprisoned, and in October was murdered in her hospital bed.

Irish women have not, however, been exempted from jailing or from the prospect of torture. Ordinarily, women have been either jailed or detained rather than interned—a legal nicety that makes little functional difference. The implication is that women who are jailed have been or will be tried under some section of the criminal code and that they will be afforded a jury trial of some sort.

In the relations between political prosecution and criminal prosecution of minority-group persons, there are too few legal safeguards to ensure that the majority of such convictions will be based on the case rather than on the disadvantage of being poor and/or a minority member. Under the Detention of Terrorists Act, presently in force in Northern Ireland, women have been jailed as terrorists (or potential terrorists) without civil trial. A frequent practice in the past was internment followed by a detention order. In 1973, the practice changed to detention orders often followed by charges, conviction, and prison sentences. In January, 1973, Elizabeth McKee, a nineteen-year-old Belfast woman, was put in detention. Later that month many other women, both Protestant and Catholic, were also detained (see Appendix for their protest). Pickets, demonstrations, and press statements attested to the sense of outrage among the nationalist population arising from the application of such laws to females. It seems to have aroused greater public displeasure than had even the detention of children aged fourteen to sixteen, which had by then become commonplace.

The violence has served in another way to undermine the prospect of equality for women. It separates into warring factions those women who would have worked together to change the system. Socioeconomic differences have been made rigid by the conflict and the way that conflict is experienced by the women in Northern Ireland.

Catholic women join various church groups (ladies sewing-circle type), or Cumann Na mBan, or the Official Republican Movement (a Marxist-oriented group that carries as part of its revolutionary program the equal rights of women), or the local civil rights organization. They may even be secretary in a local SDLP club! Protestant women have donned uniforms and carried arms (a counterpart of the Cumann Na mBan) in parades of the Ulster Defence Association, shout epithets at Catholics, decorate their homes and streets for "Orange parades," and descend savagely upon any among them who might violate their standards of maintaining a Protestant country under a Protestant queen.

Even the feminist movement (or perhaps especially the feminist population) is adversely affected by this manipulated sectarian fear and hatred. At a meeting of the Belfast Women's Liberation group in August, 1972, this destructive potential was manifest. The majority of the group (which contained only about a dozen women altogether) are either connected with Queen's University or involved in one or another professional or semiprofessional occupation. They come essentially from middle-class and Protestant backgrounds. I had been invited to attend and brought with me two young working-class women, both active in the Official Republican Movement and both eager to develop grass-roots egalitarianism within the ranks of their comrades in trade unions and neighborhood. We talked about my field research and the unspeakable family conditions in one of the most terrorized Catholic poverty areas (Ballymurphy). I mentioned having spent a night with one of the families in order to help bring some order out of the chaos. I described the pathological condition of their three small children, and a late-comer immediately said, "Well, I hope you taught them about contraception." It was so out of context that I had to gasp. She explained, in very upper-class accents, that "if you're any kind of feminist, you'd be teaching them about contraception and abortion." I said, "What do you mean?" She then said that she was a physician and ran a family-planning clinic near that area and that "the whole mess here is a product of their breeding habits!" When she heard the doctor's name, one of the young working-class women whispered to me that she'd heard "what that woman does to you when you go to that place!"

The rest of the evening was no less an example of the effects of political conflict, sectarian and class divisions on the prospect of the women's movement. War itself celebrates the "masculine mythos" of power, strength, and aggression. In this way war polarizes, it does not politicize, and in the sex-role behavior it dichotomizes rather than liberates.

Economic Exploitation

Sexism in Ireland, north and south, is the instrument for the economic exploitation of a pool of skilled and even professional workers. The Irish Women's Liberation Movement, Dublin Founding Group, published in 1971 a pamphlet listing the legal, educational, and economic facts of women's life in Ireland.[37] In many instances, of course, the discriminatory practices are no different from those of Britain or the United States. The Irish constitution, however, specifically provides for the married woman/mother the "privileged" status of nonemployability.[38] Perhaps as a kind of over-reaction to the centuries-long exploitation of young Irish girls and women in factories and mills (so eloquently described by one of the leaders of the 1916 Rising, James Connolly), the Irish Civil Service until recently dismissed female employees upon marriage. This "example" is followed by many of the private employers as well.

The economic difference between the employment of women in the Republic of Ireland and in Northern Ireland is represented by the fact that in the former women earn 54.9 percent of men's wages and in the latter 62 percent. As of 1973, women were supposed to receive equal pay for equal work in the north. Although their sisters in the south were recommended for the same privilege, it had not until very recently been initiated as legislation. Despite the ratification by Ireland of the 1969 UN Charter on the Political Rights of Women, women were not permitted until 1974 to serve on juries in the Irish Republic. In view of the restrictions on political and economic freedom of married women, especially those with children, some Dublin feminists recommended "Five Good Reasons Why it is Better to Live in Sin."[39]

The legal chains in Ulster are less blatant, but equally omnipresent. This may be attributed, at least in part, to the special relation of the Protestant clergy to the political process and power structure. As in the Irish Republic, Ulster has no women cabinet ministers and few female elected representatives. The major difference in public participation of women in militant action groups in Northern Ireland has come about through the new involvement of women with paramilitary organizations. In contrast with the present Ulster Defence Association, the older Ulster Volunteer Force had no female membership.

For well over a hundred years women in Belfast and Derry have been employed, even though the men are often unemployed (sometimes for three generations). They sweep the patch of sidewalk outside their rowhouses, they paint the curbstones (red, white, and blue in the unionist areas, orange and green in the nationalist sectors).

Certainly, the economics of racism and that of sexism are nowhere more closely related and evidenced than in the attitudes of the exploited working-class women of Northern Ireland. Interviews with Protestant women in Belfast reveal the effects of the division between Catholic and Protestant working-class women:

Q. What kind of relationships are there between Loyalist women and Catholic women in mixed workplaces, presuming they do work in certain areas together?

A. Yes, well, Loyalist women are not against Catholic women. The Loyalist women and the Loyalist men are against the IRA and the provisional terrorist, not against Catholic women. The Loyalist woman will not start a row or have a fracas with the woman next to her at work just because she's a Catholic.

Q. What sort of issues do LAW [Loyalist Association of Workers] women mobilize around in factories?

A. Well, they have to fight intimidation, and they do fight pay claims—like if they have to take a halfday off work, and they're not paid for it, the firm is closed down—Roman Catholics have remained in the firm; they haven't done any work, but they've got paid for it, you know?

Q. Do Catholic women come out in support?

A. We have Catholic members who have come out with us.

Q. I mean Catholic women outside LAW—would they come out?

A. No.

Q. Or would LAW women come out in support of any of their demands?

A. No.

Q. How do you see LAW women's role as a whole, within Vanguard [an organization composed of members of LAW and UDA, both overwhelmingly working class in composition]?

A. At the moment we are helping our women to learn to drive—in the case of civil war we'll need as many drivers as possible. We're really working on the same scale as the UDA or the Army—we have drivers, we have first-aid units, skilled nurses and doctors. If a civil war comes, it doesn't mean everybody's going to run to the front line—there's going to be people to organize children, old people, relief centers, things like that.

Q. What do you as a woman want for Northern Ireland?

A. Well, of course I want a peaceful solution, but my main point is that I want the restoration of Stormont immediately. We had a democratically elected government taken away from us by the stroke of a pen by Ted Heath [Prime Minister of Britain and head of the Conservative Party, which abolished Stormont, the seat of the mostly Unionist government in Northern Ireland, as a temporary measure. William Whitelaw, a Conservative, English politician, was installed as Secretary of State for Northern Ireland] and we will not stop in Ulster—we will take it to Ted Heath's doorstep. As you see, if you look at the south of the border, it's an underdeveloped country compared to what we were. If we went back three or four years ago, I'd be quite happy and contented. . . .

No United Ireland. Our forefathers fought and died for Ulster and we will fight and die for Ulster—there will be no United Ireland.

Q. Do you get support from any political groups in Britain?

A. I wouldn't know so much about that. There is one—what is it you call it—the National Front [a group founded by Sir Oswald Mosley, patterned originally on the Brownshirts and Blackshirts of Germany and Italy]. I can't think of any others.

Q. Would you support any of the demands that the women's movement in England is making, demands like equal pay?

A. I would say so, in equal jobs I would say equal pay. I think the women in England are rather fanatic, but then I think it's because they haven't got a basic cause to follow, they haven't got anything that's as near to the heart as we have. Their very existence isn't at stake, so some of the ambitions I've heard are airy fairy, they're non-realistic, they're silly, they're down right foolish. They're just women who think they've got a mission but aren't quite sure what it is.

Q. And you feel the women here have?

A. We have a mission, very much so, yes.[40]

Slaves of Slaves

The women of an oppressed group are oppressed not least by the men of that group. The Black and Chicano struggles in the United States early emphasized the importance of "being boys no more." They did not accept the condition of male subservience in jobs and education. Much of their rhetoric and literature were blatantly demanding that their women return to the kitchen and bedroom and leave the fighting to the men. But analyzing the role of the black woman in America provided some insights that can be extended to the relations between men and women in the minority society of Northern Ireland. Nathan and Julia Hare pointed out that

> though many black women reject the white sociologist's label of "matriarch," they nonetheless possess a keen sense of themselves as the backbone and major source of strength in the black family unit. Many feel cast into two roles, male by day and female after five, required to play the feminine role as prescribed by social custom yet driven to a masculine role by white society's harsher rejection of the black man occupationally. Thus even the positive virtues of being a black woman—easier access to jobs and financial favors compared to black men—have negative consequences in that they deprecate the black male. The more she asserts herself, the more intense her conflict with him. Accordingly, even as she may despise and regret being forced into a "matriarchal" role, she boasts of her "mother wit," which she sees as compensating for her lack of formal education or real socioeconomic power to fulfill the role thrust upon her.
> They generally must take pains to avoid the appearance of posing a threat to black men as leaders or whatever and thus feel compelled to express positive attitudes toward them. At the same time, however, they have internalized white society's low regard for black men, but they are troubled by their appraisals of black men and their performance.[41]

In the summer of 1975 I met with two young mothers in Belfast whose husbands were internees who had become sentenced prisoners. Each had been married less than five years, and neither had spent more than two of those years with her husband. They were afraid to engage in any kind of social life, even with other women, lest their husbands be informed that they were "gadding about" or "unfaithful." Their days were a ceaseless round of petty chores, which never seemed to get done, and their nights were lonely vigils. Neither of them had any interest in politics, and although they lived on meager pensions, had neither interest nor capacity to find jobs. Their conversational horizons were limited to their children and families, within which they had resumed their roles as daughters despite living outside their parents' homes. They were isolated from the social life of their communities. Even more isolated was another young woman, living in the same apartment complex, who had been born into a Protestant working-class family and had married a Catholic. Her husband had been severely tortured during many interrogations, interned and then detained. They have one child and a wall between them. He became even more politically involved and committed when he was finally released from Long

Kesh. She fought against him and his politics until they no longer had anything left to say to each other. Religion isn't the issue between them. Neither of them has any religious affinity. Both are slaves in a system where neither of them can obtain employment, develop a social life, or move freely about in either community.

What is daily life like for these women? Sometimes if they pursue a more active course, they must face a constant and often brutal challenge to their assertions of equality. A young woman, elected to the chair of a local republican club in Lower Falls, Belfast, was attempting one evening in July, 1972, to conduct an orderly meeting to discuss how such programs as the club's cooperative store and play center might be staffed and made functional. She directed criticism from the chair at the unruly behavior of some of the men present. Finally, when one "militant leader" arrived half an hour late but unrepentant and disruptive, she demanded that he be fined. The men in the group became insulting and the militant leader shouted at her that she was being a "fascist" in her manner of chairing. She immediately resigned her post and new elections were held. The young man who then assumed the chair did not even make a pretense of democratic procedure but simply resolved and commanded on every issue himself. He was never challenged for undemocratic behavior.

Men who are oppressed, who are made by the larger society into boy-lackeys for economic and political survival, cannot turn on their oppressor directly to assert their humanity: instead they assert it by maintaining a superior position vis-a-vis the women in their lives. The working-class Protestant man, with little hope for raising his standard of living or asserting power in the larger world, can instead take a superior stance toward his Catholic counterpart on the one hand or go off on the other to his Orange Lodge, where the rule is "men only." It is no accident of fate that as of 1973, there were only two women out of fifty-two representatives to the provincial government at Stormont!

It is not unusual for a man who has been interned and tortured to ventilate his pent-up anger by verbally or physically "beating" his wife. In this kind of situation, there is a complicating psychopathology. Many of these men suffered direct torture in their genitals. Others were severely beaten and believed that saltpetre was being put into their food rations at the camps. This produced a massive sexual anxiety—especially since the male reproductive function has been so valued in this society. The anxiety itself is sufficient to cripple sexuality. When they have finally been confronted with the resumption of normal marital relations, these men often do behave misogynistically.

Jimmy, aged twenty-four, was interned for ten months. He had been dragged from his home in the early morning of August 9, 1971. At that time, he had just found a job as a laborer—the first job he'd held in the three years of his marriage. He worked approximately two weeks. His wife managed during his internment to make arrangements with neighbors to keep their two babies while she visited her husband in Long Kesh. She confided, during the time he was interned, that he had been tortured in interrogation and "things had been done" to him that he wouldn't tell her about. She was anxious about his condition and would try to prepare herself for each visit by telling him about all the "little things" that were happening. He, in turn, would tell her very little about his own circumstances, but would request her to bring things from home, especially food, because he suspected saltpetre was put into the food and he wasn't going to touch any of it. She took great care then to make sure he had ample supplies and would not have to rely on the camp meals.

Just prior to his return, Patricia expressed increased anxiety over "what he'd be like." She was with him when he was interviewed and tested, two weeks after his release. She was quite subdued and, even so, he was impatient with her and asked her to leave the room while he spoke with me. He described having had electroshock applied to his genitals during interrogation and having been unable to experience any sexual interest in his wife since his return. He thought she must have guessed that he'd been "hurt," but when she showed solicitude it became too much for him to bear. He had already, for no reason he could afterward recall, hit her hard once and gone out "with the boys." He'd been drinking regularly and was still taking the pills he'd got while in "the Kesh." The pills, it turned out, were librium—a drug found to have a debilitating effect on sexual arousal.

In Belfast and Derry girls seem to marry early. Most often they marry the first boy with whom they "do a steady line." Their apparent objective is to attain identity through marriage and a "place" of their own—an often unrealized objective in a society where working-class housing is perennially short. More often, they end up living with one or the other set of parents. Lately, with the increased possibility of "squatting," the crowding of young married couples with their parents has been somewhat alleviated.

Having a baby comes to mean fulfillment and "fitting in" for these young women. Although miscarriage is not uncommon, such an event arouses grief and guilt. One very slender, quiet, nineteen-year-old confided her feelings of shame because, although her husband had been released from detention six months earlier, she had as yet not "been able to conceive." In company of her sister and sisters-in-law (all near her own age) she felt unable to join the conversation, which concerned exclusively their infants, pregnancies, and deliveries, experiences she had not shared. Her husband was charged with several offenses against the British army and, she feared, was going to be sentenced to a long imprisonment. If she could not conceive before that, her future would be totally hopeless. Without having had a baby, she could not lay claim to an identity in her reference group.

This value system places no less strain on the male within it. Because sex is "evil" and the body is "dirty" he experiences guilt feelings from thus "violating" the sanctity of the respectable wife to whom he promised protection. He is appalled by the suffering she undergoes in the pregnancy and childbirth which have resulted from his having "taken his pleasure." When his wife began to evidence a miscarriage, Pat, already at twenty-one the father of a thirteen-month-old daughter, rushed into a relative's home totally distraught and near tears. The older woman upbraided him for not having been present earlier in the day, when the physician had visited his wife, who had been feeling ill. He admitted to having been out at the time "with the lads" at a local pub, but "just for a wee moment." He quickly blamed himself for her "inadequate" medical examination and her subsequent haemorrhaging. When she was taken to the hospital he broke into tears. Because in Derry ambulances do not readily go from the Creggan to the hospital, there was considerable delay. Pat was so shaken with misery and recrimination that he was unable to care for the baby or himself during her brief hospitalization. He did not consider any reason other than his own lack of responsibility for the spontaneous abortion of a two-month fetus. The only consolation offered by relatives was that being young they'd have other chances. He never considered the miscarriage to have been related to the frequent gassings and other factors of the political scene, but simply accepted a thesis of personal guilt.

In December, 1971, the internment authorities began to grant permission for internees to take a brief, supervised leave from camp if, on medical authority, a "girlfriend" could prove that she was pregnant, and if a wedding ceremony was conducted during the leave. There was only one other basis for a temporary release, and that was to attend the funeral of a parent, child, or sibling. In this way, the role of the woman as breeder or martyr was given reinforcement, even through the machinery of internment.

In today's war in Northern Ireland the traditional role of "the mothers of Ireland" is enacted with a few up-to-date touches. Traditionally in times of civil strife, the men and "boys" have been "on the run." Some have always gone "on the run" without scenes of civil disruption—rather because this is "divorce Irish style."*

*"Divorce Irish style" consists of the man going off to England or America to find employment and, after perhaps sending home one or two pay checks, disappearing. In the Irish Republic, the wife of such a man has no legal status and cannot even obtain a job in most cases. In fact, child-care allowances from the government legally belong to the father. The wife-mother has no recourse at law, and if "him-

If they are not on the run some men are interned or detained for months or years. For the Catholic women of the north, especially the working class, it is their men who are dragged off in midnight home searches and raids; it is their children who are "accidentally killed" while throwing stones and bottles at the soldiers; it is their private solitude and misery that become glorified in songs of "female valor." Their actions? They do not act. They bang dustbin lids to warn of approaching patrols; they hide guns and bombs under their dresses; they smuggle messages into internees; they turn on their sisters and daughters who violate the sacred cause in seeking companionship "with the enemy." The viciousness to which they descend at such times is the final expression (the only one allowed them) of outrage and anger. They do ventilate their anger through loudly cursing soldiers and shouting epithets at them, sometimes with bawdy songs shouted, rather than sung, to assure command of the military ear. But their turning on one another is a final act of rage derived from feelings of worthlessness, or impotence. It is an especially poignant demonstration of their traditional predicament as biological vessels, as passive recipients, of whatever fate and men bestow. Internment, like everything else, places an additional impediment in the path of women. They wake up and wait for hours, first for transportation, then to be searched. Finally, they visit "their men" in tiny cubicles, for a half-hour under the watchful eyes of two guards.

In a society where public displays of affection between men and women are anyway exceedingly rare, the most intense and loving relationship between a prisoner and a woman has no possibility for expression. The tender emotions have no place in this world of barbed wire and fear. The internee whose experience of interrogation and imprisonment has exacerbated his anxieties about his masculinity and finally inculcated a deep-seated sense of shame and humiliation can not readily relate to the implications of a sharing relationship, with a woman.

The status of women in this society where they are "slaves of slaves," is not better in the south, where the sectarian conflict has not been as volatile. Breeding patterns were never determined by women; they have invariably been outlined or outlawed by men. In Northern Ireland, the birth rate has been a political issue. While the government social-welfare system boasts about the availability of birth control in the north, the birth rates for Protestants and for Catholics show little difference among the working-class. While interviewing several children in the Shankill (the Protestant working-class area) in December, 1971, I got into a discussion with their

---

self" should ever happen back into her life, she has no choice but to accept his presence until he should take his leave again. This is the way the sacred institutions of marriage and family life are protected in postrevolutionary Ireland.

mother about the current state of affairs and its effects on women. She told me that "these things are always hardest on the women," and then said, "but if they [the Catholics] would stop breeding like rabbits, maybe we could come to some settlements." Having earlier inquired about the number of children in this family, I was somewhat startled. "Mrs. G.," I said, "you have five children, don't you?" "Six, one just married," she said. "Isn't that rather a lot?" "If we don't—they'll outbreed us!" she exclaimed.

Women Activists

Despite seemingly overwhelming odds, women in Ireland—both north and south—have surfaced in important ways during the past decade. In 1963, Patricia McCluskey was aroused by the unwillingness of the Protestant-dominated council to move Catholics from very overcrowded housing to a group of empty postwar utility houses far superior. She organized a Homeless Citizens' League in the town, and after protests at Stormont as well as a direct action "squat-in," the Catholics were granted the tenancies they desired. In January, 1964, she and her husband, Dr. Con McCluskey, founded the Campaign for Social Justice to collect and publish information about cases of injustice in Northern Ireland.[42] For a long time, the CSJ remained the effort of a small but vocal group of Catholic professional people who intended to maintain it separate from any political party or ideology.

After the rise of Paisley and the escalating violence of unionist mobs in response to his demagoguery, the Northern Ireland Civil Rights Association was founded in 1967. Modeled after the National Council for Civil Liberties in England, for the first year it followed the same course as had the CSJ. Its members addressed their efforts to the discriminatory practices of local unionist governments in housing and jobs.

It was Mrs. McCluskey who, a year later, called the Unity Convention of Nationalists, in order to nominate a candidate for M.P. in the Mid-Ulster by-election. Bernadette Devlin was nominated. Since her appearance on the international scene, the prominence of Bernadette Devlin, who won that election, has given rise to some notion about women in Ireland as political decision-makers—as having a constituency for power. This is patently not so. No less than Indira Gandhi or Golda Meir, Bernadette Devlin's nomination for member of Parliament was a result of male rivalries that were not otherwise amenable to resolution. Although the convention through which she was nominated was called together by a woman, as Devlin herself tells us in *The Price of My Soul*, the only way she could be considered a serious candidate was through the ensuing deadlock between nationalist contenders.[43] Further, many of the men involved in her candidacy felt that she would be amenable to their "behind the scenes" direction. She proved otherwise. Far from being in her position by virtue of the support of feminists, however, she maintained her leadership in spite of the ridiculous demands placed on her to "be a lady" and conform to the stereotypes. There has of course been no acceptance on anyone's part (except her own) of the right of women as a group to achieve such independence.

Housing action was the focus of protest through which another leading figure in the current struggle emerged. Bridget Bond's efforts to secure a fair shake in housing for the Catholics of Derry mushroomed into one of the most multifaceted and mass-supported issues of any civil rights movement. Bridget and her husband Johnny had to maintain freedom from conventional marital stereotypes. Bridget has a debilitating heart disease and developed major complications. Nonetheless, the Bonds are center for everything that happens in Derry (all within the walls of their tiny prefab, two-bedroom house). With four sons now aged twelve to twenty, if they had become enmeshed in the prevalent male/female roles it is conceivable that the Catholic population of Derry would still be confined to the most inadequate, atrocious, and dangerous housing conditions in the western world (with the possible exception of Central and South America). It is also conceivable that without their teamwork factional disputes and personal animosities would by now have taken an additional death toll in Derry.

Bridget Bond is in the paradoxical position of being one of the best known leaders in the civil rights movement in Ireland and relatively unknown by people outside of Ireland. Everyone coming through Derry for a day or more is referred for information and understanding of the place to "see Bridget." When housing action in Derry, or grass-roots organizing in Derry, are written up, however, the names of John Hume, Ivan Cooper, Eamonn McCann, Malachy McGurran, and others are the ones mentioned. This seems a result of the lack of understanding about Derry social systems. Women are not "out front" in the same ways as are men, but the kind of organizing necessary to bring an alienated and downtrodden people to taking action on their own behalf is not done through the stirring speeches of middle-class males, or even the military efficiency of an IRA leader. Such organizing is the iconoclastic behavior of a respected person who is perceived as "one of our own." When Bridget refused to surrender to the prerogatives of landlords and housing authority bureaucrats telling her where she may and may not put her family for the night, she started a real revolution. Because she is of the fabric and history of Derry, because she is related by blood and marriage to many other families in that city, because she represented themselves—weakened and powerless, but determined nonetheless to proclaim her dignity and brazen her rights—Bridget Bond became a symbol of why Derry could be free.

Despite the success of the usurping culture in banishing the indigenous Irish (Gaelic) system of sex role equality from that island, the women who have led the civil rights movement in Northern Ireland have transcended stereotypes and dichotomies. Patricia McCluskey, Bridget Bond, Edwina Stewart, and Madge Davidson are descendants of the various ethnic and religious immigrants to Ireland. The dichotomies which have segregated women from men and women from other women by virtue of social class and religion have also given rise in each generation to stalwarts who reject these specious dichotomies and persist, as do these women, in being free and complete human beings.

The British Army
In Command or on the Run?

6

While going the road to sweet Athy . . .
A stick in my hand and a drop in my eye . . .
A doleful damsel I heard cry:
Oh, Johnny, I hardly knew ye!
With drums and guns and guns and drums . . .
The enemy nearly slew ye.
My darling dear, ye look so queer,
Oh Johnny, I hardly knew ye.
(Traditional Irish Nineteenth-Century Song)

With their camouflage uniforms, blacked faces, automatic weapons at the ready, the British army patrols, ubiquitous in Northern Ireland, appear perpetually engaged in a jungle big-game hunt. The insignia and colors on their berets vary from one group to another, but the regiments of the British army have all had more than one turn of service in Northern Ireland on their "peace-keeping mission." For some of the more experienced officers in the Scots Guards, the Royal Marines, and the Paratroopers, duty in Northern Ireland was a sequel to similar peace-keeping missions in Cyprus, Aden, Malaysia, and even in Palestine under the British Mandate. Among the noncommissioned and commissioned officers I interviewed in depth were many whose fathers had served in the same regiments. Also having served in certain of these regiments were Irishmen from the six counties and their fathers, many of whom were interned, detained, sentenced prisoners or on the run. The first year the British Army did not engage in operations in colonial or former colonial territories was 1968. In 1969, they became involved in Northern Ireland.

The British Army as Political Tool

The relationship of the British army to Ireland—north and south—is an old established one. British garrisons have been on Irish soil since at least the twelfth century. The relationship is not one-sided: Irish regiments have served in the British army throughout the history of the empire and in every corner of the empire. Even when the Irish Free State broke its dominion status during the Second World War, Irishmen from the Republic joined and served in the British army. In fact, that military tradition and experience is an extensive part of Irish social history. In the past, as now, many officers of the IRA acquired their military training through service in the British army.

Part of this tradition has been the practice of sending the regiments of one national group to garrison (and often to subdue) the nationalist population in another part of the empire. Thus, Irish regiments were extensively used to subdue and finally destroy the rising of the Highlanders in Scotland in the sixteenth and eighteenth centuries, and Scottish regiments are used today in Northern Ireland. In some cases, regiments serving in Northern Ireland are the same ones in which internees have served. Tragically, in one case, the son of an internee was killed by members of the same regiment in which the father had performed honorable service.

The origins of military involvement in Ireland provide a framework through which to understand the evolution of the Northern Ireland violence. In no other respect is the history so unidimensional.

Through the reign of Henry VIII, English domination of Ireland was enacted not so much through armies of occupation as through the imposition of a feudal system, with a particularly colonialist legal framework to support it, which in turn proved also to be the vehicle for what is now termed "racism." An edict of 1361, for instance, declared that "no pure-blooded Irishman of Irish nation shall be made mayor, bailliff or officer in any place subject to the king or hold a canonry or living among the English." The statutes of Kilkenny, passed in 1366, enacted, as we have seen, an "outlawry of the Irish Race." They defined as outside the "protection of the law" those who were "by blood" of the "Irish Nation."

Because the English were eager to maintain their settlement in Ireland, Henry VIII did not attempt to impose the Reformation on the Irish as extensively as he had on his subjects in England. But as he extended his imperial ambitions, he became increasingly aware of the prospect of his colonialist competitors using Ireland as a base to attack England from the rear, or to divert the profitable trade from the Indies.

The fact is that in 1580 and in the sequence of revolts in Ireland over the next 350 years military missions were sent by governments hostile to England to support the insurrectionists.

But there were other political reasons for the use of a standing army on Irish soil. From the earliest times, the English governing classes in Ireland had been so corrupt and so mismanaged their charge that in the late eighteenth century governing Ireland was costing one million pounds per annum, more than the combined American colonies. According to one scholar:

The dependence of the Irish colonial system on a frequent show of armed force found its expression in the prominence of the army in the government of the country. During the eighteenth and early nineteenth centuries Ireland's military establishment was nearly as large as that of Great Britain, and even in times of peace the Irish army could not complain of lack of work. Quite apart from its frequent intervention in riots and other disturbances of the peace, it was the mainstay of the administration in its day-to-day relations with the subject population. "The king's troops," wrote General T. A. Pitt, "have been fully employed in assisting to collect the revenue, and to carry into execution the common and statute law, in supporting the king's writ and suppressing tumultuous risings," and it was nothing but the stark truth when he added "that but for the military there would be no government at all in this country." In many places there was, indeed, little difference between army and government, and officers were freely employed as magistrates. "Our civil power is a sinecure," Peel declared in 1815, "not because there is no occasion for its exertions, but because it makes the military power perform its duties whenever it can."

The reliance of the civil authorities on the armed forces lasted as long as English rule. . . . The dictatorship of the army in Ireland was in striking contrast to its studied subordination to the civil power in England. "The guards on horseback," observed a highly placed onlooker of an official procession in 1772, "the principal officers of the household with their wards, and the pages in their livery paddling on foot through the mud, with grooms of the chambers and footmen, through the streets lined with soldiers, had an air of absolute monarchy and of military force to support it, that, had I been an Irishman, I am certain I could not have endured the sight of."

The inevitable reverse of this privileged position of the armed forces was a complete lack of discipline and a degree of corruption far in excess of the unpleasantly high norm of the period. . . . The ease with which Irish rebellions overcame the resistance of purely Irish forces and had to be quelled by British arms is sufficient evidence of the weakness and unreliability of the leadership of the Irish army, for Irish regiments acquired at the same time the highest reputation for bravery on numerous battlefields outside Ireland. . . . The cost of the army establishment was excessive even by contemporary English standards—sometimes double that of comparable English institutions.

The demoralisation of the Irish army reached its climax at the time of the 1798 rebellion. . . . Abercromby's classical description of his army as being "in a state of licentiousness which must render it formidable to everyone but the enemy," was completely borne out by its treatment of real or alleged rebels and ordinary citizens, as well as by the ignominious Castlebar Races, when a handful of French soldiers set a greatly superior force scurrying over the Irish countryside.[1]

There are many historic precedents for Faulkner's call to the army for help. Frequently when incompetent lieutenant governors or other administrators had parlayed their mismanagement into impossible dead-end conditions, as during the famine, they would communicate to their superiors their fear of incipient rebellion. This, of course, resulted in an increase of the armed force sent by the Crown. Even through the final period of the Irish struggle for independence, 1916–1921, there was a conviction in Whitehall that increasing the troop commitment would salvage the political status quo.

The threat of more troop commitment was launched at Michael Collins and Arthur Griffith when they were negotiating for the "treaty." In a sense, the outcome of that policy, which was to delay the independence of twenty-six counties of Ireland for some years more, suggests that it was a successful short-term solution to colonial problems. The escalation of violence in Northern Ireland during the past decade should stand, however, as proof that military intervention cannot permanently resolve a political problem.

Depending literally on which side of which street one has stood in Belfast or Derry, individual soldiers have been villains or heroes. For the soldier himself, it is often even more puzzling to know which side of which street he is patroling. Although the minimum age for service in Northern Ireland is eighteen, the behavior and reactions of the younger soldiers make them seem contemporaries of the adolescent stone-throwers with whom they contend.

A young freckle-faced, towhaired soldier in Belfast was standing traffic duty shortly after Bloody Friday, in the summer of 1972. He was in an "exposed position," albeit covered by a patrol from the corner. Traffic was being rerouted and his job was to wave the cars onto the detour. He had a thick Scottish "burr" almost unintelligible to my ears, but as he was explaining to me that he didn't know any of the streets for which I was looking, he was shaking and grew pale. Finally he became nearly distraught as he said, "Look, Ma'm, I've only just arrived and I don't know where I'm standing now except I was put here to move 'em on . . . and I can't understand the whole bloody mess anyhow, but if you insist on standing here and talking to me someone'll get shot for sure . . . either they'll shoot you, Ma'm, or someone'll shoot me. Please get on wi' yerself."

As frightening as it is for the isolated soldier, even if his isolation is measured by only a few yards distance from his mates, the soldier operating as part of a patrol feels the isolation no less. It's not been unusual for one man to be picked out of a patrol of eight and shot dead by a sniper. Nor is it entirely unheard of for a soldier to be separated from his patrol in foreign territory and end up dead. But the young soldiers are out to prove themselves and earn their own identity. They think they'll earn this somehow by being tough and rigid.

I was going the rounds in Lower Falls, Belfast, in the summer of 1973, introducing a Norwegian anthropologist to some of the children in my study and their parents, when we were stopped by a patrol that demanded our identification. Since such a demand is illegal in Northern Ireland (there are no requisite identity papers in Britain), I simply gave my name and she gave hers. We were then asked what we were doing "here." When we explained that we were a social psychologist and a social anthropologist, the soldiers asked, "What's that?" My colleague replied, "I study cultures." The soldiers looked puzzled and one of them turned back to her and said, "Well, you won't find any of that here."

It might have meen a humorous encounter for us, except that the patrol then followed us from place to place, and when we went into the local community social club, the patrol came in after us and persisted in running us through an identification check again. This kind of action eventually becomes harassment, especially because the patrols habitually and nervously aimed their weapons at the subject of their investigations.

Another time, en route from Derry to Belfast in an automobile belonging to the American consulate and driven by an American official, we were stopped at a checkpoint and asked for identification. I showed my passport. The young corporal looked intently at it. My companion showed his diplomatic pass and the noncom in charge of the patrol insisted that he show "one like hers." The diplomat was becoming very tense. He insisted that the pass he was showing should suffice. But no, the young soldiers were intent on doing a "thorough" job. They opened the car doors and began to reach for the diplomatic pouch. With guns trained on us and their suspicions not even allayed by the fact that the steering wheel was on the wrong side for that country, or by the U.S. State Department license plates, they were committed to their routine. At a crucial moment, their officer ran up to the car, recognized the situation, and sharply ordered them back to their posts. The soldiers were obviously confused as we drove away. Presumably, they were more thoroughly schooled by their irate officer afterward.

These experiences were among the more benign of my encounters with the British army. For even in situations of professional interviewing, or informal contact on a first-name basis, there was a remarkable lack of humor and flexibility in their approach. This rigidity, characteristic of hierarchical bureaucratic structures, complicates the very ambiguous British army situation as a peace-keeping force.

During the time I was detained in Crumlin Road jail, I was guarded by a military policeman who informed me that he was taking an additional tour of duty in Northern Ireland, not for extra pay or service medals, but because he was going to "get even with those bastards" who had wrecked the windscreen on his vehicle by throwing rocks. It had not been his private car, he said; it was an army vehicle and worth a lot of money and he would "take it out of their hides if he could get to them." When he described the area in which he preferred to serve duty—an area at the intersection of Falls and Springfield Roads—I shuddered. It was the area from which British Army personnel, located at Royal Victoria Hospital, had fired down on Dunville park the previous summer, when my students and I had taken the local children for outdoor play. We had, after that, all developed as a reflex action the capacity to flatten ourselves against the pavement at the first sound of gunfire. I wondered if he had been one of the marksmen who'd narrowly missed us.

Many, if not the majority, of the soldiers doing service in Northern Ireland have been very young men, most perhaps under the age of twenty-one because the British army recruits boys from fifteen and a half up. In 1969, the army experienced its first big upsurge in recruitment to its all-volunteer service. That period also marked a major increase in unemployment. By 1973, however, the rate of recruitment had dropped by 25 percent and a BBC Public Opinion Poll showed that 55 percent of the British people wanted their troops out of Northern Ireland.[2] A year earlier the same poll had shown that only 44 percent wanted the troops withdrawn. By 1975, the Troops Out Movement in Britain had grown to the level of mass ralleys, and several persons, well-known pacifists, had been jailed for distributing Troops Out literature near army posts.

Purpose of the Mission

When the British army was given an expanded role in the civil strife of Northern Ireland in 1969, it numbered only a few thousand men stationed there under the command of General Freeland. In July, 1972, when the British army invaded the "no-go" areas in Belfast, Derry, Newry, and Armagh, it numbered more than 23,000 men equipped with heavy motorized armored vehicles, automatic weapons, helicopters, and special counterinsurgency units.

Brigadier Frank Kitson, experienced in counterinsurgency campaigns in Kenya, Aden, and Cyprus, held a position of command in the Belfast garrison until April 27, 1972. Kitson's book *Low Intensity Operations* outlines a program for using "mobile recognizance" forces to provide intelligence information and to make random attacks in an insurgent area in order to maximize demoralization, confusion, and dissension.[3] It also provides a paradigm of military-civil collaboration in countering insurgency that advocates a philosophy of law reminiscent of that which the Nazis installed to facilitate the work of the Gestapo.[4] Whether or not the army has followed Kitson's handbook, the following conditions have been documented and repeatedly attested: (1) the army has operated to maximize confusion and disaffection in the population in order to intensify their demand for a cessation of hostilities and has exhibited a disregard for the political objectives of any of the contending parties;[5] (2) plainclothes terror units operating in the working-class ghettoes have been responsible for many of the so-called "sectarian murders"; (3) the army has used brutality in interrogation and incarcerated persons who have had no connection to violent actions; (4) the methods of so-called "riot control" utilized by the army have been often fatal, usually crippling, and have unleashed considerable justifiable fear of permanent genetic damage to the general population; (5) the soldiers themselves have been brutalized by their experience of counterinsurgency warfare. This "Friend/Foe" system of legal categorization is also consistent with the functional proclivities of the Special Powers Acts and the Emergency Provisions Acts. Such measures permit the constabulary (in this case, the British army, at first under the direction of the RUC and then as an independent quasi-constabulary) to predetermine the likelihood of an individual's "guilt" before a hostile act or charges against that person can be established. Of course, such a jurisprudential situation can be achieved only through the assumption that some segment of a society is, by its very nature, a "foe." Here is Kitson's thesis:

Broadly speaking there are two possible alternatives, the first one being that the law should be used as just another weapon in the government's arsenal, and in this case it becomes little more than a propaganda cover for the disposal of unwanted members of the public. For this to happen efficiently, the activities of the legal services have to be tied into the war effort in as discreet a way as possible which, in effect, means that the member of the government responsible for law either sits in the supreme council or takes his orders from the head of the administration. The other alternative is that the courts should remain impartial and administer the laws of the country without any direction from the government.[6]

Again, not unlike his philosophical predecessors in "Friend/Foe" jurisprudence, Kitson recognizes that from the standpoint of effective control in a situation where the will of a minority is counter to the objectives of the majority, the military organization must establish "Stability Operations." These are organizational units that tie together the civil and military measures in order to penetrate all social institutions that might provide support to the insurgent population. He cites John McCuen: "Unity of effort is extremely difficult to achieve because it represents fusion of civil and military functions to fight battles which have primarily political objectives. . . . All the political, economic, psychological and military means must be marshalled as weapons under centralized co-ordination and direction."[7]

In efforts to achieve this kind of unity in its Northern Ireland mission, the British army attempted to develop community-based outposts through which insurgents could be identified and by means of which popular support of these nonconformists could be undermined. The army set up community play centers for children in some areas with the cooperation of such groups as Women Together. Although the organization itself, like many other community-based organizations later used in the same fashion, was an entirely nonpolitical group of people whose intentions were to bring together the contending factions peacefully, their antiviolence position made them a natural political base through which to support the continuation of the extant system. These playgrounds were short-lived.

Other attempts to develop psychological operations and propaganda included the issuing of "D notices" to the news media. These are notices from the local military commander which request that a particular story not be communicated. Press releases were distributed, presenting an untrue or partial view of a particular action (this was particularly evidenced in the series of widely published releases concerning the attack of the Paratrooper Regiment on the nonviolent civil rights marchers in Derry on January 28, 1972). Cooperative arrangements with local youth groups were often established either through the Community Relations Commission projects or attempted in the RUC community relations youth programs. The object of all attempts through domestic and international propaganda has been to maintain the image of the British army as a peace-keeping mission. Thus, when BBC presents documentaries on Northern Ireland they are scrupulously "fair" in presenting "both sides"—that is, the Loyalist-Unionist side and the Republican perspective. But there are actually three sides to the conflict, and the third perspective—that of the military—is no less a political perspective than the other two, and certainly it is not that of a noncombatant role.

The British army's role in the escalation of violence has been incontrovertible. David Holloway, a lecturer in politics at Edinburgh University, writing in 1972, explained the role of the British army in Northern Ireland as a "strong arm" for implementing and supporting the policies of the Stormont government itself:

> The question of who controls the British Army is . . . vital for it depends in large measure, the Army's contribution to a settlement. When the British Army was first introduced into the crisis there was considerable confusion about who was responsible for deciding to which parts of Belfast troops

should be sent. Stormont claimed that it was entirely a matter for the G.O.C., Northern Ireland, while the Army declared that "we are in aid of the civil power. And it is at the request of the civil power that we take action." The Ministry of Defense supported this interpretation by stating that the troops were there to "give strong arm assistance to the local authority. The local authority will say where it is having the trouble. How it is to be tackled is the job of the military."

The position was formalized, if scarcely clarified in the Downing Street talks on 19th August. The Communique said that it was "agreed that the G.O.C. Northern Ireland will with immediate effect assume overall responsibility for security operations. He will continue to be responsible directly to the Ministry of Defense but will work in close cooperation with the Northern Ireland Government and the Inspector-General of the RUC." A joint Security Committee was set up . . . the fundamental ambiguity of the Army's role between giving "strong arm assistance" to the Unionist Government and "holding the ring" was to be resolved by political pressure by Westminister on Stormont for reform.

The trick of squaring this circle has now come unstuck. The British Army can hardly be said to be "holding the ring", "strong arm assistance" to Stormont is a much more accurate description of its role . . . not toward preventing Catholic and Protestants from fighting each other, . . . the Army's activities are now conducted on the basis of Stormont Legislation, in particular the notorious Special Powers Act . . . the Government of Ireland Act of 1920, which forbids Stormont to pass laws relating to the armed forces or the defence of the realm, has just been amended so that the relevant section "shall not have effect and shall not be deemed to have had effect." Stormont is now given "powers, authorities, privileges and immunities" over the army, "in relation to the preservation of peace and the maintenance of order in Northern Ireland."[8]

There would appear to be some contradiction between the rhetoric of the peace-keeping mission of the British army in Northern Ireland and the reality of the mission both from the standpoint of support for the objectives of a government that governed without consensus, or even without full enfranchisement of all its citizens, and from the view of a military role in an international "peace-keeping" mission. This contradiction is recognized even by Brigadier Kitson:

Northern Ireland affords another good example at this time of writing, because certain sections of the Unionists majority are trying to prevent their own government from giving concessions to the Nationalist minority. This process of give and take is essentially a political matter but it is undoubtedly the duty of military leaders to stress the importance of reaching agreement quickly, expecially if a pause has been achieved by the use of troops. . . .

Over the matter of identifying and neutralizing the genuine subversive elements, the army may be of more direct assistance because it can help to build up the intelligence organization. . . . It is far easier to penetrate a subversive movement when it is using non-violent means. . . . Although this can not be accepted as a reason for containing it in this form indefinitely, it is worth considering whether it should be broken up before more headway has been made towards discovering the identity of the people who are really behind it.[9]

In a later chapter, describing peace-keeping operations, Kitson makes quite a point of stating that "all too often, action or inaction is necessary from a political point of view in a peace keeping operation which runs contrary to the sort of action which soldiers would take in war."

This is in sharp contrast to the role of the military with civil authorities in "fighting subversion" which is the kind of operation Kitson exemplified as Northern Ireland.

The 39th Airportable Brigade was commanded by Brigadier Kitson for three years in Belfast. During the years 1971 through 1972, various groups and publications referred to the actions of undercover plainclothes troops as probably being from the 22nd Special Air Service Regiment (SAS).[10] Later, when some of these soldiers were apprehended and found to have military identification, the cat was out of the bag. They were from various regiments, but had been incorporated into something called the Military Reaction Force (also referred to as the Mobile Recognizance Force). These are mobile units assigned to an intelligence operation precisely like that described by Kitson. One such incident was described in the June 28, 1973, issue of the Belfast *Newsletter*, a newspaper well known for its affiliation with the unionist political establishment, under the title, "Men I Shot Had Guns, Says Soldier":

A sergeant in the Royal Military Police who is alleged to have shot unarmed men from an unmarked Army car told Belfast City Commission yesterday that two of the men had been armed and that a number of shots had been fired at his vehicle before he opened fire with a Thompson submachine gun.

Sgt. Clive Graham Williams (26), who is attached to Army Headquarters at Lisburn, said that in June last year, he had been a member of the Military Re-action Force undertaking special patrol duties in troubled areas of Belfast.

He denied the attempted murder of Hugh Kenny, Joseph Smith and James Patrick Murray on June 22, 1972; wounding them with intent to cause grievous bodily harm; and maliciously wounding Thomas Gerard Shaw, who was shot while lying in his bed in a nearby house.

The witness said that on the night of June 22, 1972, he received two radio messages from the car in the Andersonstown area that a gunman with a revolver had been seen at the Bunbeg bus terminus on the Glen Road accompanied by two other people, one of whom had binoculars and was looking at the mountain.

Just before reaching the terminus he saw a dark green car near the entrance, with a light blue car behind it. The driver's door of this car was open and kneeling behind it was a man looking through binoculars.

In front of the door by the bonnet was another man holding a pistol. A third man was standing on the far side of the car.

Sergeant Williams said he glanced away and then heard several single shots from what appeared to be a semi-automatic weapon. The third man was lying over the roof of the light blue car firing at them with a small rifle which he took to be an M1 carbine. . . .

"I dived across the back seat, got the Thompson and one shoulder out of the rear passenger window and opened fire," he said. "I fired three short bursts of automatic fire discharging 8 or 10 bullets."

The man with the binoculars fell back holding his chest; the man in front slumped over the bonnet and the man with the rifle disappeared.

Sgt. Williams denied that he had opened fire on unarmed men without any justification. Two of the men had definitely been armed.

Earlier a taxi driver told the court that his car was parked in the bus terminus at the time of the incident. . . .

There was a light blue car parked in front of him and he saw Smith, Kenny and Murray talking together. Murray had a pair of binoculars and was looking through them towards the mountain.

He heard a burst of gunfire and saw the tail-end of a car disappear down the Glen Road. Smith and Kenny were lying on the ground.

"Before the shooting I did not see anyone in the terminus who had a weapon, and I did not see any weapons lying on the ground afterwards. I did not hear any other shooting," he said.

A forensic expert gave evidence of examining swabs taken from the hands of the four wounded men, and said there was nothing to suggest that any of them had discharged a firearm. However, the lead residues from firing a weapon were easily removed. A verdict is expected today.

Earlier, in April, 1973, *Hibernia* (a fortnightly review published in Dublin) featured an article by Frank Doherty detailing incidents, discoveries, and exposés relating to the SAS, which had been uncovered during 1972. The article elaborated on the charges facing two British army captains and one NCO who would shortly stand trial in the courts of Northern Ireland for firing on civilians while out of uniform. These attacks were frequently explained away by the RUC and army as being "sectarian" attacks until other persistent investigators and forensic evidence documented the killings as the work of military personnel.[11]

It is clear from the reports of the Compton Commission and Parker Commission that the army had used interrogation methods that have detrimental effects on the psychological and physiological condition of their victims.[12] It is also clear from these reports, and from some of the evidence presented by the government of the Irish Republic and the NICRA–Association for Legal Justice (ALJ) cases in the European Commission of Human Rights, that the army was trained and prepared to administer such treatment. Apart from their earlier experience in campaigns to protect British colonial regimes in the Middle East and Africa, the troops involved in the "lifting" process had been specially trained in their camps in England and Germany several months before. The RUC, in turn, had been given training by army intelligence units to do their part. The internment round-up occurred more than twenty-four hours earlier than the plan, and nabbed a conglomerate bag of persons whose names were on army lists and persons who, by virtue of their fathers' having been interned in an earlier decade, appeared on the more extensive lists of the RUC. The premature initiation of internment was itself stimulated by army blunders in Belfast. On August 8, 1971, an army patrol had shot at a car and killed the two women occupants of it. The car had backfired. The anger aroused by the incident threatened to engulf all Belfast in anti-army actions. The lifting itself did not proceed smoothly. In Derry, for instance, masses of unarmed men, women, and children formed human barricades to impede the access of troops. The army required seven hours to proceed four hundred meters. As a last resort in many of the Catholic areas of the north, women banged dustbin lids to arouse the neighborhood and give warning. The troops made every possible effort to ensure silence. They held families at gunpoint, used CS gas and rubber bullets to disperse crowds, and showed no reluctance to wreck houses and beat up their human inhabitants.

In the first sixteen hours of rioting following the sweep, fourteen people died, including one priest. By the end of the week sectarian intimidation had intensified; Protestants and Catholics living in mixed areas were terrorized out of their homes. The immediate aftermath of the internment round-up included the temporary disorganization of the nonviolent civil rights campaign—a direct accomplishment of the objectives listed by Kitson in his directions for counterinsurgency warfare.

The bombing campaign of the Provisional IRA, which had catapulted to the foreground in numbers and actions after the July, 1970, army actions in the Catholic ghettos of Belfast, intensified, apparently not only unimpaired by the internment round-up, but rather accelerated as a consequence. Thus the vicious circle was exacerbated, with each soldier convinced that every man they lifted was an IRA man and therefore a potential danger if not already a perpetrator of death and destruction. The soldiers I interviewed during the months of the accelerated bombing campaign assured me that the bombing and shooting would stop if only the "intelligence blokes" could worm out of each captive the location of their guns and gelignite and the names of their ringleaders. The ordinary soldiers had no realization of the political rationale for the "clean-up" and saw it only in terms of military security, much as they had seen the curfew on the Falls area of Belfast the previous year as a matter of security.

The officers, Special Branch men, and intelligence commanders must have known, however, as did the politicians, that arresting patently non-violent but often well-known men would serve several necessary social functions for their political objectives. It would, for instance, satisfy the unionist population, particularly the far right of the party, that this government under the leadership of Brian Faulkner could take effective action. It would, by terming these men "the terrorists," give credence to the conviction on which the Unionist government and population had always acted as a unified group—that any age or sort of Catholic make was a violent man, a terrorist and threat to the community. It would demoralize the civil rights movement by rendering ineffectual some of its leadership, and separating them from their supporters. And finally, it must have been believed that knowledge of the torture and prison camps would serve as a deterrent to further action against the army and the civil institutions.

Two years later, when they began to round up Protestants suspected of antigovernment sympathies, the army was no less prepared to provide the "proof" for the establishment that they had the situation under control and that they were operating as a politically "neutral" third party. In fact, as related to me earlier by a major in the Light Infantry whose unit was stationed in the predominantly loyalist area of Oldpark in Belfast: "The men are becoming annoyed that they are expected to enforce the law on the Catholic community and not on the Protestants. Some of them want to get in there and make them respect the law too." In regard to accusations of army brutalities, he said, "We've had only two instances where the men have been reported to have used unnecessary force in raiding homes . . . in one instance, the report proved false, in the other, the company was quite severe in enforcing disciplinary action against the guilty party."

There had been suicides in army barracks in Northern Ireland even before the suicide in Long Kesh (which became known as the Maze Prison in 1973).

But ordinary soldiers point out the strict regimen to which they are subjected on duty in Northern Ireland and argue that to expect civil behavior from them toward the constantly threatening, obviously hostile civilian populations is "like expecting a caged animal to lick the hands of its tormenters."

There is a vast difference between the expressions of the ordinary soldier regarding his "job" in Northern Ireland and the expressions of his officers. The latter maintain that the army mission is a peace-keeping one and that they serve a community relations function. These officers, mostly from upper-class backgrounds, are quite effective in denying the use of brutality and emphasizing their desire to "be of service" to the local community. One officer regularly distributed mimeo letters to his "constituents" informing them that he knew the companies and battalions of the Provisional and Official IRA serving in that area and warning the people against helping these "criminals" in any way. Another major regularly appeared at Divis Flats tenants' meetings to proffer his services in eliminating the "menace" of "squatters."

As military men in a volunteer army that fights colonial wars, these troops, as young as they are, operate not only in a political context, but conceive of law and legal systems in terms of whether they facilitate or interfere with "getting the job done." They operated successfully under the Special Powers Act, whereby their excesses in interrogation neither negated the "confession" thus obtained nor exposed them to personal prosecution or regimental discipline. Despite the similarity between living conditions in Northern Ireland—particularly in Belfast—and their own places of origin, the combination of fear and misinformation provides an opaque screen between them and any perception of familiarity.* One young soldier said of the native population, "You see, they live just like animals. They don't know any better than killing each other and fighting all the time. Their houses are filthy with vermin, their kids go around barefoot, but they've got a piece of bunting in the window, now what do you call that?"

Many of the men are descendants of Irish immigrants to the labor markets of Britain, though they fail to identify with their ancestors' compatriots. Some find it more difficult to serve in Northern Ireland than in Malaysia. They still experience some sense of greater dread in seeing an enemy who bears such a close physical resemblance to themselves. Therefore they exaggerate the points of difference in order to create a very distorted image of the native Irish population.

From 1969 to 1972, numerous complaints were made in the military about the lack of extra pay for wartime service. As the casualties mounted, news stories about the widows and bereft mothers of men killed in Northern Ireland began to appear. As a result of complaints a medal service was instituted. But it is some of the other conditions of service in Northern Ireland that drastically undermine morale. They range from the brutality of interrogation processes to the hostility from ordinary members of both

---

*An example of misinformation is cited by the *Sunday Times* Insight Team: "The army rapidly produced a booklet called 'Notes on Northern Ireland', with the praiseworthy aim of giving its men some idea what the trouble was all about . . . the booklet printed in full what purported to be the oath of the . . . Sinn Fein. The version the army got dated from 1918, when it was forged by a group of over-heated Unionists" (Sunday Times Insight Team, *Ulster*, Harrondsworth, Penguin Books, 1972, p. 153).

communities (or the possibility of being lured by promised friendship into a death trap, as happened to three young soldiers in March, 1973). The vulnerability of the ordinary soldier was made clear when Official IRA snipers shot and killed Ranger Best, an off-duty soldier who had come home for a visit to his family in the Bogside.

Loss of Identity

For a soldier whose self-perception is defined by the ordering of a military establishment, there is no question of defining an individual or group as "the enemy." For officers and soldiers who had been schooled in anti-insurgency warfare, the torture techniques were not unfamiliar. Scots Guards, for example, undergo a series of "tests" themselves as part of their training program. Of course they undergo it with full confidence that it will be of limited duration, endurable, and that their achievement in thus "proving themselves" will be rewarded when they take on the full status of the Scots Guards. In response to several affidavits attesting to psychological tortures and physical abuse of internees, one veteran of a regiment that had also seen duty in Malaysia made the following statement: "The information given to you on the various forms of torture is probably true. However, the bit about the helicopters gives rise to disbelief, thereby distorting the truthful statements. . . . It probably makes for good reading in your science-oriented country. . . . The most simple methods can be just as effective and also cheaper."

Enlisted men—noncommissioned officers and privates—mostly come from the poorer parts of Glasgow, Liverpool, and other economically depressed areas of Britain. Membership in the military has often been the only alternative for young men who would otherwise be "on the dole" or laborers. Enlistment in the army assures them of the material benefits of a full employment and the prospect of upward mobility—a rare opportunity for men of their social class and educational background.

There has traditionally been a kind of respectability about the British armed forces, an *esprit de corps* only poorly emulated by Americans but similar to that of the Prussian and later the Nazi German army. In Britain it has evolved from a tradition of the officer-gentleman, as well as from the interaction of role and regimental tradition. Interregimental competition extends beyond the playing fields, and it has been noted by various organizations in Belfast and Derry, so that by reporting the ineptitudes and malpractices of one regiment to an officer of another, some controls have, at times, been tenuously established. Regimental tradition offers the new recruit a whole system of heroes and villains, to be quickly integrated into his new and valued identity. Typically, when interviewed, the ordinary soldier disclaims any identity prior to that he assumed with his uniform. In most cases it is the most respectable and attractive identity he has ever been able to assume. As his anger toward the IRA mounts, the soldier tends to project his own anger into the visage and behavior of every Catholic he encounters. This is not an uncommon psychodynamic pattern of prejudice.

A characteristic of the military condition is the absence of choice— the freedom from freedom. Thus the young soldier does not need to consider the rightness or wrongness of an action or possible alternatives to it. As one Scots Guard expressed it, "It's very simple really. You know that any of them could kill you or your mate, so you don't wait for that to happen, you get them first." Discipline is welcomed, since through it a soldier overcomes his own fears and ambivalence. Recognizing the strength of their own impulses to break loose (they serve a four-month tour of duty with only seventy-two hours of leave during that period), the soldiers equate the Irish situation with the anarchy they fear in themselves and in the larger society. This anarchy represents, in some ways, the normlessness of their own prior existence as unemployed beings without status. From their increasing fear issues a greater longing for bullying authority as a control.

Statements in the media suggest that soldiers experience extreme battle fatigue during their terms in Northern Ireland. There is also evidence that they have been obtaining and using Mandrax, which has recently been declared a dangerous drug. In one case that appeared in the news in 1972, a soldier shot one of his mates while in barracks and another committed suicide. After the first round of lifting for internment, the organization of the procedures was tightened, so that now depth interrogation is handled by special troops in specific places. Nonetheless, when anger erupts or some stage of drunkenness is reached, it has not been uncommon for soldiers to use physical brutality against whomever they happen to pick up and wherever they take them. In lifting anyone for interrogation and/or internment, many soldiers still operate on the assumption that anyone they lay hands on is guilty until proven innocent.

There is still a strong attitude of sex-role dichotomization in the soldiers' perception of the female. Viewing a woman as having equal potential for violence—as an equal threat—would undermine their valued male strength and act as a "weakness threat" to their prized masculine prowess. So although they hurl epithets at women (attempting thus to denigrate them, to cast out their potential for destructive "witchcraft"), they do not apply the same methods of interrogation to women. By the same token, they substantiate their own manhood by denigrating the value of another's —a feat readily accomplished in torture, whatever torture most readily breaks a man's will and endurance. This is manifest in the frequency of genital abuse. Such soldiers are not sickened by the condition of the "enemy in extremis," but rather strengthened by it.

The British establishment has seen fit to "provide this unique experience" to as many of its soldiery as possible, a major confided. That is why, he said, troops are rotated. This is a major current situation of urban guerrilla warfare, and if this form is anticipated as the struggle of the future, it becomes essential to the powers to provide for themselves an experienced army with which to counter it.

As with most armies, the literacy level of the ordinary soldier is quite low and he lacks confidence in his capacity to reason and question. Given the superior social class and experience of his officers and his own socialization into class prejudices, he becomes a willing and obedient worker. The Official IRA recognized this and in many ways has attempted to impress on the ordinary soldier that he is a victim too. They have sometimes picked up soldiers and subsequently released them when upon the promise to resign from service. The released soldiers usually fulfill that promise.

If ever there was a case of identity loss for troops in Northern Ireland, it was the incident of the "ambush" that occurred in Armagh in February, 1973. The local RUC barracks received a call on their terrorism warning line (a special number installed to allow citizens to report any suspicious actions). The caller informed them that about two dozen armed men in a van had been sighted just outside the city. The RUC dispatched a patrol to the designated spot. As the van moved into view they saw the armed men and opened a fusillade. The men shot back. In the ensuing gunfight, several constables were wounded and at least one occupant of the van was killed. The armed men in plain clothes turned out to have been soldiers. In the first press reports, the soldiers were supposed to have been on furlough and returning to base from the Irish Republic. This claim was disproved and finally an inquiry was called in Parliament. There it was established that indeed, the British army had a Mobile Recognizance Force operating in plain clothes in Northern Ireland and that these men were soldiers en route to their assignments.

Regardless of the outcry, such units continued in operation at the time of this writing. Periodically, as happened in July, 1975, an auto accident, or other mishap, exposes the identity of another such patrol to the inhabitants of a neighborhood on which it has been spying or in which it has been on a shooting spree. In the July 5, 1975, incident, the plainclothes soldier was found to have in his possession a special high-velocity automatic weapon. This particular weapon was admittedly purchased for special combat intelligence units but its service in Northern Ireland had been denied by the Ministry of Defence. Although the Minister did say that the weapon was issued to the SAS, he denied that any SAS group was operating in Northern Ireland. To the consternation of the authorities, such a weapon was found on the soldier by the angry residents of the Falls Road area that day in July.

It is of utmost importance to the soldiers to keep their identity secret, to hide from the cameras as though they were guns and to melt into the anonymity of their uniforms and armored vehicles. They may have the advantage of the same bed each night (when they are not on night patrol), but they cannot form close relationships or a sense of belonging to any community other than their regiment. They crave those few contacts they have with friendly civilians who offer them tea and biscuits, but these have become few and far between as both loyalists and nationalists increasingly find the army their common enemy and the direct rule of Westminister a "foreign dictatorship." Ultimately these men become psychic cripples, unable to conceive of themselves in terms of anything but this very singular relationship with others, and with no freedom or choice to alter that position.

The individual soldier has little access to the support given by consensual reality, which is available to other participants in the events in Northern Ireland. For every action in which the military is involved there are at least four realities, of which the soldier's is ordinarily the unpublished, undisclosed, and often, for him, fatal version. An account in the *New York Times* from Belfast reports an example:

A 19-year-old British army private was shot dead in a Roman Catholic district of Belfast, last night, and today there were two drastically differing accounts of how it happened.

Private Gary Barlow was the 156th British soldier killed in this Protestant-dominated province since 1969. His death underscores the lack of communication between the Catholics and the army. . . .

All that is known for certain is that the soldier died from two 45 calibre bullets, one of which severed his spine, after he was separated from an army patrol in Belfast's lower falls district. One account says that he was delivered to an "executioner" by a mob of screaming women; the other, that he was shot by an unknown killer as the women tried to protect him.

The two versions are by a British army officer, Capt. Martin Scrase, and by a Catholic housewife, who like most witnesses to incidents in Ulster, refused to give her name.

Capt. Scrase said that Private Barlow, a Mormon convert from Lancashire, England, was in a 12-man patrol sent in two armoured cars to follow up an intelligence report. Two men had been seen running into houses on McDonnald Street, the report said, shortly after a soldier had been hit in the hand by a sniper.

As soon as the patrol entered the houses, a crowd of about 30 housewives gathered outside shouting obscenities and creating the kind of trouble that the area is famous for, according to the captain.

The patrol decided to retreat, the captain said, but in the confusion, Private Barlow was left behind, still checking a room. The patrol drove off and Private Barlow was not missed until it returned to base.

Captain Scrase said that two distressed young women called at the post to report that a crowd was beating up a young soldier. The patrol returned to find the hostile crowd still blocking the street.

Troops fired rubber bullets to disperse it, the captain said, and the dying soldier was found sprawled in a garage driveway. The captain asserted that bruises on the soldier's body indicated that he had been beaten before being shot. His rifle and ammunition were missing.

Captain Scrase said the militant Provisional wing of the outlawed Irish Republican Army had claimed responsibility for the murder, "but the women were just as guilty as the man who pulled the trigger."

"They are normal looking housewives, but I don't regard them as human beings," the captain said. "They are foul-mouthed hags."

The housewife who gave the other version said her car had been hit by one of the armoured cars of the British patrol. "The soldiers pulled out immediately," she said, "leaving the private to stand on the sidewalk." He was very nervous, and we offered to escort him back to the army post, but he said he would wait.

"We stood talking to him and eventually we sent two women to the barracks, but the soldiers thought it was a trap. He was there at least 15 minutes and then we heard a shout, 'clear off,' and we ran for it.

"We heard shots, but de don't know where they came from. There were women near the soldier when he was hit, and they were shocked. One fainted, after whispering prayers into his ears, and when we carried her into a house the army fired a rubber bullet, thinking we were carrying away a body.

"We didn't beat him. If he had lived, he would have told how reassured he was by the women's actions."

Both accounts of the death of Private Barlow were told convincingly, the one by an officer of a regiment that has now lost its third soldier in three months, the other by a woman who insisted her version was the truth.[13]

Ordinary citizens, through a process of interaction, discussion, and communication with news media, manage to satisfy their needs for verification of their own perceptions and appraisals of reality. The army, as an institution, issues statements presenting the "official version." Both groups of the IRA and the UDA are able organizationally, and thus individually, to relate to an action or situation from their ideological perspectives. The individual soldier operating in an ideological vacuum cannot achieve even the limited comfort of expecting a true accounting for his own death.

Military Technology

It has been suggested by more than one observer that Ireland's greatest value to the British army "may well prove to be that it provided a laboratory for the development of techniques soon to be· needed at home." A paper published by the British Society for Social Responsibility in Science, distributed in 1974, echoes and analyzes a statement made by the chairman of the seminar of the Royal United Services Institute for Defence Studies, "The Role of the Armed Forces in Peacekeeping in the 1970's" (1973):

> What happened at Aldershot, what happend at the Old Bailey, reminds us that what happens in Londonderry is very relevant to what can happen in London, and if we lose in Belfast we may have to fight in Brixton or Birmingham. Just as Spain in the 'thirties was a rehearsal for a wider European conflict, so perhaps what is happening in Northern Ireland is a rehearsal of urban guerilla war more widely in Europe and particularly in Great Britain.[14]

At the same seminar, Brigadier Hudson, Deputy Director of Army Staff Duties said of military-police cooperation, "If you go to the regions and districts of the UK, this is where the contact begins and is needed."[15] It is clear that Kitson's blueprint has been accepted at the army command level in the United Kingdom.

During the first of the civil rights demonstrations in Derry in August and October, 1968, the Royal Ulster Constabulary used batons against demonstrators, members of the public, observers from Parliament, and press men alike. Seventy-seven were injured. A water cannon was used for the first time. This antiriot weapon had earlier been used by the British army in Cyprus. Such cannons were the main weapon of the Berlin police against student demonstrators of the late 1960's. The cannons used by the British army in Northern Ireland were of German manufacture (by Mayer of Hagen, Westphalia) and have an effective range of 40–50 yards. At a range of up to 30 yards, the force is sufficient to knock a man off his feet. The British army has used a dye in the water that is nontoxic although it permanently stains clothes and is difficult to get off skin. The ostensible purpose of the stain is to "identify rioters," but few so identified are ever arrested. More often, the dye serves as a means of identification of demonstrators for those among whom they may disperse.[16] In Northern Ireland, and particularly in the Derry demonstrations, this identification meant that those who escaped the batons were then subjected to further abuse when recognized by hostile Protestants.

But the purplish-blue dye and the impact of the water cannon were to prove the least lethal and least used of the military technology arsenal. By 1969, CS Gas was being used for "riot" control in Derry and Belfast. This substance, which is more poisonous than chlorine and can be metabolized to cyanide,[17] has been in regular use in Northern Ireland since then. For several years, life in the Bogside and Creggan areas of Derry included daily gassing with CS. Internees were repeatedly gassed at close range and sometimes within their barracks. My personal experience with this substance was so unforgettable that I risked further poisoning and jailing in order to carry a partially unemptied canister with me to London for analysis. Although these canisters line the streets of Derry in profusion after gassings, the army does not permit their removal. When my handbag was inspected and a CS canister discovered, I was made to return it because, as the soldier said, "it is the property of Her Majesty's Army." I told him that it had been freely given away with its contents, but that did not impress him. Children playing with canisters have been seriously damaged by the residual chemicals, but no one is supposed to remove them without authorization. Dr. Robert N. Jones, a research chemist, wrote in 1971:

An early estimate of the aerosol contraption which would kill half a group of people after an exposure of one minute was 25 milligrammes of CS per litre. This was increased to 61 milligrammes per litre. But, as Julian Perry Robinson pointed out . . . in April 1970, the toxicity depends on two other factors which can vary to an extent which renders such estimates meaningless. First, the effectiveness of a CS aerosol depends very much on particle size. The larger the particle is, the less is the penetrating power. Smaller particles can penetrate the lungs much more easily, and the amount required to kill is correspondingly less. Irritancy too is inversely related to particle size, but the relationship to toxicity is difficult to evaluate.

Second, the proportion of inhaled material retained for any given particle size is not significantly dependent on rate or depth of breathing. Hence the dosage depends on the rate of intake of air by the lungs, which can vary by a factor of 10 or more, depending on the state of activity of the individual. They become even less meaningful when applied to a population heterogeneous with respect to age, to state of health, and hence to susceptibility. This point was not lost on the Himsworth committee, as the above quotation shows.

The safety margin of CS is supposed to lie in the big disparity between the intolerable limit (an exposure of one minute to 0.007 milligrammes per litre) and the concentration expected to cause 50 per cent lethalities in a given group. This disparity, however, is not very different from that of bromobenzyl cyanide, a much more effective lachrymator than CS, but one which is correspondingly more poisonous, and which has always been considered covered by the Geneva Protocol. Moreover, the disparity is not as securely based as the figures might initially lead one to suppose.

Considerable individual variation in tolerance to CS has been demonstrated by investigators whose efforts have received support from military agencies. The size of the aerosol particles is again an important parameter. Every biologist recognizes that while a physiological response can be readily predicted and assessed in qualitative terms, quantitative predictions in the cases of an assortment of individuals with unknown characteristics cannot be made. This is why scientists go to such trouble to standardise laboratory animals; working with heterogeneous populations would undermine the meaning of many experimental results. Second, it has already been argued that the toxicity to man is not a fixed and reproducible entity, but is seen to depend on several factors. While most scientists like to place reliance on figures, this is an instance where quantitative relationships simply break down. If CS is to be regarded genuinely as a drug, then the range of dosage which an exposed person might receive cannot be left to chance, but must be worked out in advance as carefully as by a physician prescribing for a patient.

CS was the outcome of a prolonged search to discover a more effective substitute for tear gas, a compound which has disadvantages. Technical difficulties prevented the large-scale manufacture of tear gas in time for the First World War. The fact that its lethal potential was therefore not revealed on the battlefield has greatly facilitated the conception, nurture, and maintenance of a false image of tear gas as a nonlethal substance.

Once lodged in the tissues, small amounts of the material exert a necrotising action over a long period of time, and the wounds take an unusually long time to heal. Numerous instances have been reported in which the ultimate consequence of such an injury to the face is the loss of an eye. Worse, tear gas is known to have caused the deaths of several people.

As a substitute for tear gas, CS is by no means ideal; once inside the body, cyanide can be produced.[18]

By the beginning of 1971, according to official figures, more than 10,000 cartridges and 2,500 grenades had been used to disperse nearly a ton of CS. Since 1970, army patrols and armored vehicles have carried weapons specifically designed to fire CS cartridges. Fired from a riot gun at a muzzle velocity exceeding 200 mph, they have a range of 130 yards. Of course, by 1973 there were reports of newer, more "effective" varieties of gas—CR, to the effects of which tolerance could not be built up—which would produce more distressing experiences.

There are several probable cases of death resulting from CS gassings. Often the gas is fired directly into the windows or under the doors of homes, and infants, old people, and anyone with bronchial disturbance become violently ill and require extended medical treatment. There have been indications that CS is carcinogenic and that it has a deleterious effect on unborn babies, but no studies have been undertaken to prove or disprove these allegations. There are definite aftereffects resulting from eye irritation or burning and skin burning.

By June, 1973, several doctors at the Royal Victoria Hospital in Belfast issued a report on the effects of rubber-bullet injuries. The report was subsequently "classified" and withdrawn from circulation. However, during the brief time a few copies of it were available, its statistics were obtained, and they are shocking. Up to April 30, in this one hospital, four hundred injuries and two deaths from rubber bullets were logged. By June, three persons had been killed, seventeen were permanently disabled, and at least a dozen had been blinded by these missiles, which are supposed to be fired at the ground in street skirmishes at ranges up to 50 yards in front of rioters because they ricochet unpredictably. The report indicated that ninety patients went to hospitals for treatment of rubber-bullet injuries in the first two years of their use. Forty-one of these required in-patient treatment; their injuries included three fractured skulls, thirty-two fractures to facial bones, eight turned-up eye gloves (all resulting in blindness), three cases of severe brain damage; seven cases of lung injury, and one case each of damage to the spleen, liver, and intestine.[19]

Soldiers do not have to account for their use of rubber bullets, as they do for lead bullets. The BSSRS report notes:

> There is much evidence that rubber bullets are misused by soldiers. Unofficially, officers will admit that soldiers prefer to aim them directly at their targets rather than at the ground in front of them—which violates all their other training. Rubber bullets can then serve as instruments of personal revenge by soldiers. There have been repeated allegations that rubber bullets are stiffened by the insertion of objects—torch batteries in particular —to make them more painful (and dangerous).
>
> One example is this eye-witness account of the incident which resulted in the death of Francis Rowntree, aged 11½, in April 1972. "Frank and I had just come out of the Divis Flats. We approached the corner of Whitehall Place. As we rounded this corner, we could see the back end of a Sarcen sitting jutting out from the corner. Frank walked straight out down the wee path to reach the Falls Road. The next thing I heard a bang, Frank fell backward, his feet sticking out at the corner. As the bang came, I noticed splinters, this object whatever it was disintegrated. I think it was a battery, because the stuff looked like the black carbon that is inside a battery. There was no rubber bullet around that we could have seen." [It is a curious coincidence that a visitor to the Army barracks in the Creggan in early 1974 noticed that rubber bullets and electric batteries were stored right next to each other there.]

Rubber bullets are often used at shorter than the permitted range. An investigation by surgeons from the Royal Victoria Hospital of victims brought to the hospital for treatment showed that more than half of those for whom information was available had been shot from a range of less than 15 yards, and a third had been shot at less than 5 yards range. In one case a patient gave a vivid description of a soldier pressing a gun against her, followed by a bang and a smell of fireworks. She fell to the ground with a severe pain in her side. She had a rubber bullet and a massive bruise on her lower ribs to prove her story.

It is not necessary to be on the street to become a victim. A Derry youth standing in his living room was injured and taken to hospital. And Mrs. Emily Groves, mother of 11, was standing at the window of her Andersontown house when she was blinded by a rubber bullet fired at short-range by a paratrooper. Her apparent offence—playing a Republican song on the gramophone. Mrs. Groves has since received £35,000 damages from the Ministry of Defence—in May 1973 there were 13 other claims outstanding.

Although rubber bullets are no longer regarded as particularly serious by seasoned demonstrators, rubber bullets are dangerous. Despite British government assurances that intensive safety tests (never specified) have been carried out under medical supervision, evidence to the contrary is building up. A recent report commissioned by the United States National Science Foundation (the principal U.S. Government science agency) talks of there being "some risk of internal injury or death" from rubber bullets. The Spanish police have rejected rubber bullets as "too lethal."[20]

Reports indicate that CR gas, which was authorized by the British government in May, 1974, for use in Long Kesh, has indeed been used there in the rioting that broke out in the camp and in Armagh in late September–early October, 1974. According to published reports, the effects of CR· gas are not only damaging over a longer period but slower acting as well. This fact suggests that the use of military technology in Northern Ireland has some objective other than riot control. If there is no intention of permanently disabling and demoralizing the population there, then why is the effort made to develop techniques that are not only permanently disabling and fatal but which can also be used against noncombatants more effectively than against armed assailants?

Summary

The nature of the British army involvement in Northern Ireland epitomizes the paradox of the political condition of the place: it is not a part of the United Kingdom that receives the same privileges for its citizens as do those of other parts; but it is also not regarded as *outside* the United Kingdom and therefore able to demand adherence to the Geneva protocols regarding military operations of foreign occupying armies. Northern Ireland has been the laboratory for testing theses of counterinsurgency operations, such as that of Brigadier Frank Kitson, but the military involvement is presented to the rest of the world (including other parts of the United Kingdom) as a peace-keeping mission.

There are three sides to the conflict in Northern Ireland. Combatants or direct participants are not only brutalized by the ongoing violence but have also learned their tactics from the British army more often than out of their own traditions. Most of the types of weapons introduced into the campaign by the army's use have fallen into the hands of the IRA and the UDA and UVF and have been used by them. The most destructive weapon of all—torture—has become a feature of sectarian assassinations since 1974. Whether such torture victims have been mutilated at the hands of military personnel engaged in SAS/MRF actions or whether they have been put through their final agonies in the inquisition chambers of one or another sectarian paramilitary organization remains unclear.

What is certain, however, is that the use of psychotechnology in torture in Northern Ireland was introduced through the British army and RUC operation in 1971; and that the destruction of the will to resist by the utilization of modern technology has been, to date, the most effective innovation in British military strategy in Ireland for nearly four hundred years.

7 The Blood of Martyrs

If you remove the English army tomorrow and raise the green flag over Dublin castle, unless you set about the organization of the Socialist Republic, your efforts would be in vain. England would still rule you. She would rule you through her capitalists, through her landlords, through her financiers, through the whole array of commercial and industrialist institutions she has placed in this country and watered with the tears of our mothers and the blood of our martyrs.

(JAMES CONNOLLY, SHAN VON VOCHT, JANUARY, 1897)

Dublin is only about one hundred miles from Belfast as the crow flies. The distance by CIE train is more like 120 miles and requires up to three hours' travel time. Between Belfast and Dublin on that train the story of partition and the trauma of the "troubles in the north" are daily re-enacted. The Republic of Ireland, the twenty-six counties that broke away from the United Kingdom amid great violence and bloodshed, is neither immune to the reverberations of Northern bombs nor a willing participant in either republican or loyalist strategies for change. It is a tiny state whose economic survival has been based on its continued position as a neocolonial subsidiary to Britain.

In December, 1974, while on the Dublin-bound train, a group of Belfast schoolgirls were singing their way to their holiday retreat. The song they were singing was one I hadn't heard in a very long time, but which was most appropriate:

There was a boy, there was a girl
They never knew what happiness could bring
For she lived on the morning side of the mountain
And he lived on the other side of the hill.

As the verses rolled with the vibrations of the slow-moving train, I found myself thinking about Brian and Carol, a couple with whom I'd spent the previous evening in Belfast. He, a Catholic by birth, a Republican in politics, would suffer the aftermath of his internment and interrogation experiences the rest of his life. She, a Protestant who had joined him on "the other side of the hill," felt totally out of place in their own home. Neither of them practiced either religion, nor was religion an issue between them. The issue was more personal, more immediate, and more irreconcilable than that. Daily life for them and their child was a series of unending traumatic escapades. If the "Brits" weren't after Brian for "something," Carol said, the gunmen from one of the rival republican groups were at the door looking for him and ready to kill them all. As for Brian, Carol's continual hostility wore him down. The more she railed against his political involvement, the more he embroiled himself in organization work.

The girls' singing also reminded me of the figurative "mountain," or "great wall," which tries to separate the people of the two parts of Ireland to prevent them from meeting and talking. Harry Murray, leader of the Ulster Workers Council, a loyalist group, met in July, 1974, with political and community leaders from the Irish Republic at a conference at Oxford University. He reported on his pleasant surprise in discovering that they didn't "wear horns." Later he spoke on Radio Telefis (Television) Eireann (RTE) and was interviewed by the Dublin newspapers. He elaborated on his earlier remarks by saying that he found his colleagues in the south to be rational and even genial, though he had always thought of them as being dangerous lunatics out to destroy his country.

The people in the Irish Republic had, in earlier years of the Northern crisis, been able to extend their hospitality to unionists and loyalists who chanced to visit Dublin. By the summer of 1974, though, that city had had its fill of sectarian horrors. On May 17, at 5 P.M.—the moment when in London, Merlyn Rees, Secretary of State for Northern Ireland, was informing the leaders of the Ulster Workers' Council that his government rejected their ultimatum for dissolution of the Northern Ireland executive and for a new election—the first of three automobile bombs exploded on a busy street in the center of Dublin. Before the carnage was finished, twenty-eight persons had died and more than a hundred were seriously injured.

Two days earlier, on May 15, the UWC had fully effected a general strike, which brought Northern Ireland to a total standstill for two weeks. The British army was unable to meet the challenge and act against the Loyalist workers. The Northern Ireland power-sharing executive—the first government in its fifty-year history to include Catholics in decision-making positions—collapsed. Along with it, the Sunningdale triparty agreements forged between the United Kingdom, the Irish Republic, and a coalition of unionists, the Social Democrat and Labor Party (the majority of whose membership is Catholic), and the Alliance Party also collapsed. If there had been any doubt about the vulnerability of the citizens of the Irish Republic to the violence of the six counties, it was permanently resolved.

By winter, 1976, bombings in Dublin and bomb scares in the heart of the city had become part of the everyday life of its residents. The Irish government did its best to apprehend the bombers, but failed completely. They did succeed, more or less, in keeping news of the bombings from reaching the larger public—particularly their prospective tourist clientele in America. In fact, the bombings in the Irish Republic did not, during a period of five years, injure or kill as many persons as did those during the same period in Israel. Nonetheless, their vulnerability to such destruction made a very big difference in the attitude of Dubliners toward the troubles in the North. Instead of uniting them with their beleaguered Catholic cousins in Belfast, it turned many southerners actively against relationships with anyone from the north.

Irish news media publicized license plate serial letters and numbers by which to identify cars from Northern Ireland. Dubliners avoided such cars and treated their occupants with hostility, the same way Protestants in the North had reacted with bitter anger toward vehicles that were identifiably from the Republic. From 1967 through 1972, children and families taking refuge from the troubles in the north had found safe and sympathetic haven across the border. But in December, 1972, explosions rocked Liberty Hall in Dublin during the parliamentary debate about the imposition of the Offences Against the State Acts, and the heroic escapades of the IRA in the north lost some of their glamor for the southerners, and they sanctioned internment in the Irish Republic.

As the years went on and threats to their peaceful life increased, changes were perceptible in the patterns of motivational dynamics and legal socialization for the children in the south as well. Some of these changes are reflected in the test protocols of several children in the Irish Republic (Dublin) who were first tested in December, 1971, and again in 1974. The pain and problems of Ireland are reflected in the Thematic Apperception Test stories told by an intelligent and sensitive twelve-year-old girl growing up in the drab gray stone of a working-class estate in Dublin in 1971:

> This is a soldier and he's asleep and there's this child and he has led a bad life, it's his dad I suppose his soul is dead—he's not dead himself but his soul is, and as for the child—he's always coaxing him to lead a very good life but he's led a bad life himself and the child has turned his face against the man because he's telling him to do something and he's not doing it himself, and he's given a very bad example to the child. God said "this is the light," but the devil is still there and he's killing his soul, and God

can't do anything really because he has led a very bad life, and the child doesn't know what to do. It will end up that the son will go on all right, but it's so late that the father won't be able to do anything about it. It was no use.

It's a rock that goes down and up like a hill. There's no rock in the middle—it's just water and the rock has broken away and is crumbly. Somebody fell and there's bats coming out of the wall, there's bones and old garbage and stones. These stones have probably fallen out of place in the wall. It's probably so old. This man could have been chasing and accidentally slipped, anything could have happened, there's a hole where some rocks have come out and you see the sun shining. The man will die and will be buried there and not be known for a good while after.

This man's wife has died and he's trying not to cry but he is crying because he's so sad. He must have loved her and he's in his bedroom and lights are all off and she's just lying there dead and he's afraid to look again. He killed her and he doesn't know what to do now, or if he hadn't killed her he could just go on his way and have her buried or something, but now he's afraid because of what he's done and he's sorry and afraid to look.

You could really call this Our Lady, she was born without original sin and she never sinned, she has a pure white soul and because God knew she was going to lead a good life and she did.

It's a man, he's a soldier and he's following somebody and he's going along rather sorrowfully and wishing this was all over and it could have been over. There's this thick fog and it's coming in and he can't see well. There's this thick fog and it's coming in and he can't see well. There's light coming out of the houses on to the tree and he's leaning against it. He'll be shot before the war is over.

Connell, in 1971, was convinced that people struggle to be good and to make good things happen, but through no fault of their own they often fail. She demonstrated complete faith in the ultimate goodness of the Deity and the ultimate futility of fighting. Her level of legal socialization was approximately equivalent to children her age in other countries. She was somewhat behind them, however, in her sense of personal political efficacy, which is not unusual for working-class children of Dublin, who are educated in an authoritarian ambience. This is evidenced in some of her responses to the Tapp-Kohlberg questions, particularly numbers 2 and 7:

1. What would happen if there were no rules?
A. There'd be no peace in the country, there isn't peace now, but if there were no rules there'd be no countries.
2. What is a rule?
A. It's something you have to obey so everyone does. If you don't obey you'll be punished.

3. What is a law?
A. The same as a rule. Laws are made by a country, rules—nearly anybody can make a rule, the laws of church and the laws of a country.
4. Why should people follow rules?
A. To have peace.
5. Why do you follow rules?
A. Because if we didn't follow our school rules, we wouldn't be learning anything, everybody'd be telling the teacher what to do, if I follow the rule it's because I want to learn, people follow rules because they want peace in the country.
6. Can rules be changed?
A. Yes. (How?) A rule can be changed about what time you have to be in. (Who changes them?) Laws can't be changed.
7. Are there times when it might be right to break a rule?
A. I don't really think so.
8. If you could change any rule, what rule would you change?
A. Our school let-out time at night.

In December, 1971, six-year-old David, who had lived all his life in Dublin and visited his cousins in the lovely Wexford countryside during his holidays, told TAT stories that sharply contrasted with those told by his Belfast age-mates. David demonstrated great confidence in the ability of parents and others in authority to find right answers, solve problems, and generally be kind and helpful. Unlike his Belfast peers, David did not associate the word "rule" with the ruler used to discipline primary-school children in the working-class districts of Northern Ireland. He didn't know what a "rule" was, but he had some idea of "law" being associated with "police," about whom he had a positive attitude.

Tapp-Kohlberg Questions:
1. What would happen if there were no rules?
A. What is a rule?
2. What is a law?
A. The police.
   What would happen if there were no laws?
A. The robbers would be robbing.
3. Can laws be changed?
A. No.
[Unable to answer the other questions.]

TAT Stories:
1. A boy and a banjo. The boy is looking at the banjo. He's going to play it.
2. There's a man and some houses, the man is . . . it looks like a farm, the man is making a lawn and the woman's looking at the man and the man is looking at the horse. They're working and I don't know what they'll do when they're through.

3. A girl crying. Someone hit her or she fell. She'll cry for a long time. The daddy will come in.
4. The mommy's holding the baby and the girl's at the table. They got a new baby. The baby will cry and she'll give him a bottle and he'll sleep.
5. A woman is frightened the boy will call the police. The police will come to them. The police will laugh at it, and then they'll go back.
6. It's about two men and a boy and the other man has a knife killing the man and there's a gun beside the bed. The man will be dead when they kill him. The police will come to catch them and they'll take him on to hospital.
7. There's trees and a little bridge and a bee is standing on something and there's a wall and like a fish coming out of the trees. The snake's coming out after the bee and the bee will fly away.
8. A woman in bed and a man is putting his hands up to his eyes and his school books on the table and there's a picture on the wall. The man is crying, they'll call the police and the police will come.
9. On this Christmas they hung their stockings in a different way. One by the bed rail, long, one by the chimney where Santa comes out, on the following day our stockings hang full with good things. With big white things sticking up.
10. Storms. The leaves will fall off the tree and the storm blows the leaves off the trees, until it goes down (the storm keeps going until it goes down).

In the summer of 1974, while rubble from the explosions was still in evidence on the main streets of Dublin, many parents were reluctant to let their children go into town for movies, especially on Fridays. There had been several more bomb scares and some explosions, which didn't result in any injuries. The media minimized mention of such happenings, but, nonetheless, the children of Dublin had become sensitized to the idea (if not the fact) of living in a war zone.

Jimmy, a boy I had first tested in 1972, gave (at eight and a half) some new stories in the summer of 1974, which were much shorter and less optimistic than were his earlier productions:

1. His father got shot. He's sad and was crying. And his mother is going to put him into a home.
2. There's a man plowing fields and a woman standing at the tree. There's this woman and she's just standing there and a man plowing the field and another man up there with a horse, there's the woman standing against the tree, she looks weak. After they plow they'll get dinner to eat, they'll have to die sometimes.
3. She's very weak and she's sad, one of her parents are dead and she's crying. She's going out, I'd say she's going to a funeral. She'll see her father getting buried, the coffin going into the ground, and she'll go home.
4. Her husband is going and she doesn't want him to go so she's dragging him back. He'll probably get killed—the husband wherever he's going he's going to the army.

5. She's holding a baby. The woman beside her sitting down is reading. She looks sad. Her name is Jane. Her mother's going to put her into a home. She wants to take the baby with her and she can't. So she has to guard him.
6. There's this boy and his father got shot in the army and he's very sad. His father dies then he has to go into a home cause he's no parents.
7. The man killed his wife and he's weak and he's going to get put away into a home for good.
8. There's this beast who's broken through lots of walls and killed lots of people. He's breaking through another wall.
9. There's an old castle with nobody left, only him, and he dies.
10. This man lost his wife and he's dying of starvation leaning up against a lamp.

Tapp-Kohlberg Questions:
1. What if there were no rules?
A. Well, everything would be happening.
    What is a rule?
A. A person wants you to do something he wants you to keep to it.
2. What is a law?
A. The law is you're not supposed to be killing, that's one law.
3. Why should people follow rules?
A. So that everything shall be all right and nothing should go wrong.
4. Why do you follow rules?
A. So that everthing's all right.
5. Can rules be changed?
A. Some. (How?) They can be change the plans—what to do. (Who changes rules?) The King or the Queen or the Lord Mayor.
6. When might it be right to break a rule?
A. If the rule wasn't good.
7. If you can change any rule, what rule would you change?
A. If there was killing I'd change not to be killing.

When I began interviewing and testing children in working-class areas of Dublin during December, 1971, I became aware of the implications of Irish economic marginality and the politics of a nation "on the run." A family of unemployed husband, wife, and seven children lived on an allowance of £14 a week. For a couple with one child, the allowance was half that. If council houses were available for each nuclear family (and they aren't), there would still be the problem of dividing that meager income between the rent and adequate nourishment. Even inadequate quarters for a family of nine would cost upward of £26 per month, and constantly spiraling food costs make it unlikely that the children would obtain sufficient protein in the form of meat, eggs, and milk. The protein deficiency and/or the ratio of high carbohydrates to low protein, which comprises the diet of Irish people, has, in various studies (done in other places), been found to increase probabilities of mental deficiency, schizophrenia, alcoholism, premature birth, premature aging, ulcers, diabetes, and birth defects.[1]

There is also little doubt that the overcrowding resulting from doubling up of related families and inadequate privacy for the individual members of large families, combined with dietary insufficiencies, contributes to family breakdowns.

A man who is unemployed and inadequate to the task of providing food and shelter for his family, who is unable to control or ameliorate in any way the suffering of his wife or mother, whose sole source of social communion must transpire in a pub, is rendered impotent in his own self-concept. For the women (as stated in an earlier chapter) there is only the prerogative of somehow coping with a sequence of disastrous crises.

When I explained to the women (and sometimes their husbands) why I wanted to test their children—how things were in the North—they'd respond, "Well, if these women would only stay home and take care of their husbands and children instead of going out there and banging dust lids about, they'd all be better off." Or, "I don't know why those people can't get along. They've got things so much better than we have anyway; with their health service and better dole and all."

The stories told by the children of Dublin are a profound testimony to their confidence in the rectitude of established authority and their own helplessness in the face of the will of others or the whims of nature. In contrast with the Belfast children, however, they saw themselves as suffering not from the punitive behavior of their parents or malevolent others, but rather as a result of whatever fate befalls their parents. They also appeared convinced that those who are bad or who do bad things get punished. They saw punishment as the action of a just fate, whereas their contemporaries in Belfast felt they had to take on themselves the job of judge, prosecutor, and executioner.

Some of the effects on attitude and behavior in the Republic are evidenced in the findings of a study by Maynooth Professor of Sociology, the Reverend Liam Ryan. According to Father Ryan, a growing attitude among middle-class people in the Irish Republic asks: "Are we not doing fine as things stand? Why should we risk everything by seeking a united Ireland? Those Northerners will bring nothing but trouble, anyway." Father Ryan feels, as a result of his studies, that the real issue is how to integrate the Northern unionist majority into a united Ireland.[2]

The Closed Mind

The social psychological effects of eight hundred years of colonialism and fifty years of partition in Ireland are manifested in the phenomenon described as "the closed mind."[3] Northerners and southerners, Catholics and Protestants, elites and followers relate themselves to one or another of three coextensive states within this island of 35,057 square miles. They have developed their belief systems in relatively isolated contexts. Despite the illogic and contradictions inherent in each system, it forms the psychological base upon which its believers are dependent and out of which they are motivated. This is amply shown in the children's TAT stories.

The prerequisite conditions for development of a closed mind have been met in the political socialization of generations of Irish people into disparate belief systems, as dogma. M. Rokeach explains it, in the description of the closed mind: "A person may espouse a set of beliefs that are democratic in content. . . . Yet adherence to such beliefs, considered alone, is not necessarily a true guide of an anti-authoritarian outlook . . . the *way* he espouses his beliefs may be authoritarian, intolerant . . . and closed in its mode of thought and belief."[4]

Evidence of this mode of thinking appears in political and religious tracts as well as in graffiti, in the speeches of leaders and in parent-child relationships, and finally in the individual personality-test data collected from children.

There is behavioral evidence of only superficial toleration of the differences of one who is "foreign" to the immediate environs and of great reluctance to introduce onself into a new neighborhood even if it is only a mile distant. Avoidance of the different is further evidenced in self-abnegation before those of educated or wealthy status. Rokeach also pointed to this characteristic: "A person will be open to information *insofar as possible* and will reject it, screen it out or alter it insofar as necessary. . . . And if the closed or dogmatic mind is extremely resistant to change, it may be so not only because it allays anxiety but also because it satisfies the need to know."[5]

The people of Ireland exhibit a very strong "need to know." There are more newspapers per capita population in Ireland than in the United States. Television sets are more common than indoor plumbing; streetcorner speakers invariably attract audiences and school attendance is quite regular. Even so, the need to know is too often corrupted by the dogma of the educational institutions. These in turn are reacting to the threat they have experienced:

> To varying degrees, individuals may become disposed to accept or to form closed systems of thinking and believing in proportion to the degree to which they are made to feel alone, isolated, helpless in the world in which they live . . . and then anxious of what the future holds in store for them . . . pervasive feelings of self-inadequacy expressly concerned with needs for power. . . . These lead to feelings of guilt and, by rationalization and

projection, to a generally disaffected outlook on life . . . a tightly woven network of cognitive defenses against anxiety.[6]

Certain groups are, for political reasons, in positions of special and extreme threat, north and south. Therefore, both wings of the IRA and the UDA (for instance) are ideological purists, reacting with grave suspicion and even dealing out excommunication or death to those in their membership who deviate in word or action from their, dogma. As institutions, both the Catholic and Presbyterian churches have been developed in Ireland in a context of threat and feelings of helplessness, which have exacerbated their tendencies to narrow ideological prospectives and a dogmatic approach against deviance. The government at Stormont and the government at Dublin have both suffered from similar uncertainties. Nonetheless, all but the Catholic Church and the Provisional IRA profess a democratic ideology. If we apply the Rokeach thesis to the behavior of the other groups, however, we can readily recognize the closed-mindedness that underlays their professions of democratic ideology.

From his studies of open-mindedness and closed-mindedness, Rokeach distilled a number of variables that determine the ability to form new belief systems. To the extent that such factors are present in the sociopolitical groups in Ireland, they will become more consistent with the rhetoric of the groups:

1. The ability to remember or to keep in mind all the new parts to be integrated.
2. A willingness to "play along" or to entertain new systems.
3. Past experience, which determines whether a particular system is, psychologically speaking, new or not new.
4. Presenting new beliefs to be formed into new systems all at once or gradually. In closed persons the formation of new systems is facilitated when the new beliefs are presented all at once, in which case the new beliefs do not have to be reconciled with the old ones. In open persons, it makes no difference. [*ed. note—for purposes of presenting new ideas to the electorate in Ireland, it would be well to assume that one is dealing with closed minds—this will be evidenced further on in this chapter.*]
5. The degree to which there is isolation within the belief system creates the isolation—that is, the less the intercommunication between individual beliefs, the more is the formation of new systems retarded.[7] [Italics mine.]

It would be simple enough, on the basis of Irish history, to make a case to the effect that cultural survival itself was predicated on the development of a system of counterinstitutions that would be dogmatic and purist. There is even historical evidence that political, religious, and social dogmatism are of more recent origin in Ireland than in many other countries in Western Europe (see chapter 1).

As long as the Unionists and Loyalists becloud their objections to a united Ireland with the rhetoric of democratic process and social welfare systems, they are victims, with the Southerners, of economic marginality and uncertainty. They vociferously chant litanies of complaint about the antidemocratic and corrupt behavior of the government of the Irish Republic, its judicial system, the preferred role of the Catholic Church lending an authoritarian orientation to the social and educational institutions. But behind the dogmatic, closed-mindedness of all the rhetoric lies the real threat of economic disaster. This is a threat prophesied by Connolly and realized fifty years after the Government of Ireland Act removed the Union Jack from Dublin castle. Let's look at some of the facts.

According to the O'Cinneide report on Ireland, published in 1972, one-fifth of the population of the twenty-six counties is at or below the poverty level, or as a journalist put it, "below the bread line."[8] By 1971, farms of one to thirty acres accounted for 57.9 percent of all holdings in Ireland, whereas in 1960 they had accounted for 49.6 percent. During that same period the number of men working on small farms fell by 50 percent. But the rate of emigration declined between 1966 and 1971 to 4.2 per thousand whereas in 1925–1936, the estimated rate was 5.6. Unemployment in the twenty-six counties, in 1972 was 66,609.[9]

According to the Minister for Social Welfare, the only thing standing in the way of improvement in the social welfare system are "the limits of the national resources and the need to allocate additional resources becoming available as equally as possible between the many classes of people who look to the department for some or all of their income."[10]

The Irish people have, for a very long time, been accustomed to considering their island poor in natural resources. The description of Ireland that appears in the primary texts read by generations of children of that country states that Ireland is a land with few natural resources. In real fact, Ireland has been extremely rich in natural resources, which until recently were totally unexplored. Ireland's ocean shelf contains a rich lode of undersea oil and natural gas. In addition, there are metals and minerals deep in the Irish soil. None of these resources have been explored or exploited by the Irish government itself. Instead, foreign-owned companies, sometimes with a few junior partners who are Irish, have obtained the rights to these treasures without having to pay taxes on their profits or operations. Since there are so few available jobs, in fact, they have in many cases also benefited from employing cheap, nonunion labor. When their tax-free concessions are up, they depart or close down, leaving behind them not only unemployment, but exhausted deep underground caverns, which have been almost totally depleted.

The frantic cycle begins all over again, as the Irish government places ads in West German newspapers inviting more investors to "take a tax holiday in Ireland." Their objective has often appeared to be temporary. By keeping the numbers of unemployed just below the level of political threat, and rotating the unemployment by areas, the thinking goes, some-how, someday, things will come out all right.

The Irish government issues a packet to prospective investors, entitled "Ireland, Climate for Profit." On one of the enclosures, the government says that:

> In the 1960's over 500 new manufacturing industries were set up in Ire-land involving a total investment of £130 million. Three hundred fifty of these were foreign based: 40% coming from Britain, 25% coming from USA, 20% from Germany, 5% from Netherlands. Others come from Italy, Austria, Canada, Japan, Denmark, Belgium, France, Monaco, S. Africa, Sweden, Switzerland, Finland. . . . They were attracted by the package of incentives offered to new businesses setting up in Ireland to manufacture for export. The incentives include a 15 year tax holiday on export profits and generous non-repayable cash grants.

TAX HOLIDAY

· New manufacturing firms setting up in Ireland enjoy 15 years full relief from taxes on export profits and partial relief in the remaining years up to 1990.
· This is how the "tax holiday" works:

1st year of claim	Relief
1970/71	15 years full relief + 5 years partial relief
1971/72	15 years full relief + 4 years partial relief
1972/73	15 years full relief + 3 years partial relief
1973/74	15 years full relief + 2 years partial relief
1974/75	15 years full relief + 1 year partial relief

· Partial relief is
80% of the full rate in year 1
65% of the full rate in year 2
50% of the full rate in year 3
35% of the full rate in year 4
15% of the full rate in year 5

A company enjoying the tax holiday passes on a corresponding measure of relief to shareholders

Example of Tax Holiday

· A firm earning export profits over 15 years of £20,250,000 would save £11,745,000 in tax relief.[11]

What is implied in some of the materials in this packet is that Irish labor works longer for less pay than either American or English labor; and that many of the factories employ girls, almost exclusively, and that these girls, aged fourteen and up, must remain unmarried in order to keep their jobs. The artificially high turnover rate thus produced enables the employer to maintain the cheapest possible labor force with little likelihood of their requiring retirement or health benefits, or even a decent wage.

A major industry in Ireland is tourism. The troubles in the North have affected this industry adversely. These same troubles made it somewhat easier for a while to attract foreign industrial capital, since the major competitor with the Irish Republic for these industries had been Northern Ireland. Robin Baillie, while Minister of Commerce for the North, often found himself in this kind of competition. He had almost secured an agreement with a Scandinavian firm for a factory in the Derry area when internment began. The firm took quarters in the Irish Republic instead. But tourism has suffered, and Aer Lingus (Irish Airlines) has been operating at a deficit. For some peculiar reason, however, that company (which could not afford to pay full insurance on its 747's and so had them mothballed during the winter) has purchased resort-hotel facilities in two other countries! Ostensibly, the rationale is to "get the money from somewhere else if it can't come to Ireland." The implications of an Irish firm spending money in another country, paying salaries to non-Irish people, consuming products of a foreign economy, suggest that this could easily be a greater economic drain than income!

Sometimes it seems as though the future of Ireland—and particularly the future of the west of Ireland—is to be a vast, three-dimensional museum-vacationland, wherein round-cheeked, freckle-faced natives will provide cheerful service to foreign tourists, and well-preserved, uninhabited thatch-roofed cottages will dot the landscape. Hidden from the tourists' view, of course, will be the factories generating American and German capital, and mines assiduously worked by foreign investors until their tax holidays run out. Perhaps the holes in the earth will then be filled with water and stocked with trout? There's an interesting description of one town, to illustrate this prospect:

Uachtar Ard perhaps presents in perfect microcosm the problems of the small farmers in the West of Ireland. Situated on the shores of the 24 mile long Lough Corrib—with fish in it for the taking, only seventeen miles from Galway and ten from the rugged beauty of the Connamara Gaeltacht, Uachtar Ard is a magnet for millionaires. The draw is twofold —firstly, the retired British Colonel type. Secondly, there's the well-known gombeen type. That is hoteliers and shopkeepers who recognize Uachtar Ard's potential as a playground for both passing and permanent million-aires and want to develop the town and hinterland accordingly.

There are over 500 families living in Uachtar Ard parish. The town has one carpet factory which makes the most exclusive hand-tooled carpets in the country. The factory is Irish-American owned and employs twenty-one men and seven women. The town has no public toilet, four large hotels, assorted guest houses, three supermarkets, two 'souvenir' shops, a primary school and two secondary schools.

Uachtar Ard has a chronic housing problem. There are young families living in one-roomed flats in the town. The last County Council cottage that fell vacant attracted seventeen desperate applicants—an outsider was eventually given the cottage.

Uachtar Ard town is situated in the heart of small farmer's country [but] the shops are stacked with Aran sweaters and mock shillelaghs, French cigarettes and smoked salmon. The hotels with their thickly car-peted floors and endless 'musak' cater more for bourgeoisie than the farmer. Attempts to get a co-operative off the ground have been foiled by local traders, who are tied up with the big business elements in the town.[12]

The Leaders of the Crowd: South

The Irish Labour Party and the Official Republican Movement (Sinn Fein, Gardiner Pl.) both claim descent from James Connolly. Their evolu-tion into bitter political enmity encompasses the entire scope of the evo-lution of Irish party politics since the first Dail met in 1919. The Labour Party has been part of coalition governments with Fine Gael, the nation-alist party that claims descent from Michael Collins and his pro-treaty forces. The other major political party in the Irish Republic, Fianna Fail, was organized by deValera, out of a segment of the old Sinn Fein, which in the 1920's had begun to rethink its abstentionist policy. Eamon de-Valera's personal popularity as a leader of the IRA in its civil war against the pro-treaty forces carried him into the prime ministry and presidency of the Irish Republic through a political career that spanned fifty years. He became the major architect of the 1937 constitution, the declaration of the Irish Republic independence of the British Commonwealth, and finally the entrance of Ireland into the European Economic Community.

But Sinn Fein, which had been the vehicle for the political mobilization of the Irish people into nationhood, neither atrophied nor developed as a major political force. Instead, as a legal political party it sustained its abstentionist policy in the South; as an illegal party in the North, it became the political recruiting arm of the Irish Republican Army, which was banned in both north and south.

In each decade, the IRA initiated a campaign for a united Ireland. In each decade, they failed and grew less popular. Splinter groups emerged and disappeared. In 1970, Sinn Fein and IRA split yet again. The Provisional wing, under the command of Sean MacStiofain, who opposed the nonviolent Marxist strategy of the Official Sinn Fein, was led into a bloody bombing and shooting campaign in the north. The arms trial of 1970 and the removal of four government ministers from the front bench seemed to indicate a degree of collusion on the part of at least some of the government in making funds available to the Provisionals.

In December, 1972, the Fianna Fail-led government of the Irish Republic amended the Offenses Against the State Act to initiate internment to suspected IRA members in the south. The Irish Labour Party was the only opposition to that vote in the Dail. Yet there is no political party that had been more active in attempting to suppress the IRA, both Officials and Provisionals, than has the Irish Labour Party. Nor is there any party more often attacked by the Official Sinn Fein than the ILP, although the Fianna Fail Party runs a very close second. Neither of the Sinn Feins nor any of the parties in the present government will share a common platform for any kind of demonstration of unity (with, of course, the exception of the two parties to the present coalition sharing a platform).

On October 23, 1971, Tomas MacGiolla, President of the Sinn Fein (Official), and Conor Cruise O'Brien of the Irish Labour Party met in public debate in Dublin. The texts of the two position statements provide the gist of doctrinal differences. They serve to elaborate two divergent belief systems that have effectively eliminated any possibility of openness since each, obviously, perceives the other as a threat.

These texts help us to examine the dynamics of the Official Finn Sein and the Irish Labour Party—both of whom argue out of somewhat the same verbal lexicon and a value system expressed in socialist axiology. Each asserts its legitimacy as Connolly's heir and berates the other's sosialist antitheses. They accuse each other of elitism, betrayal of the working class, fascism, misrepresenting the mandate of the people, democratic process perverted into oligarchic dictatorship. The following passages constructed from their separate statements demonstrate this clash of the Irish left:

Elitism

O'Brien: . . . real power is wielded by the living military elite. They decide who is to die and when, they possess the prestige which the power to decide that confers.

Unpretentious though they may sometimes be in dress and manner, they are in fact, aristocrats. Sumarai, not ordinary people, and subject to uncommon measures. Mr. MacGiolla is the spokesman here for that military elite and for nothing else.[13]

MacGiolla: . . . instead of a mass movement they want to see elitist politics with people relying on the parliamentary system to secure improvements in their conditions. What these lackeys of capitalism fail to acknowledge is that the rules of the parliamentary system are laid down by the ruling class in our society and that . . . they have the power to alter the rules at any time or make any political opposition impossible by interning its members.[14]

Betrayal of the Working Class

O'Brien: The Dail which approved the Treaty was itself a Sinn Fein assembly, and the minority decided that the majority did not count. Why should not the Provisionals decide likewise? Why should they not exercise the right you all arrogated to yourselves—that of deciding who is a good Irishman and who is a bad one, whose vote should count and whose should not? They have decided your votes don't count. . . . There is nothing to prevent any determined group which can get its hands on guns and bombs from setting up as the true heirs of the national tradition. . . . The closer your movement approaches to success . . . the more it will be a movement dominated by the most efficient and ruthless gunmen. . . . What does matter is that these will not be people who were drawn to your movement by socialist idealism.[15]

MacGiolla: In response to this growth the Irish Labour Party was forced to adopt certain progressive slogans, though that hasn't prevented its oligarchic leadership from betraying the rank and file with proposing an alliance with the extreme right wing Fine Gael party. . . . While the Sinn Fein in the South has been active organizing people against the appalling housing situation in the main cities, against the arrogance of foreign imperialist companies, against the unequal distribution of wealth in this country, the Labour representatives have preferred to stand on the sidelines and to denounce the efforts of ordinary people to protect themselves as 'fascist'. . . . In fact, the whole pseudo-left exhibit the true signs of renegades, for while they shout loudly about socialism they make no effort to achieve it. They are essentially liberals who are afraid of the consequences of their own convictions.[16]

Fascists

O'Brien: The Republican Movement is going in that direction because Fascism is the natural destination of an anti-democratic, militarist, authoritarian, ultra-nationalist movement, whose ultimate appeal is to mystique inaccessible to reason. These elements are, in fact among the principal distinguishing marks of Fascism, and all of them are abundantly present in your movement.[17]

MacGiolla: The rabid anti-semitic utterances of Stevie Coughlan are quickly forgotten, while O'Brien demands recognition of his right of fascists like Carson, Calloper Smith, Brookeborough, etc. to mislead the working class Protestant of the North . . . let the great man speak from on high and the 'ignorant' people can follow . . . the . . . groups who upheld the right of imperialism to divide the Irish working class and confuse people by calling that socialism.[18]

Misrepresenting the Mandate of the People

O'Brien: We reject it on behalf of a socialist tradition, concerned with living realities and recognizing always that mystical politics, the language of sacred seil and the cult of the dead, are part of the apparatus of the enemy. And we reject it above all as rational beings, intent on using our minds to understand and change society, and utterly denying the right of the dead, or of their living servants, to put a vote on our thinking, on our speech or on our power of decision.[19]

MacGiolla: The Irish Labour Party is the prime example of such a group. Despite resolutions at Party conferences calling on the leadership to work for a Republican Labour alliance the parliamentary representatives have preferred to go into alliance with Fine Gael and to attack the Republican movement. . . . The Labour Party in the South can be clearly stigmatized for its failure and refusal to organize people to defend themselves either in trade union affairs or on a wide social level.[20]

Democratic Process Perverted

O'Brien: Democracy . . . is not noble, and not compatible with the ideals of a military elite. Under democracy civilians, not soldiers, have supreme power. And literally all sorts of people join in the choice of these civilians. The man who likes greyhound racing and reads the *Daily Mirror* has the same vote as a patriot who reads the *United Irishman*. People who value peace above national unification have votes. The military elite for which Mr. MacGiolla speaks decides that these votes don't count. For us, who accept democracy, all the votes count and the dead votes don't vote.[21]

MacGiolla: These Labour bureaucrats realize that genuine socialist policies are a threat to their well paid comfortable elitist parliamentary position. If people give up relying on politicians to fight their battles and start to rely on their own strength, as Sinn Fein has consistently advocated, there will be no room for the University lectures and internationally renowned liberals of the Labour Party.[22]

Ireland is not unique in having a left divided into factions more often at odds with each other than with the right. The fact that Labour did, in 1973, conclude an alliance with rightwing Fine Gael is further illustration of its condition. O'Brien reviled the Sinn Fein for "not recognizing the government" and lumped together the Provisional with the Official republicans, indicating his difficulty in reconciling his party's politics with changes that have occurred in the policy and practice of the "traditional enemy." On the other hand, Sinn Fein may also be accused of having expressed a belief system closed by its own dogmatism to recognition of the similarity between its struggle to be democratic and the problems of the Labour Party, which to a slightly lesser degree operates under the same context of marginality and system-threat. Of course a political organization which is, at most, only semilegal and is involved in urban guerrilla warfare will necessarily have a less open, less democratic process. The more threatened it is, the less democratic (or open) it is able to be. But because the Officials cherish their ideology of democratic process, they become unduly defensive when they are attacked for shortcomings in its practice.

There is the constant political problem of being a minority party, with a major potential but unaffiliated constituency—Ireland has a predominantly working-class population—and that constituency, which is only semiconscious of its class interests, has become an albatross continually threatening the candidacy of Labour Party representatives.[23]

> The Provisional line on the other hand made sense, in terms of the dominant ideology in the Republic. They were not, they claimed, out to make trouble in the twenty-six counties, they rejected Marxist language (though not Socialism) and any political alliance with Communists. They were out, they said, to liberate the six north-eastern counties of Ireland, occupied by British Forces against the will of the great majority of the Irish people. Most citizens of the Republic were conditioned to think of such a policy as well-founded and laudable. They were not conditioned to think of the Ulster Protestant as an important factor in the question, or to see that the Provisional's policy pointed ultimately to Civil War in Ireland between Catholic and Protestant. . . . It was, in fact, impossible to answer them in terms of the dominant ideology because they were the most effective and consistent champions of that ideology. Rich and influential patriots, repelled by the Marxism of the old and official IRA had a special welcome for the Provisionals: Good Catholics, good Irishmen, no threat to anyone but the British and the——Unionists. It seems that some of the rich and influential not only welcomed the Provisionals, but helped them come into being.[24]

Between the inception in 1970 of the Provisionals and the arrest of Sean MacStiofain, Chief of Staff, in November, 1972, southern cheers for

Provisional IRA northern "victories" were matched by the increasing embarrassment of the Dublin government and the growing fear of the increasing Provisional focus on operations in the South. For instance, prisoners at the Curragh Camp in the Irish Republic had, in July, declared themselves "political" prisoners and demanded status as such. The Provisionals organized rallies and demonstrations in support of them. Prime Minister Jack Lynch lost prestige when the Provisionals, in June–July 1972, dealt directly with Heath at Whitehall, thus denying the right of the Irish government to represent the interests of the Irish Republic in its status of government for the minority population in the north. There was embarrassment earlier from the alleged Haughey-Blaney direction of government funds toward the Provisionals' campaign and the publicity implicating the Irish Republic in their gun-running activities, as well as the increasingly sectarian nature of the Northern conflict.

The Provisional Sinn Fein/IRA protest against the practices of the British government in the north and the Irish government in the South. They advised their supporters against balloting in the June, 1973, assembly elections as a refusal to recognize proposed solutions from the British government. They equally vehemently denounce the Irish government for denying recognition to their republican constituency as a legitimate contender in the northern struggle. Neither their denunciations nor those of the Official IRA are permitted on radio or television in Ireland. Minister for Posts and Telegraphs Dr. Conor Cruise O'Brien has banned any broadcasting of or by either the political wing, Sinn Fein, or the IRA on RTE. Ironically, more air time is given them in Northern Ireland than in the Republic. The print media of the twenty-six counties, nonetheless, often carry IRA/Sinn Fein statements, such as this one:

> The Provisional IRA last night accused the Minister for Justice, Mr. Cooney, and the Government of planning "a new phase of coercion."
>
> A statement issued through the Irish Republican Publicity Bureau and signed, "P. O'Neill," said: "The old cliches of 'law and order' and 'one army, one government' are trotted out to condition the public mind for a policy of increased harassment and jailing of republicans."
>
> The Provisional IRA went on to say that the special powers of the Offenses Against the State Act, which Mr. Cooney found so objectionable last December, were being used to the full in order to prove to the British Government that Mr. Cooney was as good as Mr. O'Malley in hounding republicans.
>
> The statement continued: "It was ironic that Mr. Cooney's speech should come at the end of a week during which the British Army excelled itself in murder and brutality. "He spoke within hours of Mr. Edward O'Rawe being shot in cold blood in Belfast, and at a time when the people of the North are seething with rage over British Army killings in Newry and Armagh:

"There was no word of comfort for the relatives of those who died, and no call for the withdrawal of the professional killers of the British army from the streets of Irish towns and villages.

"Immediately following Bloody Sunday last year, when 13 Derry people lay dead after being shot by the British Army paratroopers, Mr. Cosgrave delivered an emotional speech demanding an immediate withdrawal of British troops from Ireland.

"Today, his Minister for Justice condones the unspeakable actions of those troops, because their conduct comes within his concept of 'law and order.'

"The Whitelaw regime can perpetrate every foul act of an occupying Power, bludgeon Irish people into accepting the White Paper proposals, and do so with the full knowledge that no Dublin politician or Churchman will raise a voice in protest. Never before in the history of our country have elected leaders shown such cowardice in the face of brutal oppression against our people by a foreign army.

"If Cosgrave and Cooney have not the courage to defend Irish people from marauding British troops, then let them end the cant and humbug of 'one army, and one government' in Ireland. There is but one Ireland and One Nation, one unlawful army—the British Army of occupation.

"If Mr. Cooney believes he can suppress the Republican Movement, he is greatly mistaken. Irish politics are littered with discredited Ministers for Justice who failed to break the Republican Movement. Republicans have paid a high price in lives and liberties for defending the people of the North and now, after three years of hard struggle, they will not be deflected one iota from fulfilling their responsibilities by the threats of a Quisling politician.

"The Dublin Government has no mandate to collaborate with British forces in Ireland, and while they may continue to mislead the people of the South, they have earned from the people of the North nothing but the utmost contempt."[25]

The British government is just as convinced as the Provisional IRA that the Dublin government cannot break the republican movement in Ireland. Periodically, Dublin tries to prove that it can. In 1973, the Irish government confiscated all copies of the Provisionals' booklet, *Freedom Struggle*, and broke up the type plates at the printing house in Dundalk that was producing the book. In July, 1975, Special Branch detectives arrested and incarcerated Daithi O'Conaill, popular leader of the Provisionals who engaged in talks that produced a year-long cease-fire between the Provisionals and the British army in the north.

Regardless of its efforts to eradicate this group, the Irish government is continually and publicly attacked by the British government for not having accomplished that which 25,000 British troops have not managed to achieve in Northern Ireland—an end to the shooting and bombing campaign.

Leaders of the Crowd: North

The development of the civil rights movement, formalized in NICRA (Northern Ireland Civil Rights Association), provided the Catholic minority of Northern Ireland a focal point for evolving new alternative institutions—newspapers, legal and welfare aid services, social and political clubs, and even cooperative production units. NICRA itself became the major alternative institution. The Protestant working class remained inarticulate, dependent on their traditional leaders who were not of their own class or interests. They had always been the bodies counted in the annual parades of the Orange Order and the Apprentice Boys; the ballots counted at the polls; the audience for evangelical crusaders. They became the armed, masked cadres blocking roadways and confronting the British army—successfully. Rarely did they speak for themselves or consider themselves an integral power. Instead, they formed into ranks behind the leadership whose legitimacy derived from membership in the old Anglo-Irish ascendancy, or who were clergymen or even successful businessmen whose fathers established factories (like former Prime Minister Brian Faulkner). This in itself was consistent with the Protestant ethic, which equates success with blessedness.

Even the Ulster Workers' Council, an allegedly grass-roots organization of Protestant workers, which through a general strike brought down the one experiment at governing that included Catholics in decision-making positions, had direction from behind by traditional leaders like William Craig, Harry West, John Laird, and Glen Barr.

The UDA (Ulster Defence Association) has tried to maintain a strong commitment to self-direction and actively fights against being manipulated by any of the traditional authority figures. Some UDA leaders have even managed to develop alternative institutions within the Protestant working class. One such person was Sammy Smyth, with whom I met several times through the years 1973–1975, to discuss his perspective. In July, 1975, Sammy summed up for me the origins of the UDA and its relationship to Ulster politics:

In the political arena it doesn't mean anything because all the political parties are opposed to me . . . possibly because I'm the only articulate, shrewd, intelligent and very experienced community candidate who poses a threat to them, and Vanguard recognized this a long time ago and branded me as a "Communist" very effectively in large parts of Belfast. They knew this to be a deliberate lie. In fact, they were challenged on it. Nevertheless it's the old saying, "tell a lie long enough and people tend to believe it." So they attempted to discredit me by saying I was a Communist. So did Paisley. The Unionist Party, Faulkner's crowd, disowned me. Of course the others did as well . . . because of my relations with the Ulster Defence

Association. So as a person, I say, and I don't think I'm being big-headed, I believe I have qualities . . . you can only praise yourself if you are among your peers because they can recognize the quality, but if you are among people who are obviously not bright, not articulate, and you are, then it's like a big tomato amongst a bunch of small ones—you're just naturally better in size. . . . They would have accepted me perhaps, if I'd been prepared to break all associations with the Ulster Defence Association, in that case any of the parties would have been glad to have me. However, I helped found the Ulster Defence Association. . . . Why? Because I know it's right. I still believe in the Ulster Defence Association and I still feel this is a vital element in the community and will be for some time to come. I do not feel that I would serve my community best if I would move into the political arena. When we were formed in 1970 and '71, the Ulster . . . Loyalist working class at that time had lost everything. The Royal Ulster Constabulary were a completely demoralized force and could offer them nothing in terms of protection or in terms of ordinary law and order. The Ulster Special Constabulary . . . [by the] propaganda put out by the IRA aided by the international press, aided by the Eire government . . . they wilted under this sustained propaganda and they couldn't answer. . . . Why they couldn't answer it heaven only knows because I could have answered it. But I was only a five-eight, a laborer at that particular time, not interested in anything but doing my daily work like the rest . . . that was the situation, and the Protestants living in the front-line areas such as Louisa St. and Bryson St. and New Barnesley, Newtonards Road . . . they were under attack by the IRA. And you had the ludicrous position of the IRA coming through the ranks of the small army posts in these areas—shooting and throwing nail bombs, generally causing violence in these Protestant areas and then driving back in through the British army, no attempt being made to stop them. So individuals among us got greatly annoyed at this and went up to the army who told us, "Our job was not to antagonize the Roman Catholic population!" So we said, "Okay, fair enough, if you're not going after them, then we will." The army commanders in each of the areas said, "If you put one foot past us we'll shoot." . . . This was ludicrous . . . we were unarmed, the IRA was coming through and attacking us, if we attempted to go after them into their own districts, the army'd shoot us. How ludicrous can you get? There were individual street vigilante groups at that time. So we made barriers to cut our streets off from 7 at night to 7 the next morning and took turns manning them. . . . The army came through with their jeeps and knocked down those barriers. You're working in the factory and buying wood to form the barriers, so you get quite annoyed. So we went up to the army and said, "What are you playing at? We're not obstructing the Queen's highway; we're doing nothing to antagonize the Roman Catholic population; we're just trying to stop the IRA from coming through. So we're putting the barriers up again." And, "As often as you knock them down we'll keep putting them up. We're not obstructing traffic during the normal daylight hours." . . . Some commanders accepted this, and some didn't. Therefore three or four of us from different areas of Belfast came together, figuring that the only way to stop these raids was for us to form an organization. This was the Ulster Defence Association. . . . We are not political. We made an agreement not to do anything political at all and anyone who was in politics would not be allowed to have any position in the UDA, not to have any say in its decision-making. So from that time until now this has been the position. Various people have tried to take over, including politicians and left-wing socialists. In the case of the left-wing socialists we simply eradicated them. In the case of the politicians we told them to "get stuffed." However, politicians were in a superb position as far as electoral position goes . . . we had to vote for them. Therefore they could disclaim us any time and they could use us anytime.

When Sammy talked about "eradicating left-wing socialists" his words have an ominous ring for people familiar with the early repetitive themes of German National Socialism. When Sammy elaborated on his statement, however, the ring was less ominous. He was not amenable to a fascist solution, but his political sophistication was not fully developed and he, knowing this, was therefore extremely wary:

If you're faced with infiltrators what do you do with them? You put them outside the organization. If in the meantime they have converted anyone who has any important position in the organization, then you must take a different method. What you do is discipline them. . . . I'm not going to spell it out, but you discipline people in different ways. The health and well-being of the organization for the community comes before any other decision. . . . For some of them we brutalized them—to put it gently, you can't afford to have that kind of take-over, because if they had taken over, the UDA would have fallen apart. It's only given support because it's non-political. . . . Eradication is a strong word and that's why I used it. They did in fact eradicate some UDA leaders who were in their way and they posed a threat. They eliminated them so as in actual fact proteges could move into the leadership . . . that was going on in early '72. . . . I am not prepared to be treated as a deviant. The extreme right and the extreme left are closer together than the middle is to either of them because both believe that the ends justify the means . . . the UDA supports a multi-party system because we embrace the left-wing socialists and the capitalists . . . and that's why we are very particular to see that no one political group takes us over. This is why some people are exasperated with the UDA. Simply because we refuse to be socialist, liberal, democrat, republican or capitalist. We have the whole range of those people . . . it's a defensive movement whose only objective is to protect the people from attack . . . and to assure that the border remains. . . . Only in that sense, in regard to the border, would you call it political. It is not a political movement.

Socially, we do a lot of social work simply because we've been forced into the position. I branched away from the military end of the UDA to handle the social aspects. Because the hard core of UDA men consider that they are here to defend, not to play nursemaid, and they regard the social end which became very large during internment and the intimidation process as not for them . . . it wasn't only Roman Catholics who were intimidated, Protestants were intimidated by the IRA.

Sammy's class-consciousness had no relationship to the kind of workers' solidarity which Bernadette Devlin or Billy McMillen, leaders of two different socialist republican organizations, advocate. It is rather a kind of populism familiar in many regions of the United States. Certain elements of a populist ideology combined with a charismatic leader and a doctrine of racial or religious superiority can mobilize into a paramilitary force and become fascism. But it would be a gross overgeneralization to equate the populist ideology of Sammy Smyth and the UDA with the kind of populist nationalism of Enoch Powell or his colleague Mosley in England.

Ulster Protestants have conceived of themselves as a beleaguered, persecuted minority. This is axiomatic to understanding the politics of Northern Ireland and the tradition of paramilitarism. A Presbyterian clergyman whose parishioners included working-class people in an estate infamous in the minority community for its loyalist associations took me to meet families in his community who had been victims of various kinds of intimidation and misrepresentation. An elementary school principal from another such area confided his own antipathy to the Unionist party and system along with his conviction that the Roman Catholic community had conspired to encircle enclaves of Protestant housing and thus force out the occupants of those districts.

From the perspective of the minority such beliefs are ridiculous. Worse yet, they are positively dangerous since they provide the rationale for the hostile aggressive actions taken by the majority. Articulating these fears and beliefs for their Protestant working-class constituency mobilizes support for Craig, Paisley, West, and other demagogues.

Against this background, the study on intimidation out of Housing, which was undertaken by Community Relations researchers Morris and Darby in 1972, was vital to establishing the empirical dimensions of this problem. They found that Catholics residing in New Barnsley Estate were intimidated out of their homes by the Regiment of Paratroopers; that in other places people had been frightened from their homes by Green or Orange extremists; and, finally, that the RUC had made no significant effort to deter such intimidation. Community Relations Commissioner David Rowlands decided unilaterally to suppress the researchers' report. It was somehow leaked to the London *Times* and several Irish newspapers.

The suppression led to more anger from all sides of the "peace line" than could ever have resulted from its publication. In discussing it, Sammy Smyth pointed to the way he became convinced that working-class Protestants have to develop their own alternative institutions:

I heard about it, so I wrote to David Rowlands and I said could I please have a copy because I am Secretary for the Northern Ireland Association of Intimidated Protestants and I have received no visits from your research team. . . . I already knew that Paddy Devlin had a copy, the *Irish Times*, the *Irish Press*, the *Irish Independent* had copies. . . . So David Rowlands wrote back and said, "No you can't have a copy." I said, "Why not?" He said, "It's not published yet." I pointed out the various people who had copies. He refused to give me it, so I then got a letter from John Darby, one of the originators of the study, "Would you please come along and discuss with me the Northern Ireland group for Intimidated Protestants." So I wrote back and said, "Who the hell do you think you are talking to. You want to meet me now and then you can alter your report to say that you interviewed me. It's just not on! . . . I have a number of contacts with persons throughout Northern Ireland who looked after intimidated Protestants. You have interviewed none of these." . . . But at the time he did this report, which was over a three-month period, incidentally, it was not over the whole period of time . . . what might have happened, in fact, was that at this particular time the authorities didn't want to know of Protestants being intimidated . . . all you had to do was put on your Pioneer badge [a Catholic organization opposing the use of alcoholic beverages], go report and you were taken in hand by various welfare bodies and helped . . . and they were registered with the Belfast Housing Trust . . . which means there is a statistical record of people who were intimidated out of their houses seeking housing. . . . Now the first Protestants who were intimidated went down to the housing executive who told them to "get lost." They couldn't do anything for them. . . . So I felt that rather than having them go down and wait for hours and get no help, it was much better if we helped them directly. So what we did is what the Nationalists did. Certain housing estates in which there were empty houses, we moved these families into them. The result was there was no statistical evidence. . . . I told this to John Darby and Geoff Morris, the authors of the report and at no time did they make any effort to confirm this . . . researchers have a duty to be objective. A researcher who refuses to be objective is not a researcher. In my opinion John Darby and Geoff Morris are both Nationalists.*

*In the spring, 1976, Sammy Smyth announced his readiness to meet with nationalist paramilitary leaders to design a system of self-governance for Northern Ireland. One week after his announcement, on March 10, he was assassinated apparently by a group of Protestant extremists.

Protestant working-class men and women, as well as adolescents, had reaped some of the benefits of the civil rights agitation even while they remained apparently unaware of it. The Community Relations Commission and its associated agencies arranged neighborhood play schemes and employed many young idealistic and talented indigenous workers, who although they operated without a clear mandate nonetheless catalyzed local self-help groups. These young people in turn also stimulated older people, like Sammy Smyth, to fill in some of the gaps in their own educations. In 1974, Sammy and a couple of his colleagues began attending a psychology course at Queen's University. He had decided to think for himself and he was looking for the necessary tools, he commented:

> Perhaps the Community Relations Commission helped us in the sense that it was set up to help the Roman Catholic community. It was not set up to help the Protestant community. When we started to make full use of it, Cooper, of the SDLP . . . suddenly closed it down. . . . Because the community was beginning to realize its own power. Prior to that, everything was a sop to the Catholics. If it was allowed to seep over into the Protestant community and we were allowed to help ourselves become more effective pressure groups . . . we would no longer be dependent on the politicians. . . . [They] rubbed out the Community Relations Commission in order to make the government come more directly over the community, thus creating that conditioning process all over again. . . . What I'd like to see is the whole new plan for schooling with different kinds of schools for different kinds of people . . . one type state school cannot care for the differences, and all schools should be available to all children . . .

Sammy's statements about the CRC typify the differences between the two population groups in their experience of government in Northern Ireland. The Catholic, or nationalist, population had felt compelled to reject (and they were rejected by) the existing government and all its functionaries. They then developed their own alternative system and organized themselves to oppose their oppression. They want equal opportunities from government resources and institutions, and their protest grew from recognition of that need. They also acquired a degree of political sophistication through having formed their own system. On the other hand, the Protestant working class has been accustomed to unquestioning reliance on the existing power system. Organizing alternative institutions came to them at a very late hour and is not yet at a level of efficiency equal to their needs.

They recognized the need for developing indigenous institutions to help themselves in dealing with the apparatus of law and government. To this end, they organized the Ulster Citizens' Civil Liberties Centre (UCCL), which, along with the Resettlement Association, is the nucleus of grass-roots campaigning to guarantee their rights. For this segment of the population, the welfare state of post–World War II Britain had become a confusing bureaucratic melange. They were aware that they were not getting the same benefits from the system as their English cousins, but for more than fifty years they had been so grateful for being allowed to remain British that they had never learned to demand treatment any more equal than the right to fly the Union Jack.

The UCCL presented a bill of rights that differs from the one proposed by NICRA several years earlier. The differences signify the different perspectives in the spectrum of political ideologies. While neither bill would allow internment without trial, NICRA would deny the government any recourse to emergency or special powers for Northern Ireland, while UCCL demands the enactment of a series of safeguards to prevent any attempt at a unilateral declaration of such powers by Westminster or Whitehall without the consent of Ulster. UCCL advocates the bill of rights as protection of its prerogatives. NICRA, on the other hand, contends that the welfare state was not originally based on democracy, but rather on a system of privileges that must be eradicated to ensure the abolition of repressive laws. The bounties of the welfare system are, they point out, not a product of equalization at all, but rather a taxing of the wage- and salary-earner while maintaining the continuity of privilege for the landed aristocracy.

From 1964 until 1974, however, the major threat to unionist hegemony in Northern Ireland did not come from the Young Unionists and progressive forces led by O'Neill or from nascent republicanism. It was not threatened by the Northern Ireland civil rights movement with its tenuous coalition of People's Democracy Radicals, Communist Party members, and Official Republicans who had become Marxists. This coalition could not have gathered the momentum to unleash the hurricane if it had not been for the efforts of the Reverend Ian Richard Kyle Paisley. Paisley symbolizes, more than any other figure, the effects of British colonialism three hundred years after the Ulster plantation.

He is the son of a Baptist minister whose ministry was located near Belfast in County Antrim. Paisley was ordained by his father in 1964. Although he tried to enter the Presbyterian Seminary in Belfast, he never achieved the admissions requirements and therefore attended as an unaffiliated student. The diploma he received did not qualify him for a ministry in the Reformed Presbyterian Church, so he began work in a less formal sect. In his quest for academic legitimacy, Ian Paisley attended the Barrie School of Evangelism in Wales and took two mail-order degrees in rapid succession from Pioneer Theological Seminary (which was subsequently closed down by the Federal Trade Commission for misrepresenting its home study courses). In 1958, Paisley took an M.A. degree by home study from the Barton College and Seminary in Manitour Springs, Colorado.

Twenty years after he completed his studies in Belfast, the Reverend Ian Paisley in 1966 was awarded an honorary doctorate by Bob Jones III, on behalf of the Bob Jones University. By then he had already earned his reputation as a man of wrath and violence.[26]

He threw a Bible at Lord Soper in 1959, to demonstrate his opposition to ecumenism. Soper, President of the Methodist Church Conference, was lecturing to a Belfast audience when Paisley terminated his appearance. The next day, when Soper made an appearance at Carlisle Memorial Church in Belfast, Paisley and his followers attempted to hang rosary beads on him, and were afterward charged in court for their disruptions. Paisley utilized that, like his many other court appearances, to stimulate further support and contributions to his anti-ecumenical campaign. In at least one instance, he had carefully laid plans for a demonstration that was to protest an expected jailing only to have his plans thrown into confusion because an anonymous woman, thickly veiled in black, paid his court fine.

Paisley's behavior during the 1960's was as often planned to embarrass O'Neill and the Unionist elite as it was directed at humiliation of Catholics. He organized demonstrations against visiting clerics who espoused ecumenism and against dignitaries from Britain who met with O'Neill on various matters of political or economic affairs. In 1965, he organized massive demonstrations to protest the visit to Belfast of Sean Lemass, then prime minister of the Irish Republic. Similarly, he demonstrated against O'Neill when the latter returned from a visit with Lemass in Dublin.

Before the civil rights movement had attempted its first march, Paisley was leading crowds of his followers through the streets of Belfast and other places shouting epithets and wielding primitive weapons. In 1964, Paisley organized a massive demonstration to protest the display of a small tricolor flag in the office window of a political candidate in Lower Falls. This march resulted in violence when the Royal Ulster Constabulary yielded to Paisley's demands that it be removed. They were armed with sten guns, rifles, steel helmets, and shields and had been ordered to restrict Paisley's mob from approaching the little office on Divis Street. Instead, they led the mob in breaking into the place to snatch the flag.[27] Four bloody nights of rioting followed that demonstration, resulting in injuries to hundreds of persons.

In 1966, Paisley began organizing paramilitary groups, The Ulster Constitution Defence Committee and the Ulster Protestant Volunteers. The same year, he founded a newspaper, *The Protestant Telegraph*. Through the newspaper and his publishing company, the Puritan Press, he flooded the province with pamphlets, treatises, and tracts—all proclaiming the false doctrine and treachery of the "Lundies" in the government; the Romeward bent of the World Council of Churches; the papistry of the Bishop of

Canterbury, who had shared his pulpit with a Catholic priest; and, of course, the danger of republicanism.

By May of that year, Orange extremists in Belfast had become so secure behind Paisley's banner that anti-Catholic shootings began. A young engineering worker, shot on the street, died of abdominal wounds. The "credit" for the kill was taken by the First Belfast Battalion of the Ulster Volunteer Force, announced by a telephone caller identifying himself to the desk of the *Belfast Telegraph* as Captain William Johnston. A month later at 2 A.M. on June 26, two young Catholic bartenders, aged eighteen and nineteen, who were working at a hotel in the center of Belfast, were shot dead and their colleague severely wounded by a group of men again identifying themselves as the UVF. Prime Minister Terence O'Neill proscribed the UVF two days later.[28] Despite Paisley's disclaimer of involvement or knowledge of the UVF, at least one of the men later convicted for the shooting identified himself with Paisley. The latter had, only ten days earlier, acknowledged the presence of the UVF at his church meeting and thanked them for their support of his antirepublicanism.

Thus started the decade of violence in Northern Ireland. Reverend Ian Paisley managed to bring down the government of Captain O'Neill, the Stormont of which he was a member, and, finally, the Assembly with its power-sharing executive, of which he was also an elected representative.

The man whose window tricolor had so offended Paisley, the RUC, and the Ulster Special Constabulary as to have precipitated a four-day riot was a steeplejack by trade and Republican by politics, Liam McMillen. In Lower Falls where he worked and sometimes lived, he was known as "Billy" or "the wee man."

Billy McMillen's lifelong dedication to republicanism and nonviolence was paradoxically ended by a burst of gunfire as he stepped outside a paint supply store on April 24, 1975. Billy and his brother Art had been interned during earlier round-ups in the 1950's. On August 9, 1971, Art was lifted, but Billy managed to escape. Despite being on the run he remained involved in the political organizing of the Official Republican Movement. Billy was the image of the Antihero. He was indeed a "wee man," standing not much over five feet, rotund, and looking—as he would put it—"older than God." He was forty-seven years old when he was killed. He had been born into a family of committed republicans. His ancestry was both Protestant and Catholic and his mother had worked for James Connolly during his period in Belfast. At the time Billy McMillen was killed he had been a member of the Ard Comhairle (Executive Committee) of Sinn Fein for ten years. He had been Officer in Command of Belfast since 1964, when his campaign for Westminster election was directed from that little office on Divis Street. The office had a sign on one wall, a quote from Yeats that expressed Billy's kind of republicanism:

Then let the Orange lily be your badge
My Patriot brother
The Everlasting Green for me
And us for one another.

Ian Paisley and Liam McMillen are a sharp contrast in typical Belfast-born leaders. They represent the conflicting and contradictory traditions of mainstream Ulster history, in which there is a strong, repetitive, and almost cyclical theme of demagoguery, bigotry, violence, and religious fundamentalism, characteristic of Paisleyism, and the equally strong current of anti-sectarianism, internationalism, and humanism, which were characteristic of Billy McMillen.

At the time of his release from Crumlin Road jail, after six years of internment, the Republican Movement had entered a new phase. The methods of physical force attempted in every decade since partition had failed miserably. And as McMillen himself put it, "the IRA was just a joke nobody wanted to know about." But McMillen had already been through two rounds of internment, having used his jail time to study the Irish language and everything else Irish. His knowledge of socialist ideology was essentially from the memory of Connolly as a personal hero, rather than from textbooks. McMillen had left school at fourteen, like most of his age contemporaries in Ireland, north and south. He worked as a steeplejack, not as an intellectual. He described his introduction to Marxist republicanism through recognition of the history of the movement:

Well, the first thing we heard was the Dublin leaders were sitting down to assess the failure of the physical force ideal in general. They decided that it was only by political involvement with the people that you'd ever get the mass support of the people. Representatives used to come down from Dublin and tell us to form Republican Clubs, get involved in tenants associations, trade unions—all this jazz. We resisted it tooth and nail! We used to spend hours at meetings trying to conjure up ideas and excuses as to why we shouldn't become involved in this type of political activity, and to tell Dublin GHQ why they were wrong. . . . The funny part of it was that the more we sat down to try and convince ourselves that GHQ was wrong, the more we saw that their policies in fact were the correct ones! . . . The basic mistake of the past . . . was that the Republican Movement concentrated on turning out soldiers. Now there's no reason in the right circumstances why we can't turn out revolutionaries. Our volunteers are now told that they must be able to get up on a platform and articulate the problems of the people; if and when the people fail to get their rights through all the legitimate channels, then they should get down from the platform, take off their politician's hat, put on their army hat and lead the people in armed struggle.[29]

Billy took his mission to combat sectarianism very seriously. He recognized that the same dynamics and pressures were at work in the division of the Republican Movement into factions like the Provisional Alliance in 1970, and the Irish Republican Socialist Party in 1974. Twice, the Provisionals tried to kill him and failed. He eschewed their violent tactics and viewed them as exacerbating the sectarian divide between Catholics and Protestants—a divide he had actively attempted to diminish. Although he argued against that organization and its activities, he was neither in favor of taking up arms against them nor willing to refuse in every situation to withhold cooperation from them.

I had known Billy for several years when I was approached by a government official (neither Irish nor British) to act as an intermediary in a typically Kitsonian scheme. I was to use my friendship with Billy and the others in his organization to persuade them into "clearing out the Provisionals from Lower Falls"—"neutralizing them"—in return for which the British army command would be persuaded to lay off the area, thus giving the Officials a degree of hegemony that could promote their political fortunes in that area. This proposition came in early 1973, when there had been accelerating incidents of dispute between these groups. I took up the matter with Billy, knowing what his answer would be, and because I felt that he should be aware that such efforts were being made to heat up rivalries. Billy took several heavy drags on his constant cigarette, his eyes twinkled, and he laughed. His comments were clear enough: "Those bloody fuckin' bastards are still trying to keep us killing each other," certainly not the eloquent prose of a political genius, but a very clear analysis nonetheless.

When Billy spoke at Bodenstown in June, 1973, at the annual commemoration for Wolfe Tone, the Protestant who founded Irish republicanism two hundred years before, he articulated his own commitment to unity: "Divided and opposed we can only benefit the rulers who have gained from our divisions in the past and who will sell you out just as soon as their interests require it."

It is tragic and paradoxical, but consistent with the rest of Irish history, that the leader who opposed sectarianism and bigotry was finally murdered by one of his own "kind." This unhappy fact was noted in the funeral oration for Liam McMillen, delivered by Cathal Goulding, Chief of Staff of the Official IRA, whose episodes of internment and narrow escapes from death by assassins from rival organizations paralleled McMillen's:

> An Orange junta sent Liam McMillen to prison because he fought for separation. The Provisional Alliance attempted to assassinate him because he held his socialist principles and fought for civil right.

The RUC and the British army of occupation harassed and hounded him because he was a socialist republican. A small, mad band of fanatical malcontents, the sewer rats of Costello and McAliskey who finally laid him low.

Goulding was referring to Seamus Costello and Bernadette Devlin McAliskey, the leaders of the Irish Republican Socialist Party, who were said to have an armed wing, the People's Liberation Army. In previous years, McMillen, Costello, and McAliskey (then Devlin) had shared the same speaker's platforms on many occasions, marched in the same cadre in demonstrations against discrimination and tyranny, and discussed as comrades the implications of socialism for a thirty-two-county Ireland. They shared the conviction that getting the British out of Northern Ireland was not the only solution, but that a democratic, socialist, thirty-two-county Ireland, a workers' republic, would end discrimination and poverty in their beloved land.

The Irish Republican Socialist Party

In 1974, Bernadette Devlin McAliskey—defeated in her bid for another term as member of Parliament for Mid-Ulster; angered by the Officials' public repudiations of her commitment and ideological unorthodoxy; desiring to remain equally part of the Provisionals and the Officials, member of neither; annoyed with the narrowness of the decisions made by hierarchies in both groups, the Moscow orientation of the Officials and the Rome orientation of the Provisionals—joined with other dissidents (many from the Official Republican Movement) to form a new political and paramilitary entity. Those who joined were too far left to be satisfied with the politics of the Provisionals and too committed to armed struggle to content themselves with the Officials' policy of political education with only defensive or retaliatory strikes against the British army.

Ideologically, McAliskey and Seamus Costello are Marxist-Leninists. McAliskey had earlier been involved with the International Socialists. Their thesis is that conducting a massive guerrilla campaign results in chaos that will shatter the capitalist economy (or exhaust it) and the people will be liberated for constructing a socialist state.

Seamus Costello had been a member of the Official Republican Movement. He had been elected to a local council seat in the Irish Republic as a Sinn Fein (Officials) candidate. However, he had never been satisfied with the cease--fire policy of that group, and he opposed the subordination of the military to the political wing and the democratic centralism of the political wing.

Like McAliskey, Costello is not vindictive toward the Provisionals. They and their group are, however, at war with the Officials. Like some of their leaders, many of the members of IRSP were part of People's Democracy, which had formed as a nonsectarian group but failed to recognize their own isolation from the working class, particularly from the Protestant working class.

They catalyzed into an organization out of their appraisal of the May, 1974, Ulster Workers' Council strike.

Shared Power

The Camelot of power-sharing didn't last a year. The period of its existence did serve, however, as a catalyst for more rapid change than had ever occurred before. That year witnessed the Sunningdale agreements, the application of the Emergency Provisions Act to intern Protestants, the split of the Unionist party, bombings in the center of Dublin, and a bombing campaign in England.

Some of the themes, schemes, and leaders interacting in this multidimensional complex emanated from the cultural and historical traditions of Northern Ireland, the Irish Republic, and Britain; others were new, and still others, like the development of the Ulster Workers' Council, were outgrowths of indigenous, unmet needs of the people whose political awareness was accelerating out of the spilt blood itself as if by jet propulsion.

In January, 1974, when the power-sharing executive was scheduled to take office, the UDA and Paisley's DUP scheduled a work stoppage and demonstration against this "abrogation" of their "traditional rights." One "right" for which they were willing to risk lives and everything else was their right to remain British. For some within these groups and for DUP, another traditional right was the right to majority rule in Northern Ireland.

While the joint commissions on law enforcement and commerce were meeting together in Belfast and Dublin, citizens on both sides of the border were challenging the constitutionality of the Sunningdale agreements. The major issue revolved around the Irish government's recognition of the right of the six counties to remain in the United Kingdom.

Kevin Boland, a leading political figure in the Irish Republic, brought suit against his government for recognizing the border in opposition to the 1937 Irish constitution. In the north, Brian Faulkner's assurances to the loyalists that he had wrung this concession out of the Irish government would rest on vapor if the Boland case proved correct. For its part, the Irish government gave repeated assurances to everyone that they had recognized the reality without abdicating their constitutional responsibility.

Those who were engaged in making this new arrangement work were unable to believe that it wouldn't survive; and those who were determined to bring it down were convinced that it would not last six months. Paddy Devlin, Minister for Health and Welfare in the Executive, was one of the most convinced participants. He had been active in Northern Ireland politics since his youthful days in Sinn Fein/IRA, when he was imprisoned along with 178 others during the 1940's. He remained in the IRA until 1950, when he became active in the Irish Labour Party and in the trade union movement. In 1956, he defeated Gerry Fitt for a seat on the Belfast Council and then joined the Northern Ireland Labour Party in 1958. By 1968, Paddy Devlin was a founding member of the Northern Ireland Civil Rights Association. He was elected to Stormont in 1969, the same year that Bernadette Devlin (no relation) was elected member of Parliament for Mid-Ulster.

In 1970, Devlin, along with five other civil rights activists, formed the Social Democratic and Labour Party (SDLP). For a long time, the party was essentially a coalition of opposition politicians rather than a coherent machine. Devlin stood to the left and Republican end of the spectrum of SDLP orientations. Gerry Fitt, a relative latecomer to labor politics, had been a leader of the small Republican Labor Party. Another SDLP leader was Ivan Cooper, who had been active in the New Ulster Movement, then in NICRA, and became in the Executive Minister for Community Relations. Austin Currie (SDLP) became Minister for Housing. He had been active in the civil rights movement since the start of the Dungannon Housing Action Committee. The SDLP as an organization and the individuals within it remained active participants in NICRA until 1972, when SDLP agreed to meet and talk with William Whitelaw. NICRA had undertaken a ban on such dialogue as long as internment was still in effect, and the SDLP, which had walked out of Stormont at the initiation of internment, had vowed against any negotiations.

The Nationalist Party, which had represented the Catholic minority in electoral politics, seldom won more than two or three seats in the Stormont government. Similarly, its record for electing representatives to Westminster was poor. The twelve representatives to which Northern Ireland was entitled in the British Parliament were almost always Unionists. The formation of SDLP in 1969 marked the end of the Nationalist Party as a political entity, although SDLP did include several of the former leaders of that party in its leadership.

During one brief period the Irish Labour Party had an active branch in Northern Ireland, sometimes led by Paddy Devlin, who also joined the leadership of SDLP after a discouraging decade of ILP efforts. Equally unsuccessful in Northern Ireland politics had been the Northern Liberal Party, which identified with the Liberal Party in England, but with even less electoral success than their English colleagues..

The Northern Ireland Labour Party usually managed to elect a few representatives to Stormont. For a long time they had been the only real alternative for Protestant voters. For a brief period they also included in their ranks a few Catholics who espoused a socialist ideology.

Before 1969, Northern Ireland had three political parties, of which only the Unionist Party was ever represented in positions of authority. Within that party there had been some factionalism, but never strong enough to split the party or even to weaken it. The younger members of the party who advocated more rapid economic growth and development seemed satisfied with the ascension to leadership of Captain Terence O'Neill in 1963.

The New Ulster Movement, formed in 1967 largely by dissident younger Unionists, became the breeding ground for the Alliance Party, which emerged in 1970, in much the same way as the civil rights movement became the catalyst for the emergence of the SDLP in 1969.

The Alliance Party, led by Bob Cooper and Oliver Napier, had been increasing in membership and influence since the upsurge of violence that accompanied internment. The Alliance Party offered itself as an alternative to both unionist and republican politics on the emotional appeal of saving lives through the restoration of peace. Its program was so consistent with the Whitelaw proposals that it would be difficult to read either without recognizing the other. From their 1972 brochure, we learn that the party was pledged to

> Support for the constitutional link between Northern Ireland and Great Britain—which is the will of the great majority of all the people of Northern Ireland and on which the standard of living of all of us depends.
>
> Getting rid of the provocative extremism—whether it comes from so-called "Loyalists," "Republicans" or "Revolutionaries." Building up universal respect for the rule of law, administered without fear or favour in every part of Northern Ireland. Rooting out discrimination and injustice.
>
> The guarantee of equal justice to all citizens regardless of their political or religious persuasion. Complete and effective participation in government and public life by people from all sections of the community.
> SECURITY FOR ALL:
> No Political Football—Alliance believes in telling the truth. Political control of our security is going to stay at Westminster. And it will have to stay there; until ordinary people on both "sides" are again strong enough to reject men of violence among them, tough, fearless and impartial security measures are essential.
>
> Alliance will not sit back and let local politicians destroy us all by using this divisive issue as their political football.[30]

After the Bloody Sunday massacre, which resulted in fourteen deaths in Derry on the last Sunday of January, 1972,* the imposition of direct rule in March of that year, and the consequent factionalism of the Unionist Party, Alliance picked up membership from among former unionists, some of whom had figured prominently in previous administrations, like Robin Baillie; and from among the professional population, persons such as Anthony Cinnamond, a barrister who successfully prepared the case against the torture interrogation of prisoners at Palace Barracks; and Basil Glass, who served as Assembly representative for a district of Belfast that includes the wealthy Malone Road as well as the working-class, Loyalist neighborhood, called Trochmona estate.

The Alliance Party and SDLP represent two of the formal systems of political alternatives that evolved out of the clash between the violent machinery of entrenched power and the traditional instruments for violent opposition. Without their formalization into political parties, the experiment in governing by power-sharing could never have been attempted. Neither party, however, had been able to mobilize the working class, which with the old Anglo-Irish aristocracy were most entrenched in their traditional and violent modes of behavior. Not unrelated to this problem was the fact that the new arrangement focused on the electoral process and the functions of the elected representatives.

The Technicians

There were no changes made at the "technological" or "bureaucratic" levels of the very large civil service organization, which actually "pushed the buttons" of government. Although members of the Executive and most of the Assembly were committed to making the scheme workable, no one polled the civil servants to find out how possible it would in fact be to achieve the reforms.

A total of forty-six seats in the Assembly was occupied by parties committed to the program. Thirty seats were held by parties opposed to the plan—VUPP, DUP, and unpledged Unionists. This one-third margin might have guaranteed success, but the majority of the civil servants in Northern Ireland had always been the staunchest supporters of the old unionist system. The problems presented by this dichotomy became apparent to me when in January, 1974, I explored the inner dynamics of two of the new ministries, Health and Welfare and Community Relations, in order to make

*Thirteen of the victims died that day. One man, seriously wounded, lingered on in comatose condition for a few months before he died.

recommendations to their ministers for programs and research. My reports to Paddy Devlin and Ivan Cooper of these respective ministries reflect the nuclear dynamics of the explosion which was then already in motion to shatter the Irish Camelot only six months later (see documents in Appendix).

I enclosed, along with the discouraging report, a memo to Paddy Devlin containing recommendations for instituting some of the necessary changes. I didn't really believe that he or anyone else could initiate necessary programs without changing the whole apparatus and population of the civil service in Northern Ireland:

Proposal for Proposing

Persons presently employed in Civil Service positions administering Health and Welfare are incredibly insensitive, rigid budgetarians, rather than being concerned and creative humanitarians. This is to be expected, I suppose. However, the only way to steer a new course with them and not violate civil service hiring-firing politics, is to set out a policy statement for the Ministry with priorities and objectives clearly delineated. Then, using consultants' services, engage these bureaucrats in finding the means to implement these policies whether or not they match those of, as Mr. Wild put it once, "the rest of the United Kingdom." Start the program with requests for statistical information regarding calls for services (broken down by areas); uses of services (broken down in the same way); statistical information on professional resources; incidence rates on various birth defects and congenital anomalies (by social class); survey rehabilitation resources including medical, psychological, half-way houses, youth services for children and youth who have either been convicted of delinquencies or are addicted to alcohol, drugs; vocational rehabilitation schemes; counseling resources; gather statistical data on upward mobility rates for welfare families—both inter- and intra-generational; records on numbers of persons who have been interned and kinds of services requested and given both during and after their internment. These statistics are a convincing argument and a necessary basis for setting program priorities. Most of these statistics can be easily and inexpensively collected in the central offices from various local records and through asking local personnel to submit reports on requests and services, etc. The information can be readily key-punched, and with simple computer operations, distributions and significance figures can be obtained. Much of the information may already be on file through National Health Service HQ. Data collection and collation should be a comfortable pursuit for bureaucrats who are budgetary minded and tend to think in abstract numbers.

When the information is together and collated, extensive consulting is in order. This will mean translating the figures into remediatory action. Once that kind of planning is in progress, a realistic budget projection may be developed. Good luck and Great Strength to Ye.

As frustrating as were my meetings with the bureaucrats of Health and Welfare, the experience of Community Relations proved even worse. Ivan Cooper, the Minister for Community Relations, had considerable experience in community organizing during his early activism in the civil rights movement. He viewed the task of his ministry as resolution of the sectarian conflict between Protestant and Catholic communities in Northern Ireland. However, his ministry existed only as the fiscal body for the Community Relations Commission, which was staffed by civil servants and had absolute independence in its operations. The commission director, David Rowlands, had been selected for the post through his high scores on university examinations. He had come to Northern Ireland from England only a few years before and had worked as a teacher of Spanish in a private secondary school. The autonomy of the CRC had not enabled it to organize much more than children's play schemes and summer holiday programs. The several research studies undertaken by the CRC proved controversial and were therefore suppressed by its director. On April 3, 1974, Ivan Cooper requested of the Northern Ireland Assembly that the Community Relations Commission be disbanded:

> I do not believe that there is any continuing necessity for an independent body to discharge the other functions, which the Commission presently exercises. The most important of these are to give grants to voluntary bodies in the community relations field; to commission items of research; and to produce relevant publications. I believe that these matters can be dealt with by my Department, and I do not see any need or advantage in having them exercised at one remove from the government.

The policies and programs relevant to the breadth of politics represented in the assembly and the executive remained on the desks of civil servants for implementation. To be a civil servant in Northern Ireland had required demonstrable evidence of support for unionist politics. The fact that Catholics did not have equal access to civil service positions had been one of the focal issues in the civil rights struggle. Thus, there was no reason to expect that these bureaucrats would respond with alacrity to programs aimed at changing their privileged status. They didn't.

When the Ulster Workers' Council began its strike on May 14, 1974, it had access to plans made by the executive to counter the massive work stoppage, and through the assistant secretaries of departments there was also a diversionary body that prevented the political leadership of the executive from receiving valuable information. Paddy Devlin notes in his account of the fall of the Northern Ireland Executive, that

> Monday night Brian Faulkner, who showed rare courage throughout the preceding week in resisting tremendous pressure to negotiate with the UWC, was rung up by a senior Civil Servant who, it is alluded, told him

that the sewage was likely to come back up into the main roads of Belfast any minute because of the intermittent flow of electricity to the pumps.[31]

Devlin's observations reveal the pathological repetition of history once again in Northern Ireland. He recognized the similarity between the 1974 fall and the dynamics of the defeat of the Home Rule Bill in Parliament in 1910–1912. After 1910, the Unionists mobilized the Ulster Volunteer Force to oppose home rule. They were armed with 40,000 rifles, several million rounds of ammunition acquired from Germany, and while they trained and drilled openly, collected over a million pounds from sympathetic Britons. The UVF then threatened to fight the whole British army to remain British. The units of the army stationed in Ireland mutinied when ordered to march against them.

In 1974, with 30,000 troops stationed in Northern Ireland there was not only no attempt made to enforce the actions of the government, but there were not even arrests made when UWC militants and armed UVF and UDA paramilitary units physically assaulted civilians, blocked transportation, and closed down businesses and took over their premises and inventories. Not a single arrest was made during the several weeks of illegal activities.

The London *Observer* commented on the UWC victory celebrations:

> With wailing fifes and huge drums shaking the landscape like cannon, 10,000 Ulster Loyalists today mounted the hill of Stormont to celebrate their victory over the British Government, and to honor the leaders of the strike. And with the bands, and the crowds wearing scraps of sponge as "Harold Wilson's spongers", came a deliberate show of paramilitary strength.
>
> Column after column each formation in its own combat uniform, and each battalion carrying its colours, marched past the contorted statue of Edward Carson, father of modern Ulster.
>
> From the platform on the steps of the Parliament building, from which the government was ejected on Wednesday, the strike organizers and the paramilitary chieftains were presented to the crowd one by one. The tone of the speeches was jubilant but vague.
>
> Mr. Harry Murray, of the Workers' Council, said that the Protestant should learn to love his Catholic neighbor, and help him cast out the evil men from his midst. Col. Brush, boss of the paramilitary Down Orange Welfare, threatened that if Ulster was further spurned it could become a 'thumb on Britain's Atlantic windpipe.'
>
> Dr. Ian Paisley came nearer than ever before to endorsing the notion of independence for Ulster. 'If English and Welsh politicians were not prepared to govern Northern Ireland like any other part of the United Kingdom', he yelled, 'then let the Ulster people do the job for themselves.'[32]

Mobilization of the Masses

The political organizing that mobilized masses of working-class Protestants to topple the power-sharing executive led to the deadlock the following year of the next attempt at forming a government for Northern Ireland—the Constitutional Assembly. It also carried within it the seeds of ongoing violence and destruction. The appeal of the mobilization has been to the one common denominator among the Protestant population— their socioeconomic privilege as Protestants. An example of this is the coalition between the Vanguard Party (VUPP), led by William Craig, whose objective is an independent Ulster (UDI), with the DUP of Paisley, whose objective is total integration within the United Kingdom. Despite their obvious contradiction they joined with yet another apparently incompatible force, the unpledged Unionists whose program is a return to majority rule through a provisional parliament connected by representatives at Westminster with the United Kingdom. The only basis for this strange collection of political bedfellows is their anti-Catholic stance. It appears to be a step backward from the earlier political organizing along social class lines and for different political objectives.

Prime Minister Edward Heath's call for a general election in February, 1974, gave this nascent coalition the stimulus for asserting its strength. Northern Ireland's twelve representatives to Westminster, a delegation including Bernadette Devlin McAliskey and SDLP leaders, fragmented their vote. The earlier unanimity that had formerly enabled the election of minority representatives had vanished through the new poltical alignments among SDLP, republicans, and independents. But the majority, always more cohesive when battling against unity with the south, had its classic basis for mobilization. Thus, in the March 1, 1974, Westminster elections, anti-Sunningdale loyalists won eleven of the twelve seats. This confirmed and bolstered the coalition, which had been in part catalyzed through the frequent regular appearances of Enoch Powell in Northern Ireland to advocate his fascist National Front line.

Despite the insistence of some observers that the power-sharing arrangement broke because of the continued Provisional IRA attacks, and the assertion of others that the development of the Ulster Workers' Council demonstrated Protestant working-class consciousness, there are too many indications that the destruction of that power-sharing government was a function of heightened fascistic activity reinforced by success. On the other hand, the Provisionals' campaign had lost so much support among the Catholic minority that, for the first time in the history of Northern Ireland, a party representing their interests had managed to attract only 8 percent of their vote. If this alternative form of government had not been provided during the period, there is much to suggest that the acceleration of sectarian murders (the majority of the victims Catholics) and the continuance of internment without trial—despite the assurances by Secretary of State for Northern Ireland Merlyn Rees to end internment—could have provided the strongest popular support for IRA violence since 1920.

As the power-sharing executive prematurely fell in disarray and Prime Minister Harold Wilson vacillated between pulling his troops out of Northern Ireland and leaving its contentious citizens to their own bloody devices and finding some new formula for conciliation, other kinds of negotiations commenced on other levels.

In the internment camps Loyalist and Republican prisoners began to join in protest, which culminated in the riots of October 16–17, 1974, that demolished Long Kesh, then renamed "The Maze Prison." While the British government called for a constitutional convention in Northern Ireland as a last-ditch attempt to organize a government, a committee of Protestant clergymen were meeting to try to find a way to stop the Provisionals' bombing campaign.

The Reverend William Arlow and others met with leaders of the Provisional IRA, including Daithi O'Conaill, in Feakle, County Clare, in the Irish Republic during November, 1974. They worked out an agreement that all internees were to be released in return for a Provisional declaration of a cease fire.

The Irish Republic had given up entirely on its plans for an all-Ireland Council and, having been excluded from the Feakle discussions, repudiated those meetings and the cease fire. In July, 1975, Dublin Special Branch detectives arrested Daithi O'Conaill, who had arranged the cease-fire meetings.

But the killings did not stop. They decreased to about a hundred fewer than had occurred the previous year. Emigration from Northern Ireland increased, and many who had been detained were brought to trial in the Special Courts and convicted.

Despite the failure of the constitutional convention to design a government, Merlyn Rees declared on December 5, 1975, that detention was at an end and that the last detainees would be released before Christmas.

Conclusion

When twelve-year-old Connel says "There's no peace now," she is articulating the consensus view of her compatriots. For whether they live in Antrim or Cork, the people of Ireland are participants in and victims of a war for survival that is entering its ninth century of devastation. Whether they are eighty years old or five, the parameters of the individual lives of

Irish people at home and abroad are being dictated by forces of greed that have yet to be repelled or to recede from the shores of that troubled island.

Under such circumstances for so long, can Ireland become a human society—one composed of individuals proud of their identity as persons, rather than as "symbols" sharing "community," rather than arguing about "communion," one wherein there are no exploiters and no exploited—an Ireland in which there is no one "on the run?"

8 Social Control
Irish Ideology and the Mass Unconscious

The institutions that comprise the social system of Northern Ireland and the Irish Republic perpetuate the unconscious ideology implanted through hundreds of years of subjection to colonialism. The social controls that enforce historical re-enactments and compel a minority-group ideology on all members of the society are embodied in the institutions and sustained and perpetuated through them.

In 1971, a member of the Royal Ulster Constabulary tried to explain to me why Lavery's Pub had just been bombed by the Provisionals and Mr. Lavery, a Catholic, blown to pieces. He said, "You see, those fellows think that if they can cause enough trouble, do enough damage, we'll be forced into becoming part of their country. . . . We're a minority group here, and we don't want to be subordinated to their rules . . . we're Protestants, but we're not prejudiced against any section of the community. We just want to stay as we are, we have a right to that, you know." Even though Protestants in fact comprise the majority population in Northern Ireland, they have been functioning as if they are a besieged minority, on the verge of obliteration.

In the same way, in the neighborhoods of Derry where Catholics form a cohesive majority, the dominant theme is signaled by the designation of "Free Derry Corner," which is an intersection surrounded by Catholic residences—a staging area for demonstrations, rallies, and barricades.

Spokespersons for each group rationalize its militant stance as "protection" from the other group. The British army, no less than the other militants, explains its aggressions as "defending the community." The Reverend Desmond Wilson recognized the part played by religious institutions in fostering the mass unconscious ideology of dependency/protection. In an interview in 1972, Father Wilson pointed to the responsibility of the Catholic Church in bringing about the demoralization and dependency of the people:

Look how the Churches establish dependency—they go out preaching, 'You're a worm of the earth. You're nothing but sod and you'll fall into sin', and when they've convinced you that you're terribly weak, they say, 'Ah! we have the means to defend you', and thus they establish control and dependency. . . . The Unionist Party have done the same with the Protestant people, convincing them of 'this terrible monster of Rome'. The Provos do the same, they run around saying, 'Who's going to protect you? Not the British Army. Not the South. Not the Government'. And when the people are all fearful and frightened, the Provos say, 'We will'. That's dependency. . . . The effects of violence on this community have been disastrous. Apathy is the result. It is terribly difficult to get people going. . . . You think north and south the Churches have far too much power. There's far too much subservience to them.[1]

Father Wilson used his insightful analysis to develop alternative institutions in the most depressed, impoverished, embattled Catholic enclave in Belfast, Ballymurphy. His criticism of the relation of his Church to its communicants culminated in a traumatic public confrontation with the hierarchy in 1975. When I interviewed him again at the apogee of his crisis, Wilson examined his own political socialization. He had, through his childhood and youth in Northern Ireland, accepted the religio-political analysis provided by his teachers. After he became a priest and a teacher, his confidence in the approved version of reality was shaken by a student's question that challenged an assumption. He began to develop a new perspective when he realized that Vatican support of the fascist government of Spain contradicted the imprisonment of Spanish priests for their antifascist activities—priests who supported their actions on grounds of religious obligation. The thought stayed quietly within him for a long while.

Father Wilson had protested the exiling of Mother Teresa and her order from their mission in Ballymurphy; the immorality of British army chaplains who turned over to the military authorities information they received in the confessional; and the unwillingness of the Bishop of Down and Connor (his ecclesiastical superior) to protest to the authorities in behalf of the victimized Catholics of Ballymurphy who were being attacked and harassed by the Paratrooper regiment.

His own experience in Ballymurphy where the hierarchy did nothing to promote the earthly well-being of his parishioners reinforced his concern about the politics of Church authority. In May, 1975, Father Wilson resigned as curate. The hierarchy, opposed to his involvement in the economic and political life of his parish, also opposed his wish to resign from the diocese and to function as a worker-priest. Wilson believes that unconcern by the institutional Church will ultimately make it irrelevant, and he is committed to the relevance, the value and necessity of his religion despite its institutional incompetence.

But the churches are merely the institutionalized social control agents of religion, which itself is only one of the agencies that serve every society as its framework and that emanate from its qualities as a social group: myths, mores, customs, language, beliefs, and morals (see Figure 1). While different social systems have different origins and metaphysical objectives, these systems are, in the words of Rousseau, "Graven neither on marble nor on brass, but in the hearts of the citizens . . . [this] creates the real constitutions of the state, which acquires new strength daily . . . preserves a people in the spirit of their institutions, and imperceptibly substitutes the force of habit for that of authority. I speak of manner, customs, and above all, of opinion."[2]

Figure 1   Institutions in a Society (Social Control Agencies)

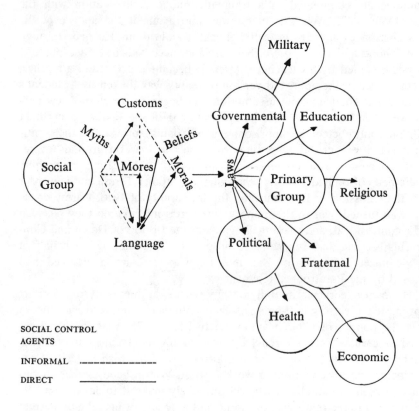

Rousseau was describing how a system of law should relate to its society. In fact, all the social-group characteristics embodied in manners, customs, and opinions do become formalized into a system of law as the social group itself formalizes to become a nation-state, or a non-state nation.* These laws are administered strictly or loosely as the values and survival needs of the society dictate. Such values and needs vary among societies as well as historically and geographically within any society. The social ordering that ensues from the application of the system provides the unconscious ideology for its human membership.

Evidences of these roots of consciousness may be found in the achievement motivation patterns of individuals within a nation-state.[3] They are also evidenced in the relations of that nation with other societies—in its foreign policy. Intrinsic to the system are both the ordering of people into and through subgroupings either horizontally or vertically in hierarchies, and the relative positions of such groups. In short, social roles and identity are formulated out of the unconscious ideology of the social mass, and enacted throughout the society. It is alleged that some nations have undergone drastic changes in adherence to political ideologies but nonetheless maintained a consistent national character. Jung attempted to explain this by reference to "racial memory" and "group unconscious";[4] but the more pragmatic explanation might be found by examining the socialization process, which is the vehicle for both cultural continuity and innovation (see Figure 2).

There are two interacting agencies for exerting social control: institutions and the socialization process itself. Societies and their mechanisms of social control can be examined either in the historical context—always *ex post facto*—or contemporaneously by examining the function or process of one or another institution. Studies of the individual within a society provide another vehicle for examining the impact of the forms of social control and their administration. Such studies of the individual in a society allow measurement of the available alternatives, of aspirations and motivations, of behavior and relationships, of the effects of interactions between the person and the system.

From Social Group to Social System

The commonalities among people—their myths, customs, beliefs, mores, language, and morals—taken together demarcate persons sharing them as

*As defined by Judy Bertelson in a series of papers presented at the International Studies Association annual meeting in 1973, 1974, and 1975, a non-state nation is a group with a claim to nationhood but is stateless. A non-state nation makes a claim in the international arena which is audible and durable.

Figure 2   Nation-State or Non-State Nation

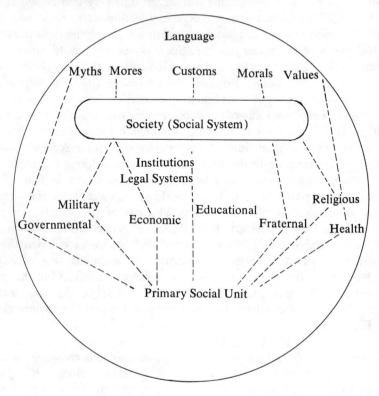

a social group. In order to function as a social system, however, these informal patterns must be formalized into institutions, and thus controlled. To carry out the institution's function, individuals with a degree of technical proficiency in the domain of the institution become its "technocrats" (sometimes called "professionals"). While they implement the mechanisms on an almost case-by-case basis, maintaining consistency over time by minimizing precedents, the informal system itself categorizes behavior and issues self-fulfilling prophecies. Political decision-making may rest with the leader or political elite of a given society, but implementation of the decisions is the domain of the technologically proficient. Complex industrial societies require a wide array of technocrats, for every institution must facilitate the scheme. Even so, it would be impossible for the institutions to facilitate a decision inconsistent with the unconscious ideology of the society. The myth system of the society, intrinsically a social control function itself, is complementary to the status of the "wise one" or technocrat (medicine man in less complex societies). Sometimes the technocrat is so well integrated into the myth system that the "Oracle of Delphi" phenomenon takes precedence over the political leader—as with King Oedipus, who could no longer be a leader to his people after his subjects were convinced of his dishonor. In that Greek myth all the elements of social control are in operation. Oedipus was cast into a role and behavior sequence foredoomed to disaster. This superordination of fate over the strivings of individuals in itself provides the basis of Greek cultural values for the present time. As defined in the mythology, the individual who challenges preordained fate invites personal and social disaster. The contemporary peasant child in Greece is socialized into accepting the vagaries of fortune as personal fate even today.[5]

In sharp contrast with the Greek myths is the Pilgrim's Progress myth system of the Protestant ethic. It glorifies the individual who struggles against all the vicissitudes of fortune in order to achieve his objective. A social control is provided through valuing as "blessed" the individual who is successful in business, family, politics, or profession. This value system is very much in evidence in Northern Ireland, where the assumption of legitimacy of authority is equated with the exertion of economic and political control. Church of Ireland religious tracts regularly document the thesis, even while the religio-politics of the Church advocate ecumenism:

> We always emphasize in our work that a change from Roman Catholicism to the Church of Ireland, which we believe to be purer in doctrine, is not of much avail unless there is also an increase in godly conduct. . . . Without seeking to disparage our Roman Catholic neighbors, they are often less concerned about truthfulness and honesty than they ought to be. We are slow to claim spiritual change until the test of morality reveals a new way of life. . . . At the rear of our Church (just off O'Connell Street, in the centre of the city) there are many neglected families with mentally retarded children, needing also physical care. These are the victims of secondary poverty, caused often by alcoholism amongst the men and inability to cope amongst the women, who are bringing up large families without a proper share of the family income. It is not surprising that one can see in large white letters painted on the walls next to the very big expensive church which sits in the middle of the houses, the hammer and sickle and commendations of Mao and Communism. One could go on to mention other statistics and accounts of life for some in the city and countryside, which reveal a community which in the main has lost heart. The majority Church which dominates most of the education in the schools and control of hospitals and institutions of all sorts, along with the Government, which makes promises of new schemes which are very slow to

appear, must share the major part of the burden for these conditions. . . .
Through a long history of development the Roman Catholic Church has
substituted superstition for sacramental significance.[6]

This tract not only reinforces the belief widely held by the Protestant
majority that Catholicism is an archaic and exploitative religion, but also
supports the belief that it leads the way to that other anti-Christ, Communism. The latter, they aver, also proscribes individual responsibility and
achievement.

Myth systems have an organic relation to mores in their social control
function. Mores are the ways of doing things that are largely accepted as
"the way" without any "why." People may act in violation of the mores of
their society and not be dislodged from it. They will be considered, however, eccentrics or "not normal." Unlike the moral dicta, *mores* are social
controls that can be violated without criminal consequence, but whose
violation does result in a kind of social ostracism. The control strength is
in the desirability of group membership and the need of the individual
human being to interact with others. Mores are subject to change and may
be gradually changed through group acceptance. There is reason to believe,
however, that such change derives from the relative status position of the
person in the group who is attempting to initiate change. It seems that this
process has been experimentally observed in lower primates as well as
among humans. Mores in their simplest form may have to do with what
substances are ingested, or the relative value of different food substances;
how these are prepared and served; who prepares them; and ceremonial
forms that accompany the consumption of foods. Sometimes the social
controls imposed by myths and mores can have far-reaching antisurvival
value for a people. The mid-nineteenth-century famine in Ireland, for instance, was most extensive in the western half of that island, where plenty
of seafood was available. As the famine wore into its third year, of course,
many of the fishermen had sold their boats and equipment in order to
purchase seed or pay their rents. At that point, food from the sea was a
negligible prospect. But the west of Ireland had long been the home of
fishermen, who were accustomed to selling their catches and continue to
do so to this day. During the famine the people did not turn to seafood for
survival.[7] Periwinkles (snail-like creatures found in abundance clinging
to the rocks along the west coast) were rarely utilized for nutrition, even
though catching them required neither boats nor nets. Other sea creatures,
shellfish close to shore or in salt-water pools, were likewise ignored. The
Irish people, says one historian, were unaccustomed to eating fish and unaccustomed also to preparing fish for eating.[8] The controls thus imposed
by this custom prevented the utilization of a major resource and resulted,
of course, in loss of lives. The myth system of the Irish had placed great

store on meat-eating, and indeed, at an early time, meat was the staple of the Irish. The seas off the west coast of Ireland had always been treacherous, and the myths had reflected their unreliability as a source of succor. Morals are a more obvious source of social control. The moral system of a society is not only a product of observation during the socialization process but is the value system which is taught directly to the young. It is a code of taboos to be observed and meritorious deeds expected of members of that society. The social controls extend to punishment for failure to meet the requirements of the moral code. At the same time, living up to the code marks an individual as a respected member of that society. Moral teaching is considered a prime requisite for the pedagogical curriculum of any society. One has only to examine the primers used in the schools of the early American colonies and indeed well into the twentieth century to see how these vehicles for the teaching of basic literacy utilized "moralisms" for that purpose.

Although the moral code reflects the basic value system of a society and provides the basis for social control, it is only the germinal substance out of which the more complex systems are evolved. From it follow ethical codes, legislation, and jurisprudence.

The myths, mores, and morals of a society are expressions, increasingly more complex, of the interpretation and meaning that group imputes to reality and the person. The control systems are means for ordering reality, stabilizing it, responding to it, and surviving in it. Language itself is one of the instruments for this purpose. We see that societies in which reality and survival are predicated on overcoming severe cold (the Eskimo society for instance) developed more words for "snow" and complex moral codes that have to do with surviving these climate conditions than others not concerned with this basic condition. The social control effect of the language itself is to administer relations with this reality, to direct conceptualization of it, and to provide an explanation. Whether or not a language is a written one has further implications for social control. An unwritten language places great value on an oral tradition, on the primacy of the technicians, on a pastoral pattern of geographic mobility and a formalized system of social life. This was the pattern of pre-Christian Celtic Ireland.[9] The Irish language tradition that persists today predicates a very different society from the dominant Anglo-Irish social system, which characterizes Ireland today, north and south.

While controls are exerted throughout the social process of every society, there is variance in their relative strength and the manner by which each is exerted. Thus, it should be possible to map a society and compare it with another by these relative differences. The social process is always a dynamic interaction, however, and, not unlike the problem we face in charting molecular behaviors, the complexity and process is only superficially apparent in two-dimensional diagrams (see Figures 1 and 2). When the network encompasses all social institutions thus having integrity as an entity, there is a nation-state or a non-state nation.[10] The entity may be defined as the former if it is a unit in interaction with other nation-states.

In a major scholarly attempt to examine the dynamic nature of social systems and the relationship of the person to the system, Talcott Parsons and Edward Shils, with several other social scientists, formulated a "theory of action" as theoretical basis for the social sciences. Within the social system, they said, the basic unit of social structures is the role:

> Role situations are situations with potentially all the possible significances.
> . . . Where the stability of the actor of the social system in question is
> maintained, there are certain "control mechanisms" which serve to keep
> the potential dispersion of the actor's reactions within limits narrower than
> would be produced by the combination of the total situation and the
> actor's personality without this specificity of role expectation. . . . Sanctions
> are not invoked against deviance within certain limits . . . like expectations
> sanctions do exert "pressures" on individual actors which . . . generate
> types of strain which in turn may have a variety of social consequences . . .
> and often result in the development of further mechanisms of social con-
> trol or the generation of pressures toward change or in both.[11]

By examining the process through this model, we can begin to deal with the issues of social control and socialization, social change and social stability, sanctions and deviance, and, finally, most important to our understanding of manipulation for destruction of one society by another, we can place the function of the technocrat as a social role into the diagram of social control:

> The equilibrium of social systems is maintained by a variety of processes
> and mechanisms. . . . The two main classes of mechanisms by which
> motivation is kept at the level and in the direction necessary for the
> continuing operation . . . are the *mechanisms of socialization* and the
> *mechanisms of social control*. The mechanisms of socialization are those
> mechanisms which form the need-dispositions making for a generalized
> readiness to fulfill the major patterns of role-expectation. . . . The mecha-
> nisms of socialization in this sense must not be conceived too narrowly. . . .
> [The process] operates mainly through the mechanisms of learning of which
> generalization, imitation and identification are . . . particularly important.
> . . . Two main levels may be distinguished . . . in the identifications formed
> through attachments of early childhood. . . . At a later stage, . . . the
> child acquires orientations to more specific roles and role complexes.[12]

Parsons and Shils do not categorize the socialization process itself as a function of social control mechanisms, but rather see them as separate but interacting mechanisms. If the socialization process were entirely a vehicle for the imposition of social controls (if such were possible for the human organism, and it is unlikely), then social change would be impossible—or at least improbable. They say:

> Even if the strains which come from inadequate socialization and from changes in the situation of the social system in relation to nature or to other social systems were eliminated, the problems of control would still persist. Tendencies toward alienation are endogenous in any social system. . . . There cannot be a society in which some of the members are not exposed to a conflict of values. . . . It is impossible for the *distribution* of the various constitutional endowments to correspond exactly to the distribution of initial or subsequent roles and statuses in the social system, and the misfits produce strains. . . . Where a sense of deprivation is associated with a collectivity or a class of individuals who come to identify themselves as similarly deprived in the allocation of roles, abilities, and rewards, the tasks of the control mechanisms and the strains on the system, become heavy indeed.[13]

There are three mechanisms of social control described by Parsons and Shils as being only an example of many such mechanisms. Each of the mechanisms is the province of specific kinds of technocrats for application and manipulation. These "middle managers" of the social system are, in effect, the "watch dogs" of the social order. The way they wield the mechanisms plays a major part in assuring either equilibrium or disintegration of a system. The following is a statement of the mechanisms as described by Parsons and Shils, and opposite them, the description of the kind of technocrat and institutional means for application.

Mechanism	*Technocrat* (Professional)
1. One of the most prominent and functionally most significant of them is the artificial identification of interests through the manipulation of rewards and deprivations. This is the exercise of authority in its integrative function. . . . Much of the integration in instrumental institutional complex is achieved through this artificial identification of interests. . . . The weaker the consensus . . . and the larger the social system, the greater the share borne by these mechanisms in the maintenance of some measure of integration.	Stockbrokers, industrial executives, government bureaucrats, legislators, educational elites (fix criteria and rewards for matriculation at each educational level)

2. Certain types of deviant behavior . . . are sealed off, and thereby their disruptive personalities are restricted . . . in . . . isolation they cannot have . . . direct effect on the behavior of other members of the society. . . . This mechanism operates with both the criminal and the ill. On the collective level, it operates in the case of "deviant" and "interstitial" "subcultures" which are not positively fully integrated with the main social system. . . . Segregation is the spatial consequence of the operation of insulation.

Legal professions, including magistrates, judges, lawyers; police; sometimes military; educators (sometimes); media specialists (by omission or definition of an individual or group); clergymen; health professionals

3. Another type . . . is contingent reintegration. The medical profession exposes the sick person so far as his illness constitutes his "deviant" behavior to a situation where the motivation to his "deviance" is weakened and the positive motivations to conformity are strengthened. What is . . . conscious or unconscious psychotherapy, is, from the viewpoint of the social system a mechanism of social control.

Health professionals, correctional workers; social workers; psychotherapists; counselors; clergymen; educationists.

Since social systems at best are not thoroughly integrated, and since personalities vary so widely within a social system, the potential for stability or change is inherent in the application of the social control mechanisms operating in conjunction with the mechanics of socialization.

What happens in a social system which changes, either through a hero-leader, as Sidney Hook would have it, or through a consensual shift in value orientations among the dominant sector? By utilizing all the machinery of social control, wielding it inflexibly and with reinforcement from some reference to the relevant aspects of the myth and mores systems, a high degree of conformity can be achieved—at least for a period. In order to sustain it, however, there must be support from the technocrats who dominate the machinery of social control. Thus, without reinforcements from the legal profession, without adherence by the health profession, without cooperation from educators, it would be impossible to implement the new system.

Nazi Germany: A Classic Example

The particulars of political ideology may vary among social systems that have wielded absolute control over their members, but one of the classic examples of this kind of social ordering is the Nazi system. Fascism is the particular political ideology in this case but a dictatorship, of the right or the left, can more efficaciously accomplish a swift and drastic reordering. Furthermore, ideology would appear to be irrelevant to the kind of closed-mindedness essential for maintaining the system.[14]

Paul Bookbinder and Raul Hilberg, in separate papers, presented at a 1973 conference on the Holocaust the jurisprudential, administrative, and bureaucratic mechanisms through which the social control system of Nazism was implemented and sustained. These papers provide evidence of two kinds of "social imperative": (1) the social system operates its control mechanisms through its institutions consonant with the governmental philosophical objective; (2) the technocrats (professionals) must be recruited by the system to sustain or even invent the control mechanisms. As Hilberg notes:

What happened then was interlocking decision making by accountants, lawyers, engineers and technocrats, one dependent on the other. When, for example, the time came for deporting the Jews, the regional or local SS and Police Officers had to procure the necessary rail transportation to bring the victims from their point of origin to one of the camps in Poland . . . the SS had to contact the German railways well in advance . . . railroad conferences were called in several German cities every few months to determine the movement of "special trains" throughout Europe. . . . Each station master along the route was notified of a . . . train passing through. . . . Imagine a transport leaving Holland or France, Italy or Greece for Auschwitz. It passed not only through various countries but also through several currency zones and in this traversal the balance of payments was invoked every time the transport passed a border. . . . We see endless correspondence on this point, starting with the so-called Special Accounts which were created at the request of the Gestapo. . . . Let us take another example. How exactly would one have gone about setting up a concentration camp or killing center? Basically, the process was begun by the acquisition of real estate and this required a condemnation proceeding. Next it was necessary to procure materials . . . rather scarce hydrogen cyanide was made available. . . . The diversity of the German apparatus and the specialized talents . . . are indication that Jewry was annihilated by processes which were legal, administrative and technical in character. . . . But not only Germans engaged in bureaucratic behavior—the Jews as well were accustomed to routines. Here too we see much that is ordinary and everyday, *that is built upon Jewish traditions, rooted in Jewish institutions, and run according to Jewish conceptions and laws.* . . . The Jewish councils were double agents, responsible to the Jewish community which they represented, while at the same time taking orders from the German destructive apparatus under which they functioned. . . . That is why ghetto life . . . appears to be such a painful exertion to preserve normality. There were hospitals, trying to heal the sick who were soon to be loaded on cattle cars; schools attempting to educate the young who would never grow up; kitchens feeding starved people who were going to be snuffed out in the gas chambers. [Italics added.][15]

Or, if we look at the jurisprudential system—courts, the legal profession, the police enforcement agencies and the prisons—we can find a synopsized, encapsulated version of the objectives and nature of a particular system. Again, we have the example of the role of the German legal institution in the extermination of the Jews. Bookbinder examines this in historical detail:

German jurists, both theoreticians and practitioners, played a clear and significant role in the persecution and eventual extermination of the Jews. . . . There are several aspects to the consideration of the relationship of the German legal system to the holocaust. The most significant aspect concerns the actions and writings of the jurists which undermined the position of the Jews during the years of the Third Reich. . . .

For centuries, from the era of Charlemagne to the period shortly before the final unification of Germany, Jews had been treated in a manner that differed from that in which other Germans had been treated. There was tremendous fluctuation from era to era with conditions deteriorating and improving depending upon the person of the ruler and his needs, general conditions of law and order, and often on economic conditions. . . .

The structure of the judiciary, their method of training and selection was fixed in 1879 and was not significantly changed until 1933. . . . The products of this six-year training process developed a more national and more uniform Weltanschauung than any other group within the nation. The jurists tended to be totally committed to the state, highly nationalistic and, in spite of the high number of Jews proportional to their percentage of the population, generally, anti-Semitic. . . . The jurists retained their privileged position within Germany during the Weimar years. The Weimar Reichstag . . . did not prove to be an effective governing body . . . this weakness gave the judiciary a great deal of independence and power. . . . The popular judicial notion of Weimar years [is] summarized by a short poem:

The law is not holy
Only right is holy
And the law is subordinate
to right.

When Adolf Hitler and the National Socialists took power, the judiciary played a different role. First, legal theoreticians provided the National Socialists with the arguments they needed to concentrate complete power in their own hands. . . . At the same time, the judiciary undermined its own position by transferring areas of legal jurisdiction to the National Socialist administration. . . . Karl Bracher states, "German legal science rushed to present the Third Reich with an airtight theory of the leader state." . . . The re-writing of early German history to fit National Socialist purposes which went on in the 1930's represents one blatant example of knowing distortion by jurists which helped to justify anti-Semitic policies.[16]

The German legal system under National Socialism instituted laws and practices, supported differential systems of treatment under law, and functioned under a jurisprudential system that has corollaries in military law and in the specific case of the Special Powers Acts and Emergency Provisions Acts, under which Northern Ireland has operated since the first day of its existence. This is not to suggest that law can consistently function over a prolonged period in contradiction to a state social system, although we see that German jurisprudence did manage to do that during the Weimar Republic. However, legal theorists and jurists can through their philosophy of the intent of law, or the underlying philosophy of jurisprudence itself, determine the nature of its application. Bookbinder points out: "Far more dangerous for the Jews was the friend-foe theory advocated by many jurists whereby society was divided into two camps. The friends stood within the legal system, the foes placed themselves outside of it."[17] This is neither new nor unique to the German legal system under National Socialism. We have already noted that one purpose of the Statute of Kilkenny, enacted in 1366, was to place the "Irish race" outside the law, and to mark them as foes of society. The later German philosophy reiterates this institutional racism:

Carl Schmitt was the chief legal theoretician who defined the friend-foe principle in the early years of the National Socialist Regime. He argued that the basis of politics was the creation and separation of groups of friends and foes. Schmitt never clearly spelled out the criteria by which the friends and foes could be identified, but he was quite clear about certain characteristics of the foe. *The foe was the national enemy.* He would live within the geographical confines of the nation, but spiritually he was always an alien enemy. . . . Schmitt was also quite clear about the relationship of the legal system to the foe. When the foe lived within the society he was not entitled to the protection of the legal system which was created for the protection of the loyal friends. Schmitt distinguished between the criminal actions committed by deviant members of the friends' group and actions committed by members of the foe. The former, which did not threaten the fabric of the society, could be handled by the legal system; the latter fell outside that framework. *Clearly such an argument provided a basis for the various protective custody regulations of the Gestapo and the SS.* [Italics added.][18]

As we have seen, this definition and use of the purpose of a jurisprudential system have counterparts in the Special Powers and Emergency Measures acts: the special courts or tribunals established to hear testimony and enact judgment in a contrary way from the regular magisterial system in Northern Ireland, and, of course, the whole issue of differences in legal systems and in application of the law between the imperial homeland and a colonial people as evidenced wherever British dominion has been established in the world.[19] The very nature of guilt itself rests on the jurisprudential philosophy of the legal system, as in Nazi Germany, where

the judiciary made at least one more specific contribution to the profession that led to the holocaust. This contribution was the re-definition of the concept of guilt. . . . Schmitt, who worked to influence the legal system on behalf of the National Socialists, can illustrate the development. In his doctoral dissertation written in 1910, he had investigated the views of the major jurists concerning the nature of guilt and the relationship between guilt and punishment. He declared that basically guilt was not psychological, philosophical, or religious; it was primarily political. *He argued that a man was guilty if he acted in a way that was inconsistent with the needs of the state and the purposes of the collective will of the people.* The extent of the guilt was determined by the value to the state of the person or object damaged by his action. [Italics added.][20]

There are many examples of such institutional functions as social control mechanisms for supporting the Nazi system in Germany. Those that emanated from the legal system are perhaps the more dramatic, but the role of jurists is paralleled by that of other professionals within the system.

Legal and Governmental Institutions

The Special Powers Acts and its successor, the Emergency Provisions Act, are predicated on a friend-foe theory of law. But the social control mechanism wielded by the legal and governmental institutions of Northern Ireland extend much further in their discriminatory application and discretionary powers. The following instances reported in the June–July, 1974, newsletter of the Northern Ireland Civil Rights Association point to some of these mechanisms and their application:

15the May   Two UDR men are cleared of the assault of James Conroy and James Tierney near Beragh, Co. Tyrone, in the spring of 1974. Following the incident in question, Conroy had required hospitalisation, but Judge Watt found that the two accused men could not be held at fault even though both were well known to Conroy and Tierney as neighbours and identified by them as their assailants.

16th May   In the High Court, Mr. Justice Gibson held that Seamus Cusack was "on the balance of probability" unarmed when shot dead by an unidentified member of the British Army on 8 July 1971. He further stated that the soldier was not reasonably justified in believing 'that Cusack was armed and that he had not given a warning before opening fire. He concluded, however, that Cusack's negligence was equal to that of the soldier for apparently participating in a riot occurring at the time of the shooting. (One is tempted to ask Mr. Justice Gibson since when has the penalty for riotous behaviour been changed from six months to the death penalty?)[21]

It is not "law and order" that has broken down in Ireland, but rather the "Rule of Law." The questions whether to arrest, whether to prosecute, what the charge shall be, and even whether the case shall be tried in court or tucked away under detention are decisions dated more often by politics than by jurisprudential systems. When a crime is believed to have been politically motivated, the case is dealt with by the judge and (or) jury in a way that more often reflects their politics than it does a relationship to evidence or legal precedent.

In many areas the Rule of Law is a function of paramilitary extremists applying coercion for infractions of their code. Such applications of punishment are rarely, if ever, challenged by the formal legal system. This merely illustrates the basic problem with law throughout the history of Northern Ireland—that is, the source of the law's authority is perceived to be external to one or the other, and sometimes to both, of the communities that comprise Northern Ireland society. As a colonial legal system, law in Ireland has been an instrument of domination rather than an articulation of the moral code and values of the indigenous social system itself. The introduction of the British army into the circle of contenders for legitimate authority did nothing to establish legitimacy. In fact, it presented a third kind of litigant, for whom yet another system of jurisprudential decision-making applied. Witness the following discussion reported in the May, 1974, NICRA newsletter:

The Course of "Justice"
In a democratic society equality before the law is one of a citizen's most fundamental rights. When double standards and discrimination are used in administering the law, and when in fact, some people are considered more "equal" than others, the system of "justice" becomes meaningless and the

law moves perilously closer to Brig. Kitson's cynical view that the law should be nothing more than a mere propaganda exercise to be manipulated by and for the political and military powers that be.

Discrimination in Granting Bail
The granting of bail is a case in point. An accused person's right to bail is meant, in part, to be a recognition that an accused person is innocent until proven guilty. But in the past in Northern Ireland flagrant discrimination in granting bail always meant that certain people were considered more innocent than others—and this continues to be true today. While many men, women and children languish in prison for up to a year on remand others charged with similar offences—most notable members of the security forces—are allowed to go free.[22]

The legal and governmental institutions have in common with the other institutions of Northern Ireland, and often also with those of the Irish Republic, the colonial characteristic of a control mechanism emanating from the political exigencies of a foreign social system. Some remarkable commonalities may thus be found in the legal and governmental institutions of Northern Ireland and India—two otherwise very different social systems. Jaggat Nahrain, a legal scholar who has studied and worked in both systems, emphasizes the impossibility of enforcement inherent in this kind of legal system. One of the problems, of which, is the lack of definition of "political crime." The effects of categorizing political opposition to an imperial regime as "criminal" is to give the movement a pre-political character.

The Enforcement Agencies: Military and Police
Whereas the major mechanisms for social control by the legal and governmental institutions are through the court and prison systems, another mechanism has, as its purpose, the conservation of established authority. In Northern Ireland, this mechanism is made up of the Royal Ulster Constabulary and the former reserve group, the "B" Specials; the Ulster Defence Regiment, a local militia affiliated with the British army as reservists; and the British army itself.

As of 1969, when rioting broke out in Derry and Belfast, there were 3,000 RUC men, of whom 10 percent were Catholic; 50 officers of whom 6 were Catholic; 120 head constables of whom 16 were Catholic.[23] The RUC had its origins in the Irish Constabulary, designated "Royal" by Queen Victoria for its success in dealing with the Fenian rising. It was formed along semimilitary lines with officers who were either of commissioned rank in the British army or who had entered the force as cadets, specially selected for their educational and class background. As in the army, a strong distinction was made between officers and men on the basis of social class origins. In the last quarter of the nineteenth century, the Belfast RIC earned a reputation for savagery toward civilians in the quelling of riots. During the 1886 riots in Belfast, they used buckshot to ward off rioting crowds. Despite the death and destruction in that year, more riots ensued the following year and twice again in the next decade. During this period, Protestant rioters were as opposed to the constabulary as were Catholics.[24] Since it was composed of an all-Irish body and the enlisted men whose regiments were often rushed to Belfast included larger proportions of Catholics than did the Belfast constabulary, Protestant demagogues whipped up their followers to oppose this "Papist invasion force." In fact, the officers of all regiments were predominantly Protestants. It was necessary in the 1880's and 1890's to augment the RIC with regular army regiments in the Shankill and Sandy Row areas where Protestant extremists usually mobilized their riot forces. In the 1893 riots, at least a hundred constables were seriously injured.

By 1913 the anti-home rule forces had mobilized into an organization called the Ulster Volunteer Force. This organization, related to the Orange Order, as well as the opposing development of an armed revolutionary force dedicated to establishing an Irish Republic, so polarized the population of three of the northern counties that the RIC emerged as the institutional force for the conservation of union with the United Kingdom. In 1920, the formation of the Ulster Special Constabulary as an arm of the Royal Ulster Constabulary reinforced the agency as the social control agency for maintaining a Protestant Ulster. On September 2, 1920, at a conference of ministers in London presided over by Bonar Law, Lord Privy Seal, Sir James Craig, the first Prime Minister of Northern Ireland, declared the political situation in Ulster was deteriorating so rapidly that civil war was threatened. He requested the appointment of an Under Secretary to Belfast and the transfer of troops and police there to his authority from that of the RIC command in Dublin. He proposed a force of 2,000 full-time special constables to assist the RIC in the six counties, to be armed and organized along military lines, and a part-time force of special constabulary be raised from the "loyal" population, which would come under the command of the RIC Divisional Commander in Ulster but be commanded by local officers. Sir Arthur Hezlet describes the mobilization of the special constabulary by Craig:

> Craig also proposed that in the event of a general rising by the rebels
> . . . or in the event of the withdrawal of the army from the North of
> Ireland, the pre-war Ulster Volunteer Force should be rearmed for the
> defence of the country.

The meeting came to the decision that it was right to separate Ulster administratively and that it was desirable to form a force of Special Constables at once. The next day the Ulster Unionist Council issued a statement demanding full and immediate protection of those whose lives and property were imperiled by the disturbances. . . .

The formation of Special Constabulary was viewed with disfavor by General Macready, who feared that it might sow the seeds of civil war and necessitate the intervention of the army, so proving a drain on his resources. . . . Sir Henry Wilson, the chief of the Imperial General Staff was also nervous about arming Special Constabulary without putting them under military discipline. . . .

From July onwards, the Unionists in Co. Armagh had begun to organize themselves for their own protection and there were indications that the Ulster Volunteer Force was being reorganized in all six counties. . . . There was friction in Lisburn in November when the RIC prosecuted some of the Special Constables for riot.[25]

Between 1920 and 1922, three hundred people were killed in the six counties, many of them by some estimated 50,000 special constables who were under arms. Three police forces existed: the Royal Irish Constabulary, which, through the administrative partition of the six counties, became the Royal Ulster Constabulary; the "A" Specials, who were mostly former soldiers; and the "B" Specials, part-time militia who were former members of the UVF—the group that had threatened to fight the British army in order to remain British and illegally shipped in weapons from Germany in 1913!

In 1969, it was the "B" Specials that were responsible for armed incursions into the Catholic areas of Belfast and Derry. The report of the Cameron Commission, investigating the August, 1969, riots, and the Hunt Commission report that followed it recommended the disbanding of the "B" Specials because, being sectarian, the members were unlikely to be able to act impartially.[26] The Stormont government rejected this recommendation, but was compelled by Westminster to accept it or be superseded by legislation from Westminster disbanding the group. The Hunt Commission also recommended an unarmed police force, but this was not acted upon. A police authority was set up, however, which did include some prominent Catholics.

As a local militia, the Ulster Defence Regiment was formed and placed under the direction of the army command. The UDR is charged with defending the border and is therefore almost entirely Protestant.

Substantiated allegations have been made that UDR members are also UDA volunteers, and that weapons in their hands become weapons legitimated in the hands of a Protestant paramilitary organization. Furthermore, the 100,000 weapons that were licensed mostly to members of the Specials were never recalled.

There is little room to doubt that gun power is an effective social control mechanism, especially when it is in the hands of established governmental authority. No bill of rights or guarantee of civil liberties operates in Northern Ireland. Gerrymandered electoral districts and property requirements for voting have functioned to eliminate any possibility of majority rule with concurrent minority rights.

The primary social control agency through which all the institutions of any society function is of course, the legal system. In the case of Ireland, the system of law has been devised to sustain foreign control over a subject people through the establishment of a network of institutions which have as their major objective the perpetuity of that status.

The Health Professional as Control Agent

Although all health professionals generally play roles complementary to the social system and supportive of its objectives, there would seem to be a less obvious or dramatic function to the role of general physician than perhaps there would be for roles of psychiatrist, psychologist, or other mental health professionals. Basic to all of them, however, are the professionalism and guild structures of the physician. Like the jurist, the physician can perform differentially according to class of patient if the guild ethic condones such actions. We have only to look at the rapidly growing literature on human experimentation to realize that a differential value is placed on the lives of prisoners and the poor in the ethics of health care.[27]

In an earlier chapter the unequal statistics of disease and mortality figures for Northern Ireland in comparison with the rest of the United Kingdom were mentioned. Such facts under the twenty-year-old national health service might be rationalized as "typical" of the failures of that scheme where unemployed and working-class populations are concerned. The facts as revealed in numerous recent studies show that this stratum of the population must expect to wait up to seven years for a simple tonsilectomy if they cannot get on a private surgery schedule! Of course, this depends on where in the United Kingdom they live. But whatever may be said about the inadequacies of the scheme in other parts, Northern Ireland has without question got the worst scores in every department.[28]

When the national health service came into being, Northern Ireland was already at the lowest health, welfare, and living standard of any part of the United Kingdom. Rather than eradicate this differential, the health care institutions of Northern Ireland as a colony were predicated on the ideology of inferiority by virtue of difference, if not by virtue of class.

To examine the institution of health care in the abstract, we must divide it into several parts: first, the training and guild structure of the professionals, or "technocrats," of this institution; second, the role of the institution as a social agency; third, the mechanisms or distribution of its control.

As of 1972, Northern Ireland had ninety-seven hospitals operating under the Hospitals Authority and practicing discrimination in the selection of specialists working in them. Of the 3,877 specialists only 31 were Catholic. Sixty-one of the specialists held teaching posts at Queen's University, but only three of these were Catholic. This is in sharp contrast with the general practice doctors, among whom nearly a third were Catholic (almost the same as the proportion of Catholics in the general population).[29]

Institutional discrimination extends beyond the hospitals' selection of specialists to the dissemination of training grants for specialists. These are determined by the Hospitals Authority on the basis of applications from general practitioners. A kind of double bind occurs in this procedure. The applicant must be accepted for the specialty training program (usually at a university in England or Scotland) before he can be eligible for a grant. An applicant, however, is not eligible for the program unless he can prove he will receive the grant funds. Thus, by delaying approval of the grant, the Hospitals Authority can void the applicant's matriculation to the program, even though he has already been deemed acceptable and qualified. In the case of one Catholic physician accepted for a specialization in Biomedical Engineering, although the grant was delayed, he nonetheless presented himself at the university to commence the program, having borrowed £2,400 to present as proof that he could support himself for the year of study. The grant was not awarded until he was halfway through the program. His was not an isolated experience.

This kind of discrimination is reflected in shortages of some specialties. During the past six years, while massive violence has been commonplace and head injuries rife, there was only one neurosurgeon in Belfast, the metropolitan area that contains one-third of the population of Northern Ireland!

Hospitals are administered by management committees. Of the 436 persons on management committees as of 1972, only 72 were Catholic. Members are chosen for their "reliability." In Derry, which has a 65 percent Catholic population, only 7 of the 21 management committee members were of that faith. In that hospital only 12 percent of the matrons were Catholic.[30]

Governing health care facilities are Medical Officers and Deputy Chief, referees, full time and half time. As of 1969, the only Catholics in this service were six part-time referees. Not one Catholic was then employed as Chief County or Borough Medical Officer, or as Deputy Chief Medical Officer. No Catholic was employed as Borough County Chief Dental Officer, or as Health Inspector at the borough level. Of the sixteen public health inspectors only three were Catholic.[31]

Royal Victoria Hospital, which is located in the midst of the heaviest concentration of Catholic population in Belfast, became the site for a major army artillery emplacement. In the summer of 1972, when I was waiting in one of the lobbies for a colleague with whom I had an appointment, the administrative receptionist told me "the reason" for the troubles. She said that it "is all because they don't know how, and refuse to control their breeding." She went on describing the derelict sexual behavior of the local population and finally, when I asked her what group she was referring to, she said "Why, the papists, of course!" She could hardly be expected to welcome and serve sympathetically hospital patients or their visitors identifiable as Catholics. But more dramatic and symbolic of the Royal was another experience that same year. The hospital staff cafeteria provides well-balanced meals at a relatively low cost. The washrooms have hot and cold running fater, paper towels, and all the sanitary amenities, including showers. Children living in ancient attached houses across the street from the hospital never experience a wholesome, well-balanced meal, hot and cold running water, paper towels, and all the sanitary amenities, including inside toilets. With several of the students who had come to Belfast with me that summer, I'd got into the practice of taking five or six Leeson Street children to the Royal for lunch—different children each time, but at a rate of about twice a week. By carefully rotating children, we figured that a goodly number might experience the wholesomeness and sanitation lacking in their lives. It was not an unorthodox approach to teaching hygiene. We had confided the nature of our program to a child psychiatrist at the child-guidance clinic associated with the hospital. He assured us that if our legitimacy was challenged we could invoke his name for the authorities. In late August, however, after my students had returned to the United States and our psychiatrist friend was on holiday, I took several Lower Falls children and two of my own children into the cafeteria for lunch. We had been seated, with our trays, less than five minutes, when the security chief rushed to our table and insisted that we leave immediately. I invoked the name of our friend and used my professional titles, but to no avail. He insisted that "this facility is for hospital personnel *who belong here*." I pointed to the armed, uniformed soldiers sitting at the table next to ours and said, "Do they belong here?" He grew angry and refused to answer. I stood up, pointed to the children, asked them to rise, and said, "Well, these children live here, belong here, and it's their hospital and their families' hospital. But it's clearly more important to the hospital that the army be well fed than that the people living here be healthy." We were then ushered out with the aid of the soldiers.

Little more hope of professional responsibility seems available from the doctors. Several have been outspoken about the treatment of prisoners. Dr. J. P. Lane, a former army surgeon and prominent gynecologist, returned his service medals after examining the effects of depth interrogation on some of his young countrymen. His eldest son was mysteriously assassinated. A colleague of his also spoke out about the brutalities. He and his two young sons were ambushed in their car, and in the shooting that followed, his eldest son was killed. Several other physicians documented in the media and professional journals the human destruction; they received warning letters from the British Medical Association about their unprofessional conduct. A young doctor in Derry en route to answer an emergency call was detained by an army patrol. He begged to have another physician called to his patient. He was not allowed to make any contact and the patient died. He protested this interference and received a written chastisement for his protest.

Most of the medical people in Northern Ireland have chosen to remain silent. A few of them comment on the positive value of expressing aggression and the concomitant decline in suicide rates. These statements are carried widely in the media.[32]

British army physicians and psychologists have been accused of utilizing their special position in relation to prisoners in order to obtain confidential and incriminating information, which is then turned over to the special branch or army to be used against that individual or group. Sammy Smyth described an incident in which he and a companion, Joe Mulvenna, were stopped at a checkpoint en route to Belfast. They were made to leave the car and despite their protests were brought into the army barracks for questioning. They became suspicious when the physician at the barracks began to question them about what they'd "really been up to" on the grounds that Sammy's blood pressure was up. There have also been incidents of examinations—made upon order by special branch—by a psychiatrist from Purdysburn Hospital (the mental hospital just outside of Belfast) of men who had been put through depth interrogation. The reports by the psychiatrist were never relaid to or discussed with these "patients" or with their families.

Besides allegations of collusion in regard to confidentiality, other allegations have been made of collusion between local physicians and the military and special branch to cover up brutalities. Father Denis Faul and his colleague Father Raymond Murray have made their special concern the documentation of brutalities inflicted on Catholics through the RUC and army interrogation and internment system. In "Doctors and Detention Centres" they relate their findings:

> We find the participation of British Army medical doctors in the conducting of interrogations . . . to be unethical. We are convinced that the chief purpose of the medical examination prior to interrogation is to ascertain the fitness of the man to stand up to brutality.. . . . These doctors

are playing a conspicuous part in the infliction of brutality upon detainees. . . .

The medical examination at the end of the 48 hours [of interrogation], prior to a removal to a place of detention, appears to be of a most cursory kind, and its main purpose seems to be to minimise or to provide false excuses for the injuries received—for example—the statement of Kevin Anderson: "When he was writing (the doctor) I heard him mutter under his breath 'fall.' "

Here in Northern Ireland the Catholic community feel that the doctor mentioned in paragraph 54 of the Compton Report, who supervised the torture of eleven "hooded" men for six days—11th August–17th August, 1971—is unworthy to remain a member of the medical profession. Likewise, the doctors who were on duty on the 9 and 10 August, 1971, in Ballykinlar Camp and Girdwood Barracks seem to our people to have fallen below the standard expected of their profession.

We regret to have to report that 2% of the adult Catholic population have been arrested and interrogated by the British Army and the R.U.C. Our community is deeply disturbed by well-proven stories of brutality and the part played in them by medical personnel.

We wish to draw your attention to internationally accepted ethical principles of the medical profession which we feel to have been violated: –

The Oath of Hippocrates: "I will abstain from all intentional wrongdoing and harm, especially from abusing the bodies of man or woman, bond or free."

International Code of Medical Ethics (adopted by the Third General Assembly of the World Medical Association held in London, England, October 1949): "Under no circumstances is a doctor permitted to do anything that would weaken the physical or mental resistance of a human being."

Declaration of Geneva, 1948: "Even under threat I will not use my medical knowledge contrary to the laws of humanity. . . ."[33]

Medical practitioners and other health professionals in Northern Ireland are members of the British Medical Society or their respective professional equivalents. A few maintain membership in the Irish Medical Society, and some psychologists in the Irish Psychological Association. The names become confusing because there is, on the one hand, the Irish branch of the British Medical Association (and of the British Psychological Society), which means that it encompasses professionals practicing in Northern Ireland; it should not be confused with, on the other hand, the Irish Medical (or Psychological) Association, which is essentially a guild of the professionals practicing within the Republic.

There is no Northern Ireland branch of the British Society for Social Responsibility in Science, a watchdog organization that, in the rest of the United Kingdom, directs its energies to issues of ethical and social responsibility within and by scientists, including health professionals as a major component. BSSRS publishes a periodical, *Science for People*, which included in its October, 1972, issue an article of mine about the use of psychology in the torture of prisoners, the general inadequacy of mental health care, and the careless dissemination of tranquillizers and sedatives in Northern Ireland. The president of the British Psychological Society was incensed at my charges and at BSSRS for publishing them. He demanded my presence in his office and castigated my BSSRS colleagues and myself with statements like, "Why I was carrying placards while you were still in diapers!" and "Our standards and practices in mental health care here in Britain are far more advanced than anywhere else in the world!" and "Of course we use electric shock treatments extensively. It's no one else's business to spy on our in-hospital treatment procedures!"

The health institution comprises a formidable social control agency for maintaining the established political and social system in Northern Ireland. Like arms of health institutions anywhere else, physicians and hospital authorities can mandate health standards and norms and thus categorize deviant behavior and provide contingent reintegration. In Northern Ireland this is done by classifying as sick those who refuse to accept the political system or who are anxiety-ridden as a result of the ongoing violence and by treating them with massive doses of tranquillizers, electric shock, or hospitalization. Yet others who are physically or emotionally harmed by the system may not have their damage adequately diagnosed or treated. Numerous cases of severe emotional damage have been induced by depth interrogation, but have not been attested by physicians, or, if attested, the physicians' appraisal has been denied.

The control mechanism exerted through the health institution has been maintained in large part by limiting access for minority group professionals to positions of authority and decision-making. Since health care in Northern Ireland is provided by the state, the only persons with access to private treatment are those who have some economic advantage. This again mediates against the religious minority group, which is severely economically disadvantaged.

As in other places, the system for mental health care in Northern Ireland mitigates against the lower classes. Since the largest percentage of the minority population is among the unemployed or marginally employed there is little chance that even under normal circumstances (without ongoing violence) this population would have adequate care.

In a review of the practices and functions of Queen's University that maintain class distinctions and discrimination in Northern Ireland, J. D. H. Downing makes some specific references to the relationships between the university, the Stormont government, and health care that document the interrelationships between institutions of government, health, and education in the colonial social system of Northern Ireland. He remarks particularly on the studied neglect of resources for the working-class poverty population:

The Faculty of Medicine at Queen's is of peculiar importance in any analysis such as this. Its predominance in the government of Queen's (as will shortly be seen), and its tangible impact on the people of Northern Ireland, both demand its examination. Hospital medicine in Ulster—and appointments to the Medicine Faculty are normally joint-appointments with the city's hospitals—is overwhelmingly Protestant: both doctors and hospital management committees have a very small number of Catholics in their ranks. Nationally and internationally, however, hospital medicine in Ulster does have a very high and justifiable reputation. This is at once its strength and its weakness. Medical practice of the highly specialized, intensive, emergency, technological and expensive kind is certainly well established at Queen's and in the hospitals. Instances are the Coronary Care Unit, the Cardiac Ambulance, the Obstetric Flying Squads, the computerised "pre-symptom" diagnoses.

This places Queen's firmly on one side in perhaps the major debate about medical practice today, which concerns the proportion of finance to be directed toward chronic and preventive care units based in the community. It is a debate that many hospital doctors find threatening since community medicine tends to de-emphasize special expertise and to reduce the scope for writing journal articles and carving out a personal career. Not surprisingly, most hospital doctors see it as lacking prestige and interest; in this respect Queen's mirrors most British teaching hospitals. Yet the specialist expertise policy is pursued in Northern Ireland, where all forms of infant mortality are 25% higher than in Britain; where eight districts of Belfast had an infant mortality rate in 1970 over 5% and where deaths from bronchitis in eight Belfast districts represented over 30% of all deaths. These forms of death are generally accepted as indices of poverty; and are also prime candidates for chronic and preventive care units based in the community. Yet the bulk of spending goes to hospitals in Northern Ireland—£55 millions out of about £70 millions.

This emphasis in favour of high-status medical specialism is reflected in Queen's medical education. Social and preventive medicine is taught for a term in the second year; there are a few lectures in the 4th year; and in the 5th year students do a small survey-project as an exercise. Student opinion on the teaching of this dimension of medicine tends to see it as patchy and dull; it probably reinforces therefore the main ethos, which is ambition for a consultancy. Further, only recently has the work of GPs been thought sufficiently significant for contacts to be organised with them for medical students. The survey of infant mortality and bronchitis deaths in Belfast was not carried out by the Respiratory Infection Unit at City Hospital (nor by the Social Studies department), but from Queen's Geography department.

In other words, the Medicine Faculty is excellent by its own criteria. Its staff operate as they would at any major British teaching hospital: their "distance" from the community is however more salient in Ulster than it is in Britain. In the final analysis, the Ulster population is treated by them as subjects rather than as participants; and their students are encouraged to perpetuate this tradition. Why this is important for the government of Queen's is that given hospital doctors' continual contact with patients as relatively powerless and dependent people (by the time they are admitted to a ward), and given their own professional self-image as expert re-creators of health, there remains only a short step to an authoritarian attitude toward people in general, and toward students and junior staff in particular. It is an easy step to take, even though some doctors do not do so.[34]

There is no doubt that health care institutions in Ireland have perpetuated the myth of defenselessness and have, through their self-interest in maintaining the status quo, been derelict in recognizing and meeting the health needs of a large segment of their community. Citizens of Northern Ireland are expected to be as defenseless against ill health as they are against unemployment. Each person is assigned to a G.P. for health care and literally must take what the G.P. gives out because in order to obtain specialist treatment, reference by a G.P. or solicitor is required. Thus the medical technocrats preserve the traditional "class control" of the British imperial system.

Symbiotic Institutions—Religion and Education

The clear objective of both religion and education as they have been nurtured throughout Ireland's colonial history has been to provide continuity of that colonial status. The destruction of the Gaelic system during the seventeenth century included the abolition of all native Irish educational institutions as well as the Catholic religion as a legitimate institution. For more than a hundred years Irish priests were trained in Paris, Lisbon, Spain, or Rome and were thus harbingers of a more cosmopolitan political and social ideology as well as functioning as purveyors of literacy and theology. After the establishment in 1795 of Maynooth, the seminary for training Catholic priests, that intrusion ended. So also, did the prospect of priests as transmitters of Gaelic tradition or republican "sedition." Students at Maynooth took an oath of support to the Crown along with their ecclesiastical oaths. This establishment ended the years of the Penal Laws, which had made it a criminal offense to perform a religious rite other than that of the Anglican communion, Church of Ireland. Presbyterians and other dissenters as well as Catholics had been forbidden their religious practices.

During the two hundred years of the Penal Laws another kind of educational division had evolved in Ireland, that between Gaelic and English language spheres. In many of the counties of the Ulster plantation as well as in the rest of Ireland, Gaelic had persisted as the dominant language and thereby the language of prayer and literacy for the many Scottish settlers as well as for the native Irish. Despite repeated attempts by the Tudor and Stuart monarchies to establish the English language and system of education, neither was accomplished until the establishment in 1832 of the National Schools. The National Board of Education articulated their perception of religious and educational ideals when they placed this verse in every National School:

I thank the goodness and the grace
That on my birth have smiled
And made me in these Christian days
A happy English child.

Several kinds of controversies were raised over the establishment of the National Schools. One of them was the issue of religion, but the other, which continued to the present time, is that of social class mobility. There was some fear lest children of the poor might, upon receiving education, become less willing to engage in manual labor. As R. B. McDowell relates it: "This attitude is reflected in the speech of the Rector of Ballymena at a school prize giving in that town in 1869 when he said: 'I greatly feared that the National Schools would prove to be educational hotbeds for stimulating to an undue and morbid extent the intellects of children. . . . Gradually these apprehensions have vanished'."[35]

The hedge-schools that had existed for the Catholic and Dissenter even in Ulster not infrequently provided joint study under the same schoolmaster. But the charter schools had been reserved for Protestant (Anglican) children only, and only a few small schools were operated by the reviving Catholic orders, and these were most often either for orphans or for prospective clergy.

It had proved impossible to eradicate, first through mandated illiteracy, and then through the establishment of Protestant free schools, the Irish legacy of learning. The danger of such a legacy was clearly recognized and fought in legislation during the middle and late eighteenth century:

In his address to the Grand Jury of Cork on 13 January 1740 Sir Richard Cox points out that: "The bad Education and obstinate Prejudices of the Old Inhabitants of this Island, and their descendants . . . still continue to be the most powerful Obstacles to an absolute Subjection to wholesome Laws," and the only way to remedy this situation was to take proceedings against Catholic schoolmasters without bothering with the ordinary legal formalities: "You are not to wait for regular Information; if the Offendors are within your Knowledge you may, and ought to, present them. Yet it is to be feared, they are too often encouraged for their Cheapness by Protestants. . . ." These are the men who lay the Foundation of that lamentable Ignorance in which the Irish Papists are bred. . . . From such School-Masters young Pedants, with very little Learning and much Vanity, transport themselves to Seminaries of Jesuits, where they learn Sophistry enough to damn themselves, and to delude un-wary and ignorant People; and then are qualified to be Irish priests, and so return to their native Soil, and become remarkably the most vicious Men inhabiting thereon. . . . To stop therefore such a Growth of idle Pernicious Drones, and to forward the Operation of the good Provisions made for the Education of Youth, it is your duty to put the Laws in Execution against Popish School-Masters."

The provisions for education he refers to are those made by The Incorporated Society for promoting English Protestant Schools. And then in 1745 came another Act of Parliament.[36]

The idea of nondenominational religious teaching was attempted through the Kildare Place Society, founded in 1911 and funded by Parliament in 1831. The Chief Secretary for Ireland, E. G. Stanley, proclaimed in a letter to the Duke of Leinster the intention of the government to establish a National Board of Education, which would subsidize mixed or united education but exclude schools based on definite religious principles:

The mixed school was to be as far as possible under mixed local direction which in turn was to be subject to a mixed Board of Education. There would, however, be separate religious instruction for the children of each denomination at times to be arranged with their pastors.
The Board was immediately attacked by some Church of Ireland Bishops on two main grounds: (1) because it deprived the Church of its statutory right to superintend national education, . . . (2) because it excluded the Bible from the schools. The Presbyterian Church also assailed it the *Orthodox Presbyterian* writing that it was "the most cunning, the most daring, the most specious attempt that has been made against Protestantism since the day of James II". Many of the Catholic Bishops on the other hand, gave a guarded approval to the scheme . . . (pointing) out that it gave priests power to give religious instruction to children of their own flock. Archbishop McHale of Tuam . . . vigorously opposed the Board all his life.[37]

Education in Ireland, north and south, remains a religious institution. In origin, this is not so different from any of the other western European societies. In fact, in the French-speaking province of Canada, Quebec, primary and secondary education are ethnically and religiously segregated in a fashion similar to Ireland's. The significant difference between Northern Ireland and other social systems that reinforce extant religious divisions through segregated and secular supervision of education has to do with the way education is used to sustain intercommunity discord and maintain the imperial framework.

In 1961 Denis P. Barritt and Charles F. Carter found in a survey that at least 98 percent of all Catholic children of primary school age attended Catholic schools.[38] In 1971, there were 174 secondary intermediate schools in Northern Ireland, exactly half of which were state schools and half Catholic voluntary schools. On the grammar school level, there are fewer Catholic schools, and slightly more Catholic pupils may be found in the state schools, but there is considerably more crowding in the Catholic grammar schools. There are no Catholic technical schools, and those who are relegated to these basic postprimary curricula of the least skilled trades function in an integrated milieu. The universities and polytechnic are not religiously segregated but teacher training institutions are almost entirely segregated with only a few Catholics attending Stranmillis, the state institution, and no Protestants attending the two Catholic teacher training institutions. Yet, at Queen's University, where admission is in large part dependent upon examination scores, in 1959–1960, only 22 percent of the students were Catholic, the majority of whom were enrolled in Arts and Law.

John Darby, former research director of the Community Relations Commission and before that a teacher in Belfast, points out that there is a clear case of selectivity in higher-education based on class origins which is much more pronounced in Northern Ireland than in other parts of the United Kingdom: "A demographic study of the two predominantly Protestant estates in Belfast demonstrates the point. In the first, where 92% of the heads of households were either managers or professionals, 100% of the children went to grammar schools; the figure was only 14% in the neighboring estate, where 60% of the heads of households were engaged in manual occupations."[39] Completion of grammar school is the requisite for university admission. When the situation of the university is itself examined, once again we see that it is a formidable agency for applying the social control mechanisms that sustain a hereditary class structure and stable proportional voting population. Despite the fact that in 1961 41 percent of the primary school age population was attending Catholic schools, indicating a potential for half the population of Northern Ireland to be Catholic voters, the proportions at Queen's University reflected the combined effects of class-tracking in education and the forced emigration of Catholics from Northern Ireland.*

Queen's University opened in Belfast in 1849, three hundred years after the founding of Trinity College, Dublin which was largely the educational domain of the Anglo-Irish Ascendancy families and the bastion of Church of Ireland social-political systems. The first president of Queen's University said at its opening that education was needed in Ireland for "the mass of middle class men." By 1920, two-thirds of the students at Queen's were Presbyterians, and the Queen's Senate and Academic Council expressed strong opposition to Asquith's Home Rule Bill in 1912. Downing traces the relationship of the University with the Unionist Party and the economic-political establishment of Northern Ireland:

> References to the formal political relationships established in 1920 are strangely devoid of content in this account: the word Orange is conspicuously absent. Yet it surely cannot be forgotten that in 1927, 94% of the most senior Stormont officials were Protestant; in 1959, despite a more than threefold increase in numbers, 94% were still Protestant; and in 1972, 95% of Stormont civil servants from deputy and assistant principal upwards were Protestant. This has been a very particular kind of "political unit", forged in highly specific circumstances. It is also worth remembering that up to 1968 Queen's sent four MPs to Stormont at each election, and so participated in its own special way in this "political settlement."

Queen's and Ulster

The story of Queen's co-operation with Stormont, its relationship with local big business, and with the community, is a long one. It should not be characterised in any facile manner as a master-servant relationship. There are though certain signal features of the relationship which must be noted. One of the most important is the re-establishment of the Faculty of Agriculture in 1924, after its demise in 1899. For some time now, the Student Representative Council has been conducting a campaign against the acceptance of military contracts by the University staff. Often the nature of these contracts has been misconceived, with those opposed to them hunting for clues to the specific military applications of the science or technology involved. In practice neither the Ministry of Defence normally contract with university departments to do work on specific applications. Their own employees work on applications, since this is better for security purposes and also helps university scientists and technologists to maintain their conventional apologia that they are concerned with basic research, the utilisation of which is beyond their control.

---

*Admission to a Grammar School is based on passing the eleven-plus exam. Northern Ireland continues to use this method to segregate and truncate intellectual development and social mobility.

The Vice-Chancellor has specifically argued that the various contracts from the Ministry of Defence awarded to the university are for non-military purposes, and are under that aegis through a historical accident. Labels can be misleading in a number of directions, however; thus since 1957 there has been a group of scientists in Queen's funded mainly by the Science Research Council and the US Air Force to research into problems of atmospheric physics. The line between civil and military research is not clearcut; as the Vice-Chancellor has correctly pointed out, the armed forces today are interested in numerous applications from electronics research, such as Skyspy, the new remote control aerial TV reconnaissance "spying saucer" developed by Short's. It is also the case that Queen's has in the recent past accepted a research grant from Porton Down, the chemical and biological warfare research institute in Wiltshire; and that in 1971 it conferred an honorary DSc on Henry Wilson, appointed chief scientist for the Army in 1969, and then Director of the Technical Centre of the Supreme Headquarters of the Allied Powers in The Hague in 1970. At the highest level, then, there is a commitment to the propriety of militarism.[40]

Downing points out that although Queen's University was founded particularly to provide higher education in the Arts, Medicine, and Law, there is more influence in its administration of military background, experience, and rank than of Law or Arts. Not unlike the decision-making process in Northern Ireland as a whole, decision-making at Queen's proceeds through a very narrow oligarchical closed structure. Downing diagrams the power structure below in Table 8.

Finally, to underscore the relationship of this oligarchy to the operational machinery exerted through the institution of education to the legal governmental apparatus of Northern Ireland, there is the case of the Fabian Tract authored by three professors of the Queen's University Law Faculty recommending replacing the Special Powers Act with a new emergency powers (security) act to cover the whole of the United Kingdom, published early in 1973. It was criticized in the press as being a dangerous contribution to the development of legalized repression.[41] In July, 1973, the Emergency Provisions Act was introduced to replace the Special Powers Act and included many of the recommendations cited by the three Queen's professors. In November, 1974, Parliament enacted the Prevention of Terrorism Act, under the provisions of which four hundred persons were detained in the United Kingdom during its first year, and another seventy were excluded from admission to the United Kingdom (nearly all of them Irish).

The technocrats who administer the mechanisms of control for the educational institution in Northern Ireland are often identical with those who administer the mechanisms of law, health, government, and economics. Their subordinates, who have primary contact with the client population, are teachers. Academic freedom is not a commonplace at any level of the educational enterprise in Northern Ireland.

The informal agencies of education, television, radio, and the press, are censored both in Northern Ireland and in the Irish Republic. In the latter, a censorship board passes judgment on print media, and, in at least one remarkable instance, the Irish government has actually destroyed the plates to a book scheduled for publication in the Irish Republic—*Freedom Struggle*, a publication of the Provisional Sinn Fein, which articulated their ideology and version of the campaign against the Stormont government and the British army. Recordings of ballads that described the conflict have also been banned from radio. Dr. Conor Cruise O'Brien, Minister of Posts and Telegraphs for the Republic, has worked through various edicts and

---

Table 8   Power in Queen's Belfast 1970–74

NAME	CONNECTION WITH QUB†	KEY SENATE COMMITTEES	ULSTER ORIGIN	OFFICE IN QUB	INTERESTS
Anderson	●	▲	■	Pro-Ch	Military
Biggart	●●●●	▲▲▲▲	■	Pro-Ch	Medicine
Black	●●●	▲▲		Pro-VC	Economics
Bryson	●	▲▲	■	Pro-Ch	Housing Tr.
Cheeseman	●●	▲▲			Medicine
Fraser	●●●●●●	▲	■		Medicine
					Military
					Business
Harrison	●●●●	▲▲▲▲		Rgstr.	Medicine
Kinahan	●	▲▲	■		Business
McKinney	●	▲▲▲▲	■	Treas.	Business
					Medicine
Neill	●●●	▲▲▲▲		Secr.	Welfare
Pritchard	●●●	▲			Medicine
Vick	●	▲▲▲▲		VC	Science
					Military
Williams	●●	▲▲		Pro-VC	Science
					Education

†Connection with QUB is measured in decades or parts of a decade.

manipulation to keep the air waves of the Irish Republic clear of any in-depth presentations sympathetic to the IRA perspective. O'Brien and others in the government have suggested that there has been altogether too much notice taken in the history books of Ireland about Irish/English enmity and the Irish struggle for nationhood. They would minimize such recollections in order to facilitate Anglo/Irish economic cooperation.

In the North, D notices provide controls for the press. Radio and television are prohibited from using live or recorded music about Irish republicanism or internment.

Conclusion

The difference between institutionalized racism and institutional racism is nowhere more obvious than in Ireland. The colonial system was predicated on establishing institutions that would totally replace any vestige of the indigenous social system and would maintain the population as dependent, subservient, and docile. The pattern of British colonialism was developed and refined through their experience in Ireland and was thereafter applied throughout the world. It has usually been successful for a prolonged period, and when the imperial armies and flag are finally withdrawn, the place remains in neocolonial status by virtue of the well-entrenched established institutions. Adding to the continuity is the institutional racism, which in many former colonies foments periodic cycles of military and economic dependency. India, Cyprus, and Palestine are other examples.

Technocrats are not only enforcement agents for the social control agencies, they are also the apologists for the system. If they are health professionals or educators they treat and diagnose pathologies in terms of the deviance or inadequacy of an individual or powerless group rather than seeking or articulating the social etiology of the disease. Thus, if very few working-class children matriculate into the universities they can demonstrate that working-class estates or working-class family life are not conducive to academic achievement or motivation. Other scholar-technocrats do attitude surveys that demonstrate that the Catholic, or minority, school system provides inadequately for the civic education of Catholic working-class adolescents and therefore such boys are prone to stoning soldiers when younger and becoming junior IRA at puberty. Media technocrats—journalists, editors, broadcasters, producers, newsmen—are apologists for sustaining institutional racism and imperial oppression when they present "fairly" the "two sides of the conflict," neglecting to present the third combatant, the British army, which represents the ultimate governmental authority on that island.* Legal technocrats—solicitors, barristers, magistrates, and judges—perform their service as they find new legal justifications for courtroom application of a jurisprudential system predicated on a friend-foe hypothesis rather than "blind justice." The religious institutions in collaboration with fraternal institutions serve themselves even while they protest injustice by preaching the parochial glories of the after life. They fail to answer the poignant question scratched on a Belfast wall, "Is there a life before death?" The clergy and church hierarchies are apologists who sustain the social system even while they interminably moralize and condemn violence, which in the final analysis only serves to desensitize the listeners to its real horror.

Why should the whole thing matter at all? Many societies, in fact half the world at least, might be justifiably, accurately described as social systems that have institutions predicated on racism. That same half and others besides are colonial, neocolonial, or imperial systems that have so incorporated inequity and unequal justice into their schema as to have these become the very adhesive of their nation-state. In fact, as the Irish poet John Montague prefaced one volume with a quotation from George Sefaris: "The Greeks say it was the Turks who burned down Smyrna. The Turks say it was the Greeks. Who will discover the truth? The wrong has been committed. The important thing is, who will redeem it?"[42]

From Prejudice to Hatred to Racism: Psychological Genocide

The effect of this system, the wrong that has been committed, has been the destruction of identity for Irish people, Protestant and Catholic, north and south. The cultural genocide initiated with the Statutes of Kilkenny in 1366 and executed by Cromwell through massacre, pillage, and enslavement three hundred years later, the Act of Union of 1800, and Randolph Churchill's playing of the "Orange card" in 1886 were the more dramatic instances of physical and cultural annihilation.

The destruction of identity proceeds more subtly on an individual basis, then becomes incorporated into the socialization process at first through the dynamics of the nuclear family. Later, of course, there is a certain consistency between the debased identity imparted through the nuclear family of a discriminated group and the dynamic interactions the individual experiences in the other institutions of that society. Being a member of a despised group takes its toll on the entire personality function. At the very least it results in the personal incorporation of a negative stereotype caricaturing one's self. The caricature-stereotype imposed on the Irish and copiously manifested in nineteenth- and twentieth-century cartoon images,

*An excellent example of this collusion has been the refusal by the media to articulate any legitimate criticisms of the 1976 government supported "Peace Movement."

is that of "the savage and often simian or porcine buffoon." *Punch* magazine depictions of this caricature were commonplace. Nor was this figure absent from the American comics of the same period.[43] The self-image imposed by this stereotype is in no way limited to the Irish Catholic or the Northern Irish. As many loyalists realized when they sought work in England or emigrated to Australia, Canada, or the United States, they were considered Irish, without hyphenations. The sense of dependency, fear, powerlessness, and inferiority inculcated throughout the socialization process has made the Irish among the most easily assimilated immigrant groups everywhere.

The Social-Psychological Dynamics

For prejudice to exist, social distance is prerequisite. For racism to exist, hereditary inferiority of the other and the danger to the survival of one's own group must be implicated.

Gordon Allport, writing in 1953, observed that prejudice unlike racism has historically been grounds for persecution, while the concept of "race" is only about a century old: "The simplicity of 'race' gave an immediate and visible mark . . . by which to designate the victims of dislike . . . the fiction of moral inferiority became, . . . so . . . an irrefutable justification for prejudice. It had the stamp of biological finality."[44] Allport traced the institution of race prejudice from the origins and popularity of Social Darwinism in the nineteenth century.

Galton and others in the infant sciences of psychology and sociology proceeded to develop "proofs" of the priority of heredity over environment in determining individual "intelligence," and finally through measures of "intelligence," proofs of the superiority of its complement in the white Anglo-Saxon Protestant race. By 1920, in fact, one prominent American psychologist had ranked the "races": "England, Holland, Denmark, Scotland, Germany, Sweden, Canada, Belgium, Norway, Austria, Ireland, Turkey, Greece, Russia, Italy, Poland. . . . The Polish it was said, were almost as dull as the Negroes."*[45] Psychologists in Britain and America early became part of the eugenics movement and through their writings, preachments, and support of discriminatory legislation served to reinforce maintenance of social distance and its resultant prejudice.

Allport defined prejudice: "Ethnic prejudice is an antipathy based upon a faulty and inflexible generalization. It may be felt or expressed. It

---

*More recently, in 1973, Hans Eyesenck, another noted psychologist, pointed out that the smartest Negroes had resisted enslavement and therefore only the least intelligent blacks were brought to America, where they bred more unintelligent Negroes. On the other hand, he said, conditions in Ireland were so bad that only the least intelligent Irish stayed there. He claims that this explains why the British have had such a difficult time governing that island.

may be directed toward a group as a whole, or toward an individual because he is a member of that group."[46] He described the progressive enactment of prejudice in five steps varying in degree or negative action from the least energetic to the most:

1. *Antilocution* . . . people who have prejudices talk about them. With like-minded friends, occasionally with strangers they may express their antagonism freely. But many people never go beyond. . . .
2. *Avoidance* . . . the bearer of the prejudice does not directly inflict harm upon the group he dislikes. He takes the burden of accommodation and withdrawal entirely upon himself.
3. *Discrimination* . . . makes detrimental distinctions of an active sort. He undertakes to exclude all members of the group in question from certain types of employment, from residential housing, political rights, educational or recreational opportunities, churches, hospitals, or from some other social privileges. . . .
4. *Physical attack*. Under conditions of heightened emotion prejudice may lead to acts of violence or semi-violence. . . .
5. *Extermination*. Lynchings, pogroms, massacres, and the Hitlerian program of genocide mark the ultimate degree of violent expression of prejudice.[47]

In the works of Allport and other social psychologists studying the phenomenon of prejudice, such as Lewin and Nevitt Sanford, the occurrence of prejudice is seen as an outgrowth of the individual's conceptualization of affiliative relationships.[48] By virtue of this cultural identity the individual becomes part of an "in-group," has a "reference group," and recognizes an "out-group(ness)." Group loyalties may, but do not necessarily, include hostility to other groups. For those whose personal identity includes a reference group or an in-group characterized as "superior," however, hostility toward and distancing from the out-group become imperative. When that distancing is abetted by geographic distance as in colonialism, or by residential, employment, and educational segregation as happens in institutionalized discrimination, there is little chance for contradictions of stereotypes to be experienced.

There is considerable evidence from experimental social psychology that even after the categorization/generalization/stereotype development has been contradicted, unless that contradiction is strongly reinforced, the cognitive dissonance thus engendered will resolve itself into the original perception.[49] Festinger and others experimenting with cognitive dissonance and discriminatory behavior conclude that the prejudiced individual fails to recognize the cognitive contrast.[50]

Milton Rokeach and his associates carried the study of prejudice beyond the earlier landmark studies of the authoritarian personality syndrome and examined open-mindedness and closed-mindedness as a precipitating dynamic in the phenomena of prejudice. They concluded that affective-cognitive belief systems developed in *relatively isolated contexts* produced the "closed mind."[51] Thus despite the illogic and contradictions inherent in such belief systems when confronted with reality, they form a psychological system upon which the believers are dependent and which motivates them.

The consequent development of personality and corollary behaviors is essentially "crippled." The relationship between a master and a slave cannot, by its very definition, provide many alternative behaviors for either of them. They become victims together of their limited choices and the compulsive responsibilities of their roles. The relationship between the prejudiced and the victim is not only a role restriction, but, as Allport and others point out, underlying personality dynamics compound the effects.

While several possible reactions to oppression are available to the oppressed (which we will deal with shortly), there are few alternative modes of perception available to the prejudiced. According to "psychodynamic" theories of personality, the prejudice itself is a product and a symptom of neurosis—much as is a phobia or a compulsion. Social psychological experimenters suggest that the authoritarian personality aggresses from anticipation of punishment for frustration-induced aggression directed toward the in-group; and that a prejudiced personality suffers from decreased perceptual discrimination under stress.[52] Prejudiced persons have been found to have authoritarian attitudes that originated in the experience of the harsh and punitive discipline from parents for independent, autonomous behavior. They received approval only for imitative, conforming behavior.

In describing the personality syndrome of the prejudiced person, Allport lists four kinds of frustration as common corrolaries: constitutional and personal, as a direct frustration of self-esteem; frustrations within the family, rejective atmosphere and harsh treatment as concomitant to the authoritarian personality syndrome; near-lying community, a blend of school and home usually incorporating economic frustration and resembling the frustration-aggression-displacement sequence; remoter community, frustrations arising from high levels of societal competition for "scarce commodities." In addition, the prejudiced person, like any other neurotic, is the first victim of his own fear, anxiety, shame, or guilt.[53] These conditions are clearly evidenced in our studies of the colonial system operating in Ireland.

Gardner Murphy regards status hunger as the root of ethnic prejudice. This reflects the poor self-image of the prejudiced person. The person who is frustrated and uncertain is ego-threatened, of course, and grasps the straw of a less favored out-group to symbolize his own relatively higher status. Through status hunger the working-class Protestant in Northern Ireland grasps Paisley's proffered straw of anti-Catholic bigotry.

There is strong experimental and clinical evidence to indicate that the prejudiced person has experienced a high degree of sexual frustration and anxiety. It is certainly corollary that sex-role dichotomization and hierarchies are prevalent among groups feeling threatened and that the sexual double standard is more readily applied in societies in which authoritarianism and prejudice are prevalent. This is consistent with the need of the prejudiced person to dichotomize everything. As we have seen, sex-role dichotomization in Ireland has reinforced social controls and been reinforced as a social control mechanism.

Clinically, a prejudiced person or group experiences extreme internal ambivalence and disorder. Consequently a strong need exists to order the outside world, accept shibboleths, support vigorous social control, moralize, and rigidify. The prejudiced person feels a lack of control over personal destiny and thus requires external controls. Most of all, the prejudiced person is looking for certainty and adheres to abstract higher principles embodied in supernationalism. The egocentricity turns to ethnocentricity with a frantic and fanatic adherence to perceived in-group or reference-group values.

This is neither a comfortable psychological state of being nor is it a physically healthy condition. For along with the psychological repression of the prejudiced person may be found psychosomatic disorders such as ulcers, asthma, neuritis, and colitis.

But let us look also at the psychodynamic condition of the victim of the prejudice. He has two possible paths—psychological change and psychological resistance:

Psychological Change
1. Change toward being the expected image; long term role playing produces actual psychological change.
2. Wanting to be like the dominant group; emulation of the master group, usually with a concomitant hatred and denigration of one's own group.
3. Direct psychological effects of living in a low-opportunity environment; effects especially on intellectual development, achievement, aspirations, physical health and well-being.

Psychological Resistance
1. Open resistance or revolt.
2. Passive resistance; especially the use of the put-on both as passive resistance against the dominant group and as a technique to maintain one's own sense of dignity.[54]

The consequences of membership in an oppressed group are readily apparent through studies of child development. Eric Erikson claims that the child's development of mastery is truncated at the level of shame and self-doubt.[55] Within a group victimized by such status, self-hatred flares into factionalizing, low morale, and often cultural suicide, as the group increasingly attempts to adhere to reference-group behavior in order to achieve higher status. Examples of such victimizing by the victims abound in studies of interaction between waves of immigrants to the United States. Oftentimes an earlier wave from the same point of origin resented, abandoned, and disavowed the newer arrivals who demonstrated unacculturated forms of behavior and reminders of the despised heritage.

The effect of prejudice on the exerter as well as the victim, on the individual as well as on the group, and hence on the total societal context in which it occurs is dehumanization through a depersonalization. It sets the stage for what Herbert Kelman aptly calls "Sanctioned Massacres."[56]

Genocide-Sanctioned Massacre

We have come to associate genocide with violence. Indeed, the most profound examples remain those in which masses of lifeless and mangled bodies represent the deliberate decimation of a group. The repetition and extension of sanctioned massacre is sufficient indication that we lack real knowledge of the nature of the human organism and of the social and political dynamics of national units where violence is incorporated into public policy and the policy is aimed at objectives for the "public good." Sometimes the violence is couched in moralisms relating to "self-defense." In this way, the Armenian minority of Turkey was viewed as a prospective ally of the Russian enemy and therefore had to be exterminated in order to save the majority of the Turkish population. So also were the Jews presented as "polluters" of the Aryan race and "Bolshevik" threats to the economic survival of the German people. The victims of the My Lai massacre were viewed as "gooks" cooperating with "Commies" to thwart the "pacification" program. In all such cases, the destruction of helpless civilian populations has had moral sanctions and been viewed as promoting the general welfare. The designated targets are usually powerless and numerically inferior. Sometimes a historical hostility toward a particular group provides a kind of moral sanction for its destruction. But, as Kelman points out, considerable evidence from social psychological experimentation and studies suggests that sanctioned massacres under circumstances of violence do not require that the perpetrators have a hostile attitude toward the victims or that as individuals they have sadistic personalities. Some research on the frustration-aggression hypothesis implies that a population whose aims and identity needs are frustrated may turn to aggressive behavior. This hypothesis certainly explains the more violent episodes of racial conflict. As Kelman says:

> Sanctioned massacres certainly involve a considerable amount of hostility toward the victims, traceable both to historical relationships and to situational dynamics. Hostility toward the target, however, does not seem to be an instigator of the violent actions. Historical relationships provide a reservoir of hostility that can be drawn upon to mobilize, feed and justify the violent actions, but they do not cause these actions in the immediate case. . . . The expressions of anger . . . serve to provide the perpetrators with an explanation and rationalization for their violent actions and appropriate labels for their emotional state. They also help to reinforce, maintain, and intensify the violence . . . rather than by creating powerful forces that motivate violence against these victims.[57]

It is important to note that the antecedent conditions of genocide include all the dynamics concomitant with colonialism, prejudice, and racism. The condition of violence conceived by Kelman as instrumental in the enactment of genocide may or may not be engaged through one or the other circumstances. Also in common with colonialism, prejudice, and racism, genocide as sanctioned massacre requires "authorization." Studies by Stanley Milgram and Phillip Zimbardo that explored the social dynamics of aggression directed by authority figures and of aggression accruing to role, respectively, have broadened our knowledge of the relevance of "authorization" in dehumanizing the victim in order to perpetuate hostile behavior toward him/her.[58]

An authoritarian social ordering provides the maximal environment for "authorization" of hostile actions, and extremist loyalty to an ideology, be is fascist or democratic, precludes acceptance of deviations, so the dehumanizing of the victim is facilitated by its "ordinariness."

In Milgram's experiments, the subject given directions for rewarding or punishing the victim was led to believe that he would, by administering massive doses of electric shock, actually be aiding the victims' learning process. Since a learning experiment is consistent with the functions of a psychological laboratory, and since conditioning or reinforcement learning is standard procedure, the subject found no outstanding inconsistency between the directions (authorization) and the task (role). Distancing of the subject from the victim was crucial in maintaining the imposed perceptual set.[59] In Northern Ireland all the institutions contrive a "set" through which no one in the social system may perceive the dissonance inherent in the authoritarian, rigid oligarchical social ordering imposed under the rhetoric of democracy.*

Each new generation inherits through the experience of its parents a preview of imminent and constant threat to its survival. The preview of destruction and the experience of ongoing violence and prejudice serve to "desensitize" the participants from any of the normal human emphatic reactions. The prelude to the violent action itself performs a kind of immunization function.

Where all of these prior circumstances apply, it is conceivable that there is not even a need for the authorities to negotiate an immediate environment of violence in order to authorize (sanction) genocide.

Psychological Genocide

The United Nations conventions on genocide include in their definition the phrase "causing serious mental harm"† and other statements that relate to the destruction of ethnic groups by means less dramatic than wholesale slaughter. It is possible that the intent of these conventions was to encompass the various crimes against humanity which were prelude to the sanctioned massacres. Nonetheless, these conditions are stated specifically *in addition to* the definition of genocide as mass physical destruction.

Psychological research provides data suggesting that the destruction of individuals and social groups through serious mental harm can proceed without scheduled massacres, but with only intermittent reinforcement of fear that such may ensue. Research on intelligence and nutrition provides insights into the prospect for genetic mutation through inadequate nutrition and without the dramatic effects of nuclear explosions. Sociological research suggests that debilitating cultural patterns evolve within groups that suffer political and social oppression, and that these retard accension for individuals from such groups and for the groups themselves. History proceeds from the definitions of dominant groups to the extinction of losers. Since history is written by the winners, it rarely dwells on the survival mechanisms and positive values of the losers, although sometimes anthropologists explore those crevices.[60]

We find ourselves in a vast gray area. The definition of genocide in the context of violence is so consistent that we tend to place changes in the

*This is exemplified in Northern Ireland by the consistent use of corporal punishment in the schools.
†According to Raul Hilberg, this codicil of the convention was introduced by Nationalist China (Republic of China) in consideration of the damage done to the Chinese people by Great Britain through the opium trade (personal communication).

nature of groups by means other than annihilation into categories labeled "natural forces" or "social problems." The dynamics of destruction is too often relegated to a social darwinist explanation as the product of the survival of the fittest.

Just as there are institutions and agencies within a society that have the objective of effecting personality changes in the individuals within them, cultures and societies themselves provide through their common terms of reference the norm system against which the individual measures self and others. The values that comprise the common culture of a tribal, social, or national group carry the unique statement of that identity and its relation to out-groups. When that group identity incorporates victimization by out-groups, the variety of behavior patterns available to its membership is restricted. Likewise, the individual in such a group has behavioral limitations imposed for personal survival. These restrictions may go so far as to include restrictions against both fight and flight—the two psychological mechanisms for dealing with confrontation. Finally, adaptation for physical survival may require that group identity be discarded, as has been the case in forced conversions, or that the individual victim join with the oppressors in aggression against the group of origin. Through various restrictions imposed on the oppressed group its members may be compelled in every circumstance, ranging from food choices to ceremonial functions, to the diminution of their alternatives.

What then is the difference between assimilation/acculturation and psychological genocide? For thousands of years human groups have adapted to restrictions of the natural world and of their human adversaries in order to resolve the dilemma by change. With the advantages of hindsight we can theorize about the relative merits of such adaptations, but we can hardly challenge their necessity. Most of these adaptations have occurred through the exertion of one or another form of social control. Social control mechanisms range from the informal systems, such as the mores and traditions of a group, to the technical systems represented by legislation and jurisprudence. The difference between psychological genocide and adaptation processes is that although both proceed through all the levels of social control, *psychological genocide is the mandated destruction of a group as such, with the sanctions of the social control systems and the objective of "outlawing" their capacity for perpetuating their own identity.* This is accomplished by massacre in some cases, by intermittent annihilation in other cases, or by a prolonged, sustained subjugation to adversity. In the case of the Irish, it has been accomplished by a combination of these methods.

Several studies have suggested that in-group loyalty and esteem are corollaries to the suffering, cost, and effort endured in group membership. If this is the case, then despite access to assimilation the group maintains an identity. The endurance of a "lachrymose" identity as a product of such a history would not in itself indicate the psychological destruction of a group. In fact, as Walter Zenner suggests, it might enhance ethnocentricity.[61] But the divisive forces of continued aggression against the group in combination with sanctioned destruction through the social control mechanisms can result in the psychological and cultural destruction of the membership.

It has been the contention of this book that such a process has been imposed upon the Irish people and that, individually and as a group, they are classic victims of psychological genocide.

Appendix

A Lawyer's Critique of the Detention of Terrorists Order (NI) 1972

The Order provides that the British Secretary of State can appoint any number of Commissioners to adjudicate on persons so arrested. A Commissioner must have held judicial office in any part of the United Kingdom, or be a Barrister, Advocate or Solicitor of not less than ten years standing in any part of the United Kingdom. Part I to the Schedule to the Order which deals with the status of Commissioners does not indicate whether a Commissioner has any security or tenure of office. The matter seems to be left deliberately vague and merely says that a Commissioner shall hold office and vacate his office in accordance with his terms of appointment. If a person appointed to exercise judicial functions is removable at will by the Executive, he is not deemed to be an independent judicial officer as his independence is presumed to be impaired where he is removable at will by the Government.

It may be for this reason that the status of a Commissioner is left deliberately vague and it is presumably the intention of the Secretary of State to remove Commissioners at will (the Judges sitting in the Special Criminal Court in Dublin at present under the Offences Against the State Act are removable at will by the Government).

The Commissioner "shall inquire into the case for the purpose of deciding whether or not he is satisfied" that the person arrested has been concerned in terrorist activities and that his detention is necessary for the protection of the public. Where a Commissioner is so satisfied, he makes a Detention Order for the detention (without limitation in time) of the person in question. Otherwise, he must direct his discharge and release.[1]

Detention Order

A Detention Order, therefore, takes the place of the previous Internment Order, but its effect is precisely the same. A person is kept in prison without having an opportunity to test his innocence or guilt by normal judicial processes and his detention is unlimited in terms of time.

The process before the Commissioner can in no sense be described as a judicial process or in compliance with the requirements of the European Convention on Human Rights in relation to the right to a fair trial. The arrested person can be given as little as three days within which to prepare his Defence before the Commissioner, the proceedings are held in private and, although the prisoner can be represented by Council or Solicitor and may adduce evidence, the whole procedure violates judicial processes in the following way:

1. The Commissioner is not bound by any laws of evidence and can admit evidence that would be inadmissible in a Court of law (hearsay evidence of police officers who have no personal knowledge of the matters they are given evidence about can, therefore, be admitted to the prejudice of the prisoner).

2. The Commissioner can actually exclude the Prisoner and his Counsel and Solicitor from any part of the proceedings if he thinks he contrary to the interests of public security so to do and thus evidence can be given (on a hearsay basis or otherwise) about which the prisoner and his legal representatives have no knowledge and by witnesses whom they have no opportunity of cross-examining. The Commissioner is empowered "insofar as the needs of the public security and the safety of persons permit" informing the prisoner and his representatives of the substance of the evidence in question, but he is not obliged to do so and has a complete discretion as to concealing evidence or statements prejudicial to the prisoner upon which he will ultimately make his finding.

3. Persons giving evidence against the prisoner are permitted to do so behind a concealed curtain, so that their name and identity is unknown. Several cases have been heard on this basis. Where a Detention Order is made by the Commissioner, he must state the grounds upon which he makes it and a copy of the Detention Order shall be sent to the prisoner, but there is no time laid down for serving a copy of the Order—notwithstanding that the prisoner has only twenty-one days from the making of the Order (as distinct from its service on him) to appeal against it.

Appeal Tribunal

A person who is the subject of a Detention Order may appeal to an Appeal Tribunal within twenty-one days of the making of the Order, indicating the grounds of his Appeal and whether he intends to introduce any fresh evidence on the hearing of the Appeal.

The Appeal Tribunal consists of such number of members as the Secretary of State decides, and a member must hold the same qualifications as the Commissioner listed above. The tenure of the office of each member is left vague as in the case of the Commissioner.

A quorum of the Tribunal shall consist of three members and it shall decide by majority verdict.

The same rules apply to its procedure as to the hearing before the Commissioner, i.e. evidence or statements which would be admissible in a Court of Law are permitted to be taken into account, the prisoner can be excluded from any part of the hearing if the Tribunal so decides etc.

If the prisoner wishes to introduce fresh evidence on the hearing of the Appeal, he can only do this with the consent of the Tribunal. He has no right to it.

If the Tribunal "are of the opinion that the Commissioner's decision should be set aside" they shall allow the appeal, otherwise they dismiss it.

Powers of Secretary of State

Not withstanding the procedure laid down for hearings before Commissioners and the Appeals Tribunal, the British Secretary of State still has the power to direct the discharge at any time of any person detained under an Interim Custody Order or any person detained under a Detention Order, but he has the extraordinary power of being entitled to "re-call to detention" any person whom he releases under a Detention Order. This means that the Secretary of State can imprison, release and re-imprison people at his will without giving any reasons and a person so treated is deemed to be held under the original Detention Order—which means that he has no right to appeal again to the Appeal Tribunal and, since the Appeal Tribunal have no function once they have dealt with a case, a person in this situation becomes almost the personal prisoner of the Secretary of State and can only be released on his personal decision.

Conditions of Imprisonment

A person detained under this Order shall be detained "as nearly as may be as if he were a prisoner detained in a prison on remand." Where a prisoner is detained under a Detention Order (whether made by a Commissioner or by the Appeal Tribunal) the Secretary of State has power to refer his case back against a Commissioner, but it is not clear from the Order whether a person whose case is thus dealt with has again a right of appeal to the Appeal Tribunal if the Commissioner decides he should not be released.

Male Members of the Security Forces May Not Search Women

Arrest

The Army can arrest anyone by saying "I am arresting you as a member of Her Majesty's Forces." They may hold you for four hours for screening. Then you must be released or handed into RUC custody. Relatives should phone the Army Post for information.

Relatives should insist on being present at the interrogation of their children, and to accompany them to the Army Post if they are available.

IN A LETTER IN THE IRISH NEWS FATHER PAUL GIVES THE FOLLOWING ADVICE TO PEOPLE ARRESTED FOR 72 HOURS UNDER THE EMERGENCY PROVISIONS ACT.

1. When brought in say, "I want my solicitor," and name him "Patrick O'Neill, of O'Neill St." If he is not available, say "I want Sean Quinn of Quinn St." and so on.

Everyone should carry in his head, or a piece of paper the names of two solicitors who are willing and not afraid of the RUC.

2. When they ask you any question say, "I want that question in writing, and when my legal representative is present, I shall answer your question in writing, when my solicitor has checked it."

3. Do not sign your name to any piece of paper for the full 72 hours unless you are advised to do so by the solicitor of your choice.

4. Always get yourself medically examined by your own doctor during your detention and always after the 72 hours are up. As a general rule, do not trust Army or Police doctors.

5. Ignore all documents presented to you as confessions of your friends implicating you. These are usually forgeries. Ignore threats and suffer patiently when they beat you up. Do not accept bribes or promises. Do not trust them.

6. Be patient for 72 hours: sit and think good thoughts: they cannot deprive you of your legal rights or liberty any longer.

7. Do not hold any conversation with them on politics, the troubles, civil rights etc. It is all being taken down and will be produced in court against you.

We believe that the RUC are illegally stopping lawyers getting in to see men detained under Section 10 of the Emergency Provisions Act. If this happens to you ask your solicitor to challenge it in court.

If you have a complaint of your treatment by the police or army

1. Get a medical certificate of your condition
2. Get a solicitor
3. Inform NICRA
4. Make a formal complaint to the RUC

IT HAS BEEN PROVED THAT IT IS ALMOST IMPOSSIBLE TO GET SATISFACTION ON COMPLAINTS LOCALLY, THEREFORE ALL CASES OF BRUTALITY AND HARASSMENT ARE BEING TAKEN TO THE INTERNATIONAL COURTS.

Harassment has not stopped; in fact it has got worse since the Emergency Provisions Act was passed by the British Parliament. Every citizen should know their rights, and how best to protect themselves.

The Census

This is illegal, and army headquarters at Lisburn has denied giving any orders for it to be taken. When the army raid, any person in the house at that time must give his name and address. You do not have to say who else lives in the house or give any other information. The Army may retaliate by making more visits to your house. In that case phone NICRA, 23351 or contact a local civil rights person, and we will contact Army Headquarters, and have this harassment stopped.

Being Stopped by the Army in a Public Place

The Army have the right to ask your name and address. Give it and carry some identification with you.

Searches

The Army has the right to search any person, place or vehicle, as a member of Her Majesty's Forces. Always insist on accompanying them during a search. Make sure all damages done is listed in the damages claim form. The office to claim at is now Londonderry House, and not Bedford House. You should be given two copies of the form, one to send to Londonderry House, with an estimate of what it will cost to repair the damage. Keep the other copy carefully.

Statement by Rona Fields, PhD., Associate Professor, Clark University, USA, Psychologist and Sociologist—Author of "On the Run," a Psychology of Northern Ireland

Ann Walsh, at the age of eighteen, has endured all the variety of "treatments" designed to break the morale and commitment of dissenters in Northern Ireland. The effects of these treatments have taken their toll on the mental and physical condition of this young woman. In an interview and clinical examination by an American psychologist, Ann attempted to compensate for the effects of her torture experience. She made an enormous effort, but, nonetheless, her test performance indicated she has suffered some damage to her central nervous system, probably as a result of being subjected to the "noise treatment" during interrogation.

The effects are such that her memory has been impaired and she is extremely nervous.

It is hard to tell whether the effects of the noise treatment or, perhaps, the many beatings she has sustained (which have included blows to her head) have produced the sensory problems evidenced in periodically blurred vision and temporary loss of hearing from which Ann suffers.

Of course the repeated harassment which preceded Ann's arrest last March could have been responsible for the kind of tension and anxiety which result in extreme fatigue, hallucinations, and irritability.

Since her imprisonment, Ann has experienced repeated bouts of depression exacerbated by the conditions of her prison environment. There is some question about how long she can continue to tolerate these conditions without experiencing a severe nervous breakdown.

Medical and psychiatric treatment for Ann had been prescribed as early as November, 1972, following the evident effects of her noise treatment interrogation. She had received some medical specialist treatment for her hearing disability prior to her March arrest, but since that time she has been denied all specialist services despite her family's repeated requests. In such cases—where treatment of damages to central nervous and sensory systems is delayed—the possibility of restoration is slight.

In an interview with the psychologist who examined Ann, Dr. Rona Fields stated that "the continued imprisonment of Ann Walsh is a contradiction to the obvious need of a sick person to receive humane and ameliorative treatment." Dr. Fields testified on her findings before the Tribunal hearing on Ann Walsh. The barrister for the Crown was unable to contest Dr. Fields's findings, but accused her of "political and sectarian" allegiance in her admission of membership of N.I.C.R.A. She was subsequently the subject of a decision by the Ministry of Home Affairs, which was articulated by a Mr. Wilson, not to be allowed further access to examining prisoners in any Northern Ireland institutions.

Since Dr. Fields had already evaluated 125 victims of interrogation, and has completed a book on the effects of interrogation and internment (to be published by Penguin in October), she is highly qualified to testify on these effects.

The decision by the Ministry of Home Affairs is an indication of their determination to sweep under the carpet of their legal system the living evidence of their brutality. (Northern Ireland Civil Rights Association, July, 1973)

We Are Not Recognized (Armagh Jail, 1973)

There are now six women interned in Northern Ireland so far and at present being held at Armagh Prison. We feel that the public must know that we are being denied our basic rights as Internees, by the Ministry and through them the Prison staff. We are not in the same category as remand or sentenced prisoners although the Prison Authorities constantly tell us we are to be treated as Remands. Naturally we refuse to recognize this, as none of us have had either charge or trial. At the moment the only privilege we have are extra food parcels and an extra visit, plus segregation from criminals. We have asked for a visiting box and the answer is "A visiting box and you lose your extra visit." In fact we are living under the threat that if we speak out about our rights we shall be moved to a Military Controlled Camp (like Long Kesh), or what little rights we have may be jeopardised.

We are locked up four times a day, we have no education facilities, the games we have are a broken table-tennis table, net-ball posts but no ball. These we share with twenty political prisoners who are serving two to twelve years. Before we asked to be segregated from non-political prisoners and the Governor told us he would have to have the Ministry's permission, the Ministry look on us as not a few Internees but hundreds moving. Therefore the Ministry have admitted we are Internees but yet have refused to treat us as such. We know that Whitelaw will deny other young girls their freedom by Internment but will he persist in denying them their rights. Remember segregation is only a small part in Political Status. That is all we have got.

STRENGTH & LIBERTY

Signed: Elizabeth McKee   Angela Nelson
Teresa Holland   Aine Walsh
Margaret Shannon   Maire Delaney

Northern Ireland Assembly: Official Report, Vol. 3, No. 1, April 3, 1974: Extract from Speech on Estimates by Mr. Ivan Cooper, Ministry of Community Relations

. . . I have looked at both the statutory framework of the Community Relations Commission and at its practical performance. The main activity into which the Commission has chosen to put its energies and its resources has been fieldwork. The Commission employs a staff of about 15 field workers whose task is to help voluntary groups to set about tackling local problems, where necessary with Government assistance. The objective was to build up a body of responsible opinion and constructive local leadership. . . .

The statutory framework for the Commission's activities was provided by the Community Relations Act 1969. This Act gave the Commission the overall duty of encouraging good community relations. To this end it gave the Commission powers and responsibilities in relation to publications, conferences, educational programmes and the giving of grants to organisations concerned with community relations. It also gave the Commission an advisory function in relation to Government business which had a bearing on community relations.

The Commission was established as an independent body, not part of Government although set up by Statute and therefore not another voluntary group. In the circumstances of 1969 it was right that the independence of the Commission and its existence apart from Government should have been featured for there was an underlying assumption that in many areas a direct Government presence would not be acceptable. This assumption was made explicit by the Commission in preparing its plans for its field work. It was agreed that this was something which necessarily had to be done by an independent body. It was claimed that Government itself could not perform this role, since Government were a party to the conflict which it was trying to solve.

One of the things which I have been at pains to do in reviewing these matters had been to consider fully and fairly the role which the Commission might properly play in the different circumstances in which we find ourselves today. In many respects the slate has been wiped clean and a fresh start has been made. This is very obvious in the field of local government. . . .

The present situation is therefore rich in potential. We have made a new start in Government and we could be at the beginnings of a new era in community relations. The need is to capitalise on the opportunities which are before us as a community. But how best to do it? This is the problem which I have been wrestling with over the past weeks.

The conclusions which I have reached only after much hard thought—and I confess it was a very difficult decision to make—is that in the changed circumstances of today the format and range of activities of the Commission are no longer the most appropriate. It is therefore my proposal that the present Commission should be replaced by a new body, one which would be larger and which could thus be more broadly based and more widely representative. . . .

What I have in mind, therefore, is an advisory council with a substantial membership. Its terms of reference would be to advise me on matters affecting community relations in Northern Ireland. About one-third of its members would be district councillors; another one-third would be drawn from the ranks of leaders of grass-roots community associations, and the remaining one-third would be people who had a generally recognised interest in and a contribution to make to better community relations. This, I hope, would include some of the members of the present Commission, whose experience and knowledge, as I say, I would be anxious to retain.

As far as the Commission's executive functions are concerned these, too, require a rather different treatment if they are to be developed properly. It is my belief that in the present-day situation it is not only desirable but necessary that these executive functions should be directly administered by Government agencies. I see the Commission as having demonstrated the value of a variety of strategies, as having pointed the way which should be followed. But I believe that these functions, in their scale and in their importance, need a new base from which they can be further developed. . . .

Moreover, I do not believe that there is any continuing necessity for an independent body to discharge the other functions, which the Commission presently exercises. The most important of these are to give grants to voluntary bodies in the community relations field; to commission items of research; and to produce relevant publications. I believe that these matters can be dealt with by my Department, and I do not see any need or advantage in having them exercised at one remove from Government.

I believe that it is better that they should be within Government, where I believe that their influence and their relevance would both be heightened. In order to give effect to the proposals which I have outlined this afternoon I will in due course be bringing before the Assembly a draft Measure which would provide for the Commission to be discontinued, and for these present functions to be transferred to Government.

Proposals and Report on Reorganization of Ministry of Health and Welfare, January 17, 1974

Proposed: Investigative research and action to evaluate and reduce consumption of tranquillizers and sedatives. Specific: Obtain per capita statistics on dissemination and compare these with available figures for England, Scotland, and Wales.

Develop: A drug education program and in-service training material to alert GP's who may be overusing prescriptions for these drugs.

Response by Mr. Wild (Chief Administrative Officer): These statistics are available. We operate in the same fashion as the rest of the United Kingdom. There are no funds for new programs, etc.

When asked to locate the statistics, Mr. Wild was uncertain about where to look for them or if they were collected.

Proposal: To meet the increased need for professional services and not exceed budgetary limitations; also in order to upgrade job skills: Develop training programs for paraprofessionals. These would be geared to persons with

Leaving Certificate level educational background and the interest, ability, and maturity to become health aides; lay counselors . . . ; play scheme leaders; tutors; legal aides, etc. These paraprofessionals . . . would be provided paid on-the-job training under professional supervisors in each respective profession. These paraprofessionals would carry responsibility in their home locales, meet together regularly to upgrade job skills and have sufficient job flexibility, mobility to allow them status, recognition, responsibility and pay increases for experience and additional training. To this proposal, Mr. Wild and his associates responded that persons trained thus would want only to move on to full professional status and thus there would always be a gap at this level. Further, they remarked, that experience with "volunteers" had indicated that persons lacked confidence in the semi-trained personnel. He admitted that "volunteers" were untrained, unpaid, and self-selected (hardly likely to inspire confidence in themselves or anyone else). They also doubted that there would be budget for such programs and that professionals would welcome such assistance.

Proposal—Mobile Health Units: This is intended to alleviate that barrier between themselves and the services provided in the standard institutions as perceived by working-class persons in Northern Ireland. This kind of service could also provide a scheme for Preventive Medicine by allowing people ready access to information and advice. As part of this mobile service a dietician could offer small group discussions on meal preparation; a physical therapist might give exercise groups for those in normal health and also for those with some kind of handicap—including the aged, overweight, amputees, etc. The mobile unit would include a Counselor, Social Worker, and a Legal Aide as regular staff. Each mobile unit would spend two days per week in a specific area and establish itself as regular "staff members" of that community on the assigned days. At regular intervals, the units would include TB x-ray facilities, dental units, eye-examination or hearing testing facilities.

Objections: Mr. Wild and his associates mentioned that there are regular stationary health clinics in communities and that these are heavily attended and serve the purpose. However, they lack any kind of statistical documentation for this claim. They also claim that working-class people are not put off about attending reggular medical facilities and that there is no need for a reach-out program since the quality of health in Northern Ireland, like the rest of the United Kingdom, is amongst the best in the world.

Personal comment: I disagree—at least insofar as West Belfast is concerned, and I strongly disagree insofar as the Bogside and Creggan Estates in Derry are concerned.

Proposal for Ex-Internees: There are special health and welfare needs for individuals who have been interned and their families. These are (or become) multi-problem families requiring considerable aid—especially as related to the effects of disabilities suffered through interrogation and internment. An initial survey should be done to obtain figures on the number of persons who have been through this process in order to begin realistic planning for health and welfare needs. Specialists' services are necessary . . . in the areas of psychology and neurology. Aid is also needed for re-employment, correcting educational deficiencies arising from having missed part of full years of secondary or vocational or apprenticeship training during internment. This kind of program could and should be extended as well to all who have been imprisoned. . . .

Objections: Mr. Wild and his colleagues say that there is no proof that internees have special needs. Furthermore, they are dispersed after release into new areas and new communities and therefore are able to commence new lives. Further, we should consider then, he says, that all prisoners or ex-prisoners would require the same special services. He is also not convinced that interrogation techniques have left a permanent effect on the majority of persons in terned. . . .

Summary: For entertainment and to prove that the test evidence of brain damage indicated a real difference, and also because I felt desperate to achieve some kind of consensual validity with these men, I administered a Bender-Gestalt test of psychomotor function to three of these men. They all performed well indicating . . . they are all of normal intelligence and have not been brain damaged. I suppose they are therefore capable of learning and of behaving in new ways. However, it will not be easy!

After some discussion with Ivan Cooper, I worked out a new scheme for organizing community relations to meet the objectives he envisioned:

Organization Scheme for Community Relations

Objectives: Grass roots involvement in decision-making, implementation; providing training programs and services within and between communities; changing social class and sex-role stereotype patters.

Structure: Community level multipurpose agencies coordinated by area to the next level—town or city; to a county level; and then at the province-wide level.

Personnel and Relationships: At each level there should be two bodies—a professional staff and a community advisory board.

From each advisory board persons are elected to an "area" board; from the "area boards" they are elected to a regional board, etc. This will assure that persons serving at the top level were elected at grass roots level and are therefore accountable to their peers. Professional staff should be responsible to their community advisory boards. Each such board enacting the intermediary role between those performing the service and the recipients of service—essentially a "bridging" function in communication and advisement.

Training programs should be carried out at an "area" level, thus enabling commonality of experience for two locales and their shared investment in the training program. For example, Lower Falls in Belfast could be teamed in an "area" with Sandy Row.

Services Performed: Recreation programs for all age groups; paraprofessional skills training and service in health, education, welfare, legal aid, counseling and vocational rehabilitation. The staff will be prepared to carry out surveys and other information-gathering services. . . .

A tutorial program in addition to play schemes can be staffed at an "area" level.

Relationships between existing private welfare agencies and public agencies: As approved by each local advisory council the particular programs of private welfare agencies may be incorporated into the local or area scheme. For example, if an agency is primarily concerned with treatment of alcoholism it may present its program to a local advisory group or to an area advisory council. If approved by them, the professional staff persons of the private and public agencies will plan together to implement programs and services on a local level. . . . If an institution of higher education wants to carry out side its own campus then they will provide the lecturers and materials. . . . The local agency will recruit prospective students, place for classes. . . .

Paraprofessionals: Whenever possible local people would be employed in local and area agencies while in training and afterwards. They will be supervised by appropriate professionals. . . .

Proposals: There were two basic proposals for Community Relations: the first involved a reorganization scheme. . . . The second proposal relates to personnel and recruitment policies. . . .

What Happened: Mr. Slinger [Chief of Staff for the Ministry] allocated fifty minutes to our discussions. His reactions to my suggestions were of two sorts: first, that I made a case for selling my own services as a consultant. . . . Second, and most important, that the Ministry and the Commission are separate entities with the former having no controls over the latter except to sign checks. . . . Mr. Slinger asserted that the Commission was entirely proper in exerting controls of all sorts on research publication of studies carried out under its auspices. He, personally, had no knowledge of the Intimidation Report, and properly, no one else ought to have such knowledge if the Commission declined to disseminate it. . . . The Director . . . could act . . . to prohibit . . . any influence which might be prejudicial in his eyes or to Commission policy. . . . As for qualification for personnel, that was up to the Commission to establish. . . .

Problems and Prognosis: Mr. Slinger has apparently been able to deal with problems and issues relating to Community Relations by emphasizing the autonomous nature of the Commission. In this fashion any coherent policy-making attempt is thwarted. . . . There is no recourse for Community Relations workers or the recipients of its services to make changes or utilize resources. Obviously Mr. Slinger cannot be made to disappear overnight, neither can he be made to relate the Ministry with the actions of the Commission. The only possibility would be to use outside consultants . . . with access to CR workers, ministerial staff, and data about the population . . . to appraise the structure, objectives and actions with a view to change. . . . Mr. Slinger did admit to awareness of the grumblings amongst CR workers with regard to the administration of the Commission. There could be a total and . . . public disintegration of the Commission if the administration continues its policies. My own appraisal, based on discussions with committed and creative CR staff, suggests that their morale is sustained by their own cohesion as a group, but that it would not require much more . . . for the group to break down and find other channels. . . . That woud leave the Commission with the same kind of civil service bureaucracy as has the Ministry. . . .

The other course of action might be for the Ministry to organize a parallel system—such as that outlined in the discussion . . . which would itself be contracting for the services of the Commission in the form of staff personnel and research.

Notes

1. Introduction

1. Conor Cruise O'Brien, *States of Ireland* (New York: Pantheon Books, Random House, 1972).

2. Karl Marx and Friedrich Engels, *Ireland and the Irish Question: A Collection of Writings* (New York: International Publishers, 1972); Padraig O'Snodaigh, *Hidden Ulster: The Other Hidden Ireland* (Dublin: Clodhanna Teo, 1973); T. A. Jackson, *Ireland Her Own: An Outline History of the Irish Struggle* (New York: International Publishers, 1970); T. W. Moody, *The Ulster Question: 1603-1973* (Cork: Mercier Press, 1974); Constantine Fitzgibbon, *Red Hand: The Ulster Colony* (New York: Warner Paperback, 1973).

3. T. D. Williams, "John Devoy and Jeremiah O'Donovan Rossa," in T. W. Moody, ed., *The Fenian Movement* (Cork: Mercier Press, 1968).

4. Robert Kee, *The Green Flag: The Turbulent History of the Irish National Movement* (New York: Delacorte Press, 1972).

5. Nora Chadwick, *The Celts* (Harmondsworth: Penguin Books, 1970); Kenneth Nichols, *Gaelic and Gaelicised Ireland in the Middle Ages* (Dublin: Gill-Macmillan, 1972).

6. Leonard P. Liggio, "The English Origins of American Racism," paper delivered at the Columbia University Seminar on Irish Studies, New York, Feb., 1974, pp. 11-12.

7. T. M. Healy, *The Great Fraud of Ulster* (Dublin: Anvil Books, 1971); Sean Cronin and Richard Roche, *Freedom and Wolfe Tone Way* (Dublin: Anvil Books, 1973); Owen Dudley Edwards, *The Sins of Our Fathers The Roots of Conflict in Northern Ireland* (Dublin: Gill-Macmillan, 1970).

8. Chadwick, *The Celts.*

9. Ibid.

10. Louis Hyman, *The Jews of Ireland: From Earliest Times to the Year 1910* (Dublin: Irish University Press, 1972).

11. Ibid., p. 13.

12. Edmund Curtis, *A History of Ireland* (London: University Paperback, 1950).

13. Eric Strauss, *Irish Nationalism and British Democracy* (New York: Columbia University Press, 1951).

14. Curtis, *History of Ireland*.

15. Sean O'Faolain, *The Great O'Neill* (Cork: Mercier Press, 1970); see also John J. Silke, *Kinsale* (Liverpool: Liverpool University Press, 1970).

16. Padraig O'Snodaigh, *Hidden Ulster*.

17. Ibid. See also Michael Hechter, *Internal Colonialism: The Celtic Fringe in British National Development, 1536–1966* (Berkeley and Los Angeles: University of California Press, 1975).

18. Chadwick, *The Celts*.

19. C. P. J. Dowling, *A History of Irish Education: A Study in Conflicting Loyalties* (Cork: Mercier Press, 1971).

20. Ibid. See also O'Snodaigh, *Hidden Ulster*.

21. M. Rokeach, *The Open and Closed Mind* (New York: Basic Books, 1969).

22. Maurice Ashley, *England in the Seventeenth Century* (Harmondsworth: Penguin Books, 1952).

23. Kee, *The Green Flag*.

24. Curtis, *History of Ireland*, pp. 336–37.

25. Kee, *The Green Flag*.

26. Cecil Woodham-Smith, *The Great Hunger: The Horrific Story of the Irish Famine* (London: New English Library, Times-Mirror, 1970).

27. Kee, *The Green Flag*.

28. Andrew Boyd, *Holy War in Belfast: A History of the Troubles in Northern Ireland* (New York: Grove Press, 1969).

29. David Boulton, *The UVF 1966–73: An Anatomy of Loyalist Rebellion* (Dublin: Torch Books, 1973).

30. Kee, *The Green Flag*; Sean Edmonds, *The Gun, The Law and the Irish People* (Ireland: Anvil Books, 1971); Desmond Ryan, *The Rising: The Complete Story of Easter Week* (Dublin: Standard House, 1949).

31. Kee, *The Green Flag*, p. 562.

32. *What Dunne Saw in Ireland: The Truth About British Militarism in All Its Brutality!* by an eyewitness, Hon. Edward E. Dunne (New York: 1919); *Two Years of English Atrocities in Ireland*, anon. pamphlet, circa 1919.

33. Cf. poems by Padraic Pearse: "The Fool," "A Mother Speaks," "The Mother," "An Dord Feinne"; or William Butler Yeats, "The Rose Tree," 1916.

34. Kee, *The Green Flag*.

35. Brig. General Reginald Lucas, *Col. Saunderson, MP* (London: privately published, 1908).

36. Ken Griffith, narration in film biography of life of Michael Collins, ITV, 1973.

37. John A. Murphy, *Ireland in the Twentieth Century* (Dublin: Gill-Macmillian, 1975).

38. Liam de Paor, *Divided Ulster* (Harmondsworth: Penguin Books, 1970), pp. 106–7.

39. Alfred McClung Lee, "To What Is Ireland's Civil War Relevant?" *Holy Cross Quarterly*, vol. 6, no. 1–4, *The Irish Issue*, ed. E. Van Etten Casey, 1974.

40. Hechter, *Internal Colonialism*.

41. De Paor, *Divided Ulster*.

42. Lars Rudebeck, *Guinea Bissau: A Study of Political Mobilization* (Upsala: Scandinavian Institute of African Studies, 1975).

43. W. B. Yeats, "Leaders of the Crowds."

44. Frank Kitson, *Low Intensity Operations: Subversion, Insurgency and Peace Keeping* (London: Faber & Faber, 1971).

45. Boyd, *Holy War in Belfast.*

48. Vahakn N. Dadrian, "The Common Features of the Armenian and Jewish Cases of Genocide: A Comparative Victimological Perspective," in *Victomology: A New Focus*, ed. I. Dropkin and E. Viano (Lexington, Mass.: D. C. Heath, 1975); Marjorie Housepian, "The Unremembered Genocide," *Commentary*, 42, Sept. 1966.

49. Robert M. Yerkes, "Psychological Examining in the United States Army," *Memoirs of the National Academy of Sciences*, 15 (1921), 790–91.

50. On American Indian genocide, see F. C. Battey's Introduction to *Our Red Brothers*, by Lawry Tatum (Lincoln: University of Nebraska Press, 1970), and Vine Deloria, *Custer Died for Your Sins* (New York: Macmillan, 1969).

51. Carey McWilliams, *North From Mexico: The Spanish Speaking People of the United States* (New York: J. B. Lippincott Co., 1949).

52. Netta Dor Shev, "Some Psychological Characteristics of Survivors of the Holocaust and their Children," paper delivered at the International Conference on the Effects of Stress in War and Peace, Tel Aviv, Israel, Jan., 1975.

53. Herbert C. Kelman, "Violence Without Moral Restraint: Reflections on the Dehumanization of Victims and Victimizers," *Journal of Social Issues*, vol. 29, no. 4, 1973.

54. Kelman, "Violence Without Moral Restraint," *Journal of Social Issues*, vol. 29, no. 4.

2. Psychological Genocide

1. Leo Eitinger and Axel Strøm, *Mortality and Morbidity after Excessive Stress* (New York: Humanities Press, 1973).

2. Robert Coles, *Children of Crisis: A Study of Courage and Fear* (Boston: Atlantic Monthly Press, 1964); Bruno Bettelheim, *The Informed Heart* (Glencoe, Ill.: The Free Press of Glencoe, 1960).

3. Anna Freud and Dorothy Burlingame, *Infants Without Families* (New York: International Universities Press, 1944); *War and Children* (New York: Medical War Books, 1943).

4. William Ryan, *Blaming the Victim.*

5. Hannah Arendt, *A Report on the Bandity of Evil* (New York: Viking Press, 1963).

6. Cf. Nathan Glazer and Daniel Patrick Moynihan, *Beyond the Melting Pot* (Cambridge, Mass.: Harvard-MIT Press, 1963).

7. Hannah Arendt, *Report.*

8. June Tapp and L. Kohlberg, "Developing Senses of Law and Legal Justice," *Journal of Social Issues*, vol. 27, no. 2, Fall 1971.

9. *The Northern Teacher*, Winter, 1973; see R. Cathcart, "To Build Anew," and John Malone, "Schools and Community Relations."

10. Morris Fraser, *Children of Conflict* (London: Secker & Warburg, 1973).

11. Ibid.

12. Morris Fraser, "The Cost of Contention," *British Journal of Psychiatry*, March, 1971, pp. 18–19.

13. Quoted in the *Belfast Telegraph*, Dec. 20, 1971.

14. H. A. Lyons, "Psychiatric Sequelae of the Belfast Riots," *British Journal of Psychiatry*, March, 1971.

15. P. P. O'Malley, "Attempted Suicide Before and After the Communal Violence in Belfast, Aug., 1969," *Journal of Irish Medical Association*, vol. 56, no. 5, 1971.

16. James L. Russell, *Civic Education in Northern Ireland: Report to the Northern Ireland Community Relations Commission* (Belfast: The Commission, 1972).

17. S. L. Neilsen, "Intergroup Conflict and Violence, Belfast 1968," *Psychosocial Studies*, no. 4, University of Bergen, Norway, 1972.

18. Personal observation and communication with several U.S. journalists who had just given coins to a group of children to reward them for throwing the rocks.

19. *Northern Teacher*, Winter, 1973.

20. Magda B. Arnold, *Story Sequence Analysis* (New York: Columbia University Press, 1961).

21. Tapp and Kohlberg, "Developing Sense of Law and Legal Justice."

21. Jeanne Knutson, "Personality in the Study of Politics," in *Handbook of Political Psychology*, ed. J. Knutson (San Francisco: Jossey-Bass, 1973).

23. Arnold, *Story Sequence Analysis*.

24. Ibid.

25. Tapp and Kohlberg, "Developing Senses of Law and Legal Justice."

26. Gordon Allport, *The Nature of Prejudice* (Garden City: Doubleday, 1958).

27. Ibid.

28. Covenant of the Prevention and Punishment of the Crime of Genocide, adopted Dec. 9, 1943, Article 11: "In the present Convention, genocide means any of the following acts committed with intent to destroy, in whole or in part, a national, ethnical, racial, or religious group, as such: (a) Killing members of the group; (b) Causing serious bodily or mental harm to members of the group; (c) Deliberately inflicting on the group conditions of life calculated to bring about its physical destruction in whole or in part; (d) Imposing measures intended to prevent birth within the group; (e) Forcibly transferring children of the group to another group."

29. Bettelheim, *Informed Heart*.

3. Psychotechnology

1. Report by British Society for Social Responsibility in Science, 1972. Cf. Ned Opton, *The Mind Breakers* (New York: Random House, scheduled for publication in 1977); James Marshall, *Law and Psychology in Conflict* (New York: Bobbs-Merrill, 1966); Jay Katz, *Experimentation with Human Beings* (New York: Russell Sage Foundation, 1972); Jessica Mitford, *Kind and Usual Punishment: The Prison Business* (New York: Vantage Books, 1974); "Patuxent as a Progressive Step Forward," *The New York Times Magazine*, Sept. 17, 1972.

2. Examples which relate to internees experience (excerpted from *Psychological Abstracts*): P. Hocking, *Extreme Environmental Stress and the Significance for Psychopathology: American Journal of Psychotherapy*, 24, no. 1

1970, 4–6: Describes some of the immediate and long-term effects of a number of situations involving severe to extreme stress, semi-starvation, sensory deprivation . . . in people subjected to extreme forms of environmental stress, suggests that permanent psychological disability may result and . . . personality characteristics may do no more than determine how long an individual can withstand prolonged streme stress (*Physiological Psych.*, vol. 44, 12074).

Kohlshun, Osatu, Kikachi, Trijji, and Murai (Nigata University, Japan), *Studies on Sensory Deprivation*, vol. 6, part 2: Effect of sensory deprivation upon memory processes . . . investigated the effect of sensory deprivation of recall in long and short-term memory. In long-term memory the effect was inhibitory rather than facilitative. This result suggests the need of differentiating respondent recall from spontaneous recollection. In short-term memory a deteriorative effect if sensory deprivation was seen not on the rote-learning function, but in the organizing function of memory (*Experimental Psych.*, vol. 43, 13073).

Marjana Vodanovic, *Effect of Fatigue on Conformity of Free Associations*: A list of 94 randomly used words . . . was applied immediately after Ss had completed 7½ hour mental work. . . . It appears legitimate to conclude that, on the average, fatigue led to statistically significant increases in conformity of answers (*Experimental Psych.*, vol. 43, 13646).

3. Tim Shallice, writing a report for BSSRS in 1971 stated: "After being held for two days at Regional Holding Centres they were transferred to an interrogation centre at 6:30 a.m. on August 11th, held there until 15.45, transferred again to Crumlin Road Jail for service of detention and removal orders and then returned to the interrogation centre by 19.00, all on the same day. While the prisoner was held at the interrogation centre he was subjected to these procedures while not actually being interrogated: 1. *Hooding*—his head was hooded in a black bag of tightly woven or hessian cloth. 2. *Noise*—the room in which he was held was filled with a noise described as 'like the escaping of compressed air' or the 'whir of helicopter blades'—presumably white noise of 85–87 db (Compton Report, p. 16). 3. *Wall standing*—the internee was made to face a wall with hands high above his head on the wall and legs apart. If he moved or collapsed he was forced or lifted to regain position. Periods of wall-standing up to 16 hours at a stretch (Compton Report, p. 10). 4. *Sleep*—none allowed for the first two or three days. 5. *Inadequate diet*—diet was severely restricted to occasional administration of dry bread and a cup of water."

4. From the prologue to the American Psychological Association Code of Ethics.

5. Frank Kitson, *Low Intensity Operations: Subversion, Insurgency and Peace Keeping* (London: Faber & Faber, 1971).

6. Parker Commission Report (1972), *Report of the Committee of Privy Councillors Appointed to Consider Authorized Procedures for the Interrogation of Persons Suspected of Terrorism*, HMSO, C 4901. Compton Report (1971), *Report of the Inquiry into Allegation against the Security Forces of Physical Brutality in Northern Ireland*, HMSO, Cmd 4823.

7. Parker Commission Report.

8. Ibid.

9. Compton Report.

10. Tim Shallice, "The Ulster Depth Interrogation Techniques and Their Relation to Sensory Deprivation Research," *Cognition*, 1, no. 4 (1973), 383–405.

11. D. Faul and R. Murray, *Brutalities* (Belfast: Association for Legal Justice, 1972).
12. Shallice, "Ulster Depth Interrogation Techniques."
13. Ibid.
14. See Katz, *Experimentation with Human Beings*; Herbert C. Kelman, *A Time to Speak: On Human Values and Social Research* (San Francisco: Jossey-Bass, 1968); 1975 Revised APA Ethical Code on Experimentation with Human Subjects.
15. Faul and Murray, *Brutalities*.
16. P. P. O'Malley, personal communication, July, 1972.
17. Kelman, "Violence Without Restraint," pp. 13–15.
18. H. D. Rankin, "On the Psychostasis of Ulster," *Psycho-Therapy and Psychosomatics*, 19 (1971), 160–74. Rankin analyzes the assimilation by Ulster Protestants of Irish Catholic myth systems and forms.
19. Cf. Richard Rose, *Governing Without Consensus* (Boston: Beacon Press, 1971). Rose sets out a model to explain how a system of government has been maintained in Northern Ireland in an apparently democratic format without representing the majority of the people and still remaining impervious to rebellion.
20. A. Bandura and R. H. Walters, *Social Learning and Personality Development* (New York: Holt, Rinehart & Winston, 1959).
21. P. P. O'Malley, "Attempted Suicide Before and After the Communal Violence in Belfast, Aug., 1969," *Journal of the Irish Medical Association*, vol. 65, no. 5 (1972); Morris Fraser, *Children in Conflict* (London: Secker & Warburg, 1973).

4. Social Control Mechanisms

1. Rona M. Fields, *A Society on the Run: A Psychology of Northern Ireland* (Harmondsworth: Penguin Books, 1973).
2. J. McGuffin, *Internment* (Republic of Ireland: Anvil Press, 1973).
3. Ibid.
4. D. Faul and R. Murray, *Whitelaw's Tribunals* (Armagh, Northern Ireland: 1973).
5. Jonathon L. Freedman, *Crowding and Behavior* (San Francisco: W. H. Freeman, 1975).
6. Parker Commission Report (1972), *Report of the Committee of Privy Councillors Appointed to Consider Authorized Procedures for the Interrogation of Persons Suspected of Terrorism*, HMSO, Cmnd 4091.
7. The Report of the Diplock Commission, Dec. 20, 1972, states, "We would not condone practices such as those described in the Compton Report and the Parker Report. . . ."
8. Most notably, Seamus O'Tauthail, *They Came in the Morning* (Belfast: NICRA, 1971); *Sunday Times* Insight Team, *Ulster* (Harmondsworth: Penguin Books, 1972); D. Faul and R. Murray, *Brutalities* (Belfast: Association for Legal Justice, 1972).
9. *Irish Times*, Dec. 22, 1971, statement quoted from Richard Sharples, Minister for Home Affairs.
10. Henry Murray, *The Thematic Apperception Test*, Manual (New York: Psychological Corporation, 1943, 1971).

11. D. McClelland, "Methods of Measuring Human Motivation," in J. Atkinson, ed., *Motives in Fantasy, Action and Society* (Princeton: Van Nostrand, 1958).

12. Magda B. Arnold, *Story Sequence Analysis* (New York: Columbia University Press, 1961).

13. F. K. Graham and B. S. Kendall, *Memory for Designs Test: Revised General Manual* (Missoula, Montana: Phychological Test Specialists, 1973).

14. For a more complete description of the "field dependent-independent" personality prototypes and concomitants, see H. B. Lewis, *Shame and Guilt in Neurosis* (New York: International Universities Press, 1971).

15. The conditions of normlessness and unrelatedness are more thoroughly defined and described by Erich Fromm, *Escape from Freedom* (New York: Holt Rinehart & Winston, 1941).

5. Women of Ireland

1. James Connolly, *The Re-Conquest of Ireland* (Dublin: New Books, 1914).

2. R. Thurneysen, Nancy Power, Myles Dillon, Kathleen Mulchrone, D. A. Binchy, August Knoch, John Ryan, S.J., *Studies in Early Irish Law* (Dublin: Royal Irish Academy, 1936).

3. Donald S. Connery, *The Irish* (New York: Simon & Shuster, 1970).

4. Leonard P. Liggio, "The English Origins of Early American Racism," paper delivered at the Columbia University Seminar on Irish Studies, New York, Feb., 1974.

5. See *Studies in Early Irish*; Nora Chadwick, *The Celts* (Harmondsworth: Penguin, 1970); Sean O'Faolain, *The Great O'Neill* (Cork: Mercier Press, 1942).

6. Elizabeth Gould Davis, *The First Sex* (Baltimore: Penguin Books, 1971).

7. Nora Chadwick, *The Celts.*

8. Friedrich Engels, *The Family, Private Property and the State* (New York: International Publications, 1972).

9. *Early Irish Law*, passim.

10. Ibid.

11. Sean O'Faolain, *The Great O'Neill.*

12. O'Faolain, *The Great O'Neill*, 1970 edition, pp. 116–21. (Italics added.)

13. *Early Irish Law.*

14. J. Ryan, "*The Cain Adomnain*," in *Early Irish Law*, p. 170.

15. *Early Irish Law*, passim.

16. Rudolph Thurneysen, "Die Realiesistungun des Mannes und der Frau," in *Early Irish Law.*

17. *Early Irish Law*, passim.

18. Nancy Power, "Classes of Women . . . ," in *Early Irish Law.*

19. Ibid., p. 87.

20. Ibid.

21. Ibid., p. 86.

22. See ibid., pp. 95–96, for a discussion of these relationships.

23. Myles Dillon, "The Relationship of Mother and Son, Father and Daughter . . . ," in *Early Irish Law.*

24. Maud Gonne MacBride, *A Servant of the Queen* (London: Victor Gollancz, 1974).

25. James Connolly, ". . . none so fit to break the chains . . . ," *The Re-Conquest of Ireland*, 1914.

26. Lillian Conlon, *Cumann Na Ban and the Women of Ireland* (Kilkenny People, Ltd., 1969).

27. Ibid.

28. Ibid., pp. 503–8.

29. D. P. Barritt and C. F. Carter, *The Northern Ireland Problem: A Study in Group Relations* (London: Oxford University Press, 1962), pp. 34–36.

30. H. D. Rankin, "On the Psychostasis of Ulster," *Psychotherapy and Psychosomatics*, 19 (1971), 160–74.

31. Ibid., p. 166.

32. Ernest Jones, cited by H. D. Rankin, "Psychostasis."

33. Rankin, "Psychostasis," pp. 161–67.

34. Connery, *The Irish*, p. 192.

35. Engels, *The Family, Private Property and the State.*

36. From personal communication.

37. Dublin Founding Group, Irishwomen's Liberation, *Irishwomen: Chains or Change?* (Dublin: 1971).

38. Constitution of the Republic of Ireland.

39. Dublin Founding Group, *Irishwomen.*

40. "Loyalist Association of Workers, Belfast," interview in *Irishwomen Speak* (New York: Hanna Sheehy Skeffington Club, 1973).

41. *Transaction Magazine*, "Women's Issue," article by Nathan and Julie Hare, Oct. 1971.

42. Richard Rose, *Governing Without Consensus* (Boston: Beacon Press, 1971).

43. Bernadette Devlin, *The Price of My Soul* (London: Pan, 1969).

6. The British Army

1. Eric Strauss, *Irish Nationalism and British Democracy* (New York: Columbia University Press, 1951), pp. 1–65.

2. BBC Poll, taken in 1973, reported in the *Irish Echo*, Nov., 1973.

3. Frank Kitson, *Low Intensity Operations: Subversion, Insurgency and Peace Keeping* (London: Faber & Faber, 1971).

4. O. C. Giles, *The Gestapo*, Oxford Pamphlets on World Affairs, no. 33 (Oxford: Oxford University Press, 1940).

5. *Low Intensity Operations.* For a description of these tactics, see chapters 3, 4, 5.

6. Ibid., p. 69.

7. Ibid., citation from John McCuen, *The Art of Counter Revolutionary War* (London: Faber & Faber, 1968), p. 69.

8. David Holloway, "The British Army in Northern Ireland," *New Edinburgh Review*, no. 17, 1972.

9. Kitson, *Low Intensity Operations*, p. 88.

10. *Belfast Newsletter*, June 28, 1973.

11. Frank Doherty, "The SAS in Northern Ireland," *Hibernia Fortnightly Review*, April, 1973.

12. *Report of the Inquiry into Allegations against the Security Forces of Physical Brutality in Northern Ireland* (Compton Commission), HMSD, Cmd 4823, 1971; *Report of the Committee of Privy Councillors Appointed to Consider Authorized Procedures for the Interrogation of Persons Suspected of Terrorism* (Parker Commission), HMSD, Cmd 4901 (1972).

13. *The New York Times*, March 6, 1972.

14. Holloway, "The British Army in Northern Ireland."

15. Ibid.

16. BSSRS, *The New Technology of Repression: Lessons from Northern Ireland*, paper 2, London, 1974.

20. Ibid.

7. The Blood of Martyrs

1. Roger Lewin, "Starved Brains," *Psychology Today*, Sept., 1975.

2. Cited in Michael MacGrail, *Tolerence and Prejudice in Ireland* (scheduled for publication, 1977).

3. Milton Rokeach, *The Open and Closed Mind* (New York: Basic Books, 1960).

4. Ibid., p. 15.

5. Ibid., p. 68.

6. Ibid., p. 69.

7. Ibid., p. 398.

8. *Sunday Independent* (Dublin), July 30, 1972.

9. Betty Sinclair, *Unemployment* (Belfast: pamphlet, 1972).

10. O Cinneide report, *Sunday Independent*, July 30, 1972.

11. Irish government economic affairs pamphlet, circa 1972–73.

12. *United Irishman* (Dublin), March, 1972.

13. Conor Cruise O'Brien, *States of Ireland* (New York: Pantheon Books, Random House, 1972), p. 318.

14. *United Irishman*, Oct., 1971.

15. O'Brien, *States of Ireland*, pp. 311–12.

16. *United Irishman*, Oct., 1971.

17. O'Brien, *States of Ireland*, pp. 320–21.

18. *United Irishman*, Oct., 1971.

19. O'Brien, *States of Ireland*, p. 320.

20. *United Irishman*, Oct., 1971.

21. O'Brien, *States of Ireland*, p. 318.

22. *United Irishman*, Oct., 1971.

23. A condition in Scotland similar to that of the Irish Labour Party is discussed in Charles A. Powell, "Contemporary Scotland as a Non-State Nation," paper delivered at the annual meeting, International Studies Association, March 14–17, 1973.

24. O'Brien, *States of Ireland*, pp. 208–9.

25. *Irish Times*, April 13, 1973.

26. Patrick Marrinan, *Paisley: Man of Wrath* (Republic of Ireland: Anvil Press, 1973).

27. Ibid.
28. David Boulton, *The UVF 1966–1973: An Anatomy of Loyalist Rebellion* (Republic of Ireland: Torch Books, 1973).
29. An interview with Rosita Sweetman, in *On Our Knees* (Ireland: 1972; London, Pan Special, 1972), pp. 195–96.
30. Alliance Party leaflet, Belfast, 1972.
31. Paddy Devlin, *The Fall of the Northern Ireland Executive* (Northern Ireland: privately published by author, 1975).
32. Neal Ascherson, "Strikers Celebrate," *The Observer*, June 2, 1974.

8. Social Control

1. From an interview with Father Desmond Wilson, reported in Rosita Sweetman's *On Our Knees* (London: Pan, 1972). Father Wilson, in interviews with me, and in numerous articles of his own appearing in *The Community Forum* and other publications, elaborated on this thesis.
2. Jean Jacques Rousseau, *The Social Contract*, vol. 1.
3. Harry and Pola Triandis, "The Building of Nations," *Psychology Today*, Feb., 1967.
4. Carl Jung and C. Kerenyi, *Essays on a Science of Mythology* (New York: Pantheon, 1949).
5. Triandis and Triandis, "The Building of Nations."
6. *Banner of the Truth in Ireland* (pamphlet), May–Aug., 1971.
7. Cecil Woodham-Smith, *The Great Hunger: The Horrific Story of the Irish Famine* (London: New English Library, Times-Mirror, 1970).
8. Ibid.
9. Gearoid MacNiocaill, *Ireland Before the Vikings* (Dublin: Gill-Macmillan, 1970).
10. Judy Bertelson, "The Non-State Nation," a series of papers citing theory and case studies based on this model, presented at annual meetings of the International Studies Association, 1972–75.
11. Talcott Parsons and Edward Shils, eds., *Toward a General Theory of Action* (New York: The Free Press of Glencoe, 1951), pp. 24–25.
12. Ibid., p. 227.
13. Ibid., p. 229.
14. Milton Rokeach, *The Open and Closed Mind* (New York: Basic Books, 1960).
15. Raul Hilberg, "The Holocaust as an Administrative Phenomenon," paper presented at the Conference on the Holocaust, Hebrew College, Brookline, Mass., April, 1973, pp. 3–7.
16. Paul Bookbinder, "The Crime of Being: The German Legal System and the Jews," paper presented at the Conference of the Holocaust, Hebrew College, Brookline, Mass., April, 1973, pp. 1–13.
17. Ibid., pp. 13–14.
18. Ibid., p. 14.
19. Roger N. Hill, *The Irish Triangle: Conflict in Northern Ireland* (Princeton: Princeton University Press, 1976).
20. Bookbinder, "The Crime of Being," pp. 15–16.
21. Northern Ireland Civil Rights *Bulletin*, June–July, 1974.

22. Ibid., May, 1974.

23. *Campaign for Social Justice in Northern Ireland*, pamphlet, 1970, published in Northern Ireland.

24. Andrew Boyd, *Holy War in Belfast* (New York: Grove Press, 1969).

25. Sir Arthur Hezlett, *The 'B' Specials: A History of the Ulster Special Constabulary* (London: Pan Books, 1972), pp. 19–21.

26. John Cameron, *Disturbances in Northern Ireland: Report Of The Commission Appointed by the Governor of Northern Ireland*, CMC, no. 532, 1969.

27. *Campaign for Social Justice in Northern Ireland.*

28. Ibid.

29. Ibid.

30. Denis Faul and Raymond Murray, *British Army and Special Branch RUC Brutalities* (Cavan, Northern Ireland: A Bey Printers, 1972).

31. J. D. H. Downing, *Inquiry* (London: private publisher, 1974), pp. 7–8.

32. C. P. J. Dowling, *A History of Irish Education* (Cork: Mercier Press, 1971).

33. This is from Faul and Murray, *British Army*, pp. 389–390.

34. Downing, *Inquiry*, pp. 7–8.

35. R. B. McDowell, 1964, *The Irish Administration*, p. 63.

36. Dowling, *History of Irish Education*, pp. 78–79.

37. McDowell, 1964, *The Irish Administration*, p. 63.

38. Denis P. Barritt and Charles F. Carter, *The Northern Ireland Problem: A Study of Group Relations* (London: Oxford University Press, 1962).

39. John Darby, in *The Holy Cross Quarterly: The Irish Issue*, Spring, 1974, pp. 81–82.

40. Downing, *Inquiry*, pp. 6–7.

41. Gil Behringer, *The Tribune* (Belfast), May 25, 1973.

42. John Montague, *The Rough Field: A Book of Poems* (Cork: 1974).

43. E. Curtis, *History of Ireland*, p. 408.

44. Gordon Allport, *On the Nature of Prejudice* (Garden City: Doubleday, 1968), p. xi.

45. C. F., Racism, *Intelligence and the Working Class*, 1973, PLP, or Loen Kamin, *The Science and Politics of IQ* (Halstead Press, 1974).

46. Allport, *On the Nature of Prejudice*, p. 10.

47. Ibid., pp. 14–15.

48. Nevitt Sanford, *Self and Society: Social Change and Individual Development* (New York: Atherton, 1966); Kurt Lewin, *Field Theory in Social Science* (New York: Harper & Row, 1951).

49. Leon Festinger, *A Theory of Cognitive Dissonance* (Stanford, Calif.: Stanford University Press, 1957).

50. Ibid.

51. Rokeach, *Open and Closed Mind.*

52. Sanford, *Self and Society.*

53. Allport, *Nature of Prejudice.*

54. E. E. Sampson, *Social Psychology and Contemporary Society* (New York: Wiley, 1971), p. 218.

55. Eric Erikson, *Identity, Youth and Crisis* (New York: W. W. Norton & Co., 1968).

56. Herbert O. Kelman, "Sanctioned Massacre," *Journal of Social Issues*, Spring, 1975.

57. Ibid., pp. 37–38.
58. Stanley Milgram, *Obedience to Authority* (New York: Harper, 1974); Phillip Zimbardo, 1973.
59. Milgram, *Obedience to Authority*.
60. Terence Des Pres, *Survivors* (New York: Harper & Row, 1975).
61. Walter Zenner, "Lachrymose Identity," paper presented at International Studies Association Meeting, Washington, D.C., 1975.

Appendix

1. A new book—Kevin Boyle, Tom Hadden, and Paddy Hilyard, *Law and the State* (London: M. Robertson & Co., 1975)—describes in depth the paradoxes and contradictions of the laws.

Index